London Transport
Since 1933

Part One
1933-1962

London Transport Since 1933

Part One
1933-1962

Michael H. C. Baker

Ian Allan
PUBLISHING

Originally published as:
London Transport 1933-1962, 1996
London Transport Since-1963, 1997

This combined edition first published 2000

ISBN 0 7110 2702 1

Published by Ian Allan Publishing

an imprint of Ian Allan Publishing Ltd, Terminal House, Shepperton, Surrey TW17 8AS.

Printed by Ian Allan Printing Ltd, Riverdene Business Park, Hersham, Surrey KT12 4RG

Code: 0001/A1

Contents

Introduction

London Transport 1933–1962

I gave up collecting London bus numbers at the end of 1950 when I decided there was practically nothing but STLs and members of the RT family to record. I suppose it had something to do with the disappearance of the last STs and LTs, types which I had known all my life. Forty-five years on this seems a rather odd decision for I had a great liking for the STL, the successor of the ST and LT and which, as the most up-to-date standard London bus, I considered the bee's knees, the cat's pyjamas. This decision didn't lessen my interest in London buses, or trams, trolleybuses and trains for that matter. And if I didn't mark off numbers in my *abc* any more, I made a mental note of each batch of RTs which arrived, spanking new, to operate one of our local routes. Local was Croydon. But buses also operated into the town from Elmers End which was also pretty local and, a bit further afield, Catford, Bromley and Sutton, which were all outer suburban. We also got buses from closer in to the West End and the City from Streatham, Norwood, Old Kent Road, Nunhead, Camberwell and from the other side of the river, Chalk Farm. Then there were all the Country Area garages which sent their green double-deckers and single-deck Green Line coaches into Croydon, Chelsham, Godstone, East Grinstead, Dunton Green, Reigate, Crawley, Dorking, Guildford, Leatherhead, Hemel Hempstead, Amersham and Tring. Pause for breath; then on to tram depots at Thornton Heath, Telford Avenue and Brixton Hill and, sometimes, Purley, and finally two trolleybus routes whose vehicles lived at Carshalton and Hammersmith. All of which goes to show how such a wonderfully rich variety could not fail to engage the interest of any schoolboy remotely aware of public transport.

Many of us with an interest in public transport keep an eye out in the cinema for familiar buses passing behind the leading lady, and London, featuring probably more than all other cities in the kingdom put together, provides a rich harvest. Who doesn't know that familiar shot — particularly familiar around now as I'm writing this at the height of the VE-Day 50th anniversary celebrations — of a roof-box STL in Parliament Square in 1940 amongst a convoy of tanks? Hollywood, especially in black and white days, often passed off the most outrageous artefacts as genuine London vehicles, but one film which did get it right was the Fred Astaire, Ginger Rogers classic, *Top Hat*. Fred is driving Ginger across Westminster Bridge in a hansom cab and they pass in a brief but fascinating sequence, NSs, LTs, STs and an E3 tram on a Kingsway Subway service. The E3 is fitted with driver's screens and, *Top Hat* being released early in 1935, this feature and the liveries suggest these second unit scenes must have been filmed around 1933-4 when our book opens.

Within these pages we record the types, the changes, the liveries, the contractions and expansions, some of the people and a few personal reminiscences of the more than 30-year history of the largest urban transport undertaking in the world.

Michael H. C. Baker
July 1996

Below:
Southgate station, on the Piccadilly Line extension to Cockfosters, under construction. *Topical*

1933

The London Passenger Transport Board (LPTB) came into existence on Saturday 1 July 1933, less than three months after the bill setting it up had received the Royal Assent. It created the largest passenger transport operating organisation in the world. A total of 9,500,000 passengers was carried daily. For some areas of its operations great changes were in store; one thinks initially of the replacement of the trams by trolleybuses, but such diverse aspects as architecture and publicity would also come to the forefront. The underground and tube networks would expand, and buses and coaches, powered by diesel in future rather than petrol, carrying the London Transport name would penetrate far into the countryside of Kent, Surrey, Sussex, Middlesex, Buckinghamshire, Hertfordshire and Essex. Its operating area of some 2,000 square miles was defined as extending between 20 to 30 miles from Charing Cross.

Although a huge number of operators were absorbed by LT, many were very small, sometimes one-man only businesses. Inevitably it was the few big ones, the London County Council (LCC), the Underground Electric Railway Co and its subsidiary, the London General Omnibus Co (LGOC), which were to influence policy. There was a mixture of continuation in some areas and innovation in others.

For the trams 1933 was a year which suggested they might just have a future. The previous year the LCC had completed updating all its trams by fitting upholstered seats downstairs and at least partly upholstered ones upstairs. In the spring of that year tramcar No 1 emerged from Charlton Works. This splendid vehicle was based on the HR2 of 1930 but considerably more modern. It had concealed interior lighting, separate heated driver's cab, air and magnet brakes, air-operated doors, and was to be the prototype of a new generation of trams. In 1931 London United Tramways (LUT) and the Metropolitan Electric Tramways (MET) had put into service what was perhaps an even more revolutionary tram, the Feltham, or UCC class. No less than 40ft 6in long over fenders, these tremendous vehicles also had air-operated doors at back and front — allowing fast boarding and alighting — air and electromagnetic brakes, and ran so smoothly that they could coast considerable distances with power off. Both No 1 and the 100 members of the Feltham class were in truth in advance of any bus then in operation and there is evidence of preparations to build many more of them. In some respects both No 1 and the Felthams were still ahead of any other PSV when they were withdrawn from the streets of London in 1951-2 and sold for further service in Leeds.

Unfortunately most of the 2,465 (plus 165 in store) London trams were ancient and out of date, although still quite serviceable. While no tram services were withdrawn in 1933, the success of the Kingston area trolleybuses put into service by the LUT in 1931 had convinced LT that this was where the future of electrically powered road vehicles lay. Nevertheless just one day after LT came into existence a virtually new tram entered service, on 2 July 1933. This was No 1370. 'Virtually' needs some amplification, for its

Left:
One of the handsome and comfortable bus shelters designed by Charles Holden. Although the LPTB had nothing to do with the design of either the passengers or the houses beyond, both are standard for the period too. *IAL*

Right:
STL1, a very upright vehicle, poses for its official picture. *Topical*

origins are complex in the extreme. It had started out as LCC Class M car No 1446, dating from 1910 and was a four-wheel version of the standard E1 class bogie car. Most of the Ms (not the LCC's most successful tram because their riding could be uncomfortably nautical), were withdrawn in 1932 but three were converted to ME3 bogie vehicles. No 1446 was the third of these. It was given a brand new top deck — virtually identical to that of No 1, although the number and destination screens were different — flush lower deck sides, an aluminium-framed windscreen, and Hurst Nelson bogies. However, just before it was ready to enter service, an E1 car, No 1370, crashed outside the Oval, probably because the driver was trying to catch a glimpse of one of Jack Hobbs's last innings. This was deemed a write off; the money for its replacement was credited to the rebuilding of No 1446 which assumed No 1370's number. The story doesn't end even there, for some parts of the original 1370 were salvaged and were used up in yet another new, very similar car, No 2, which took up work in February 1935.

January 1933 saw the entry into service of the double-deck bus which was to be the London standard until the war. This was STL1. It wasn't a pretty vehicle. Its body was a development of the Bluebird LT Renown six-wheeler and ST Regent four-wheeler, but it did not share their handsome proportions. This was because it managed to squeeze 60 seats into its 26ft length. Until the previous year 25ft had been the maximum length allowed for four-wheel chassis and the 49-seat ST had been the standard Central Area double-decker. The upper deck of the STL projected ahead of the cab, being in line with the radiator and, as there was virtually no slope back or front, 34 seats were squeezed in upstairs, 26 downstairs. Lightweight materials were used wherever possible to keep the laden weight down to 10 tons, and whatever the original STL lacked in elegance, its design showed much originality. It was well built; indeed, one of the bodies lasted on a much later chassis until 1954, 21 years being a remarkable lifespan for a London bus in those days, particularly one which had suffered nearly six years of wartime neglect.

Another variety of STL was also in production in 1933. This was the Thomas Tilling version. Thomas Tilling, one of the most famous names in the British public transport industry, had been operating buses in London since 1847. Although keeping its independence it had been a member of the London

Left:
Oxford Street in late 1933. A brand new 'leaning back' STL on route 6 bound for Hackney Wick loads up outside Selfridges ahead of an LT on the 15. Both carry the legend 'General' as worn in LT's first months. *Author's collection*

Below:
Former Tilling STL80 from Catford Garage on the 36. Years of practice have removed all danger of the conductor losing his grip and dignity as he assumes standard nonchalant pose for rounding Marble Arch. *LT*

Right:
55, Broadway, the hub of the world's greatest urban transport system. *Topical*

Left:
Tram No 1 outside Holloway depot on a special working. It ran from this depot until 1938 when it was transferred southside to Telford Avenue. This picture was taken during a postwar visit to its old haunts. *IAL*

Below:
Tram No 2 in postwar days at the Catford terminus of the 52. The elegant top deck is somewhat compromised by the crude fitting of the windscreen to the dash. *IAL*

Right:
Two NSs give way to a tall-funnelled steamer at the West India Docks. *Author's collection*

Below right:
No 2376, an archaic looking former LUT U-class bogie car of 1902, heading towards Hampton Court on route 57. *Author's collection*

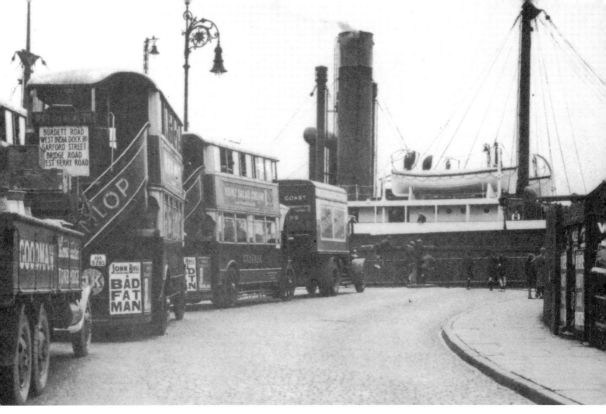

Left:
No 2280, a relatively modern ex-MET G-class bogie car, stands ahead of Feltham No 2092 in Finchley Depot.

One bus which appeared wearing the title General, even though it wasn't completed until August 1933, was STL203. This was a 56-seater, the standard number for so many highbridge double-deckers of that period. It differed in many other respects from its immediate forebears and was well on the way to the standard STL. It was not yet there because its front, although more pleasing than that of the first LGOC STLs, sloped back and was not entirely smooth, and it had a petrol engine. The back was a fine piece of design, curving out gently from the base and then equally subtly to the roof line and the domed roof. In this respect the standard STL had been reached and in the author's opinion was more elegant than either the RT or the RM. This batch was completed with the entry of STL252 into service in November 1933, and was immediately followed by STL253, which was very similar but had a smoother frontal appearance.

On the Underground rebuilding of stations — Chancery Lane on the Central Line for example — continued. The final stage of the Piccadilly Line tube surface extension from Finsbury Park from its last but one station, Enfield West, to its impressively modernistic enclosed terminus at Cockfosters, designed by Charles Holden, was opened on 31 July. At that time tube trains were painted, like buses and trams, in a red and off white livery, unlike the all-red of modern surface stock, as the larger Metropolitan and District Line trains were known.

1934

While changes certainly took place in 1934, in retrospect it was a relatively quiet year, when the indelible image which LT was to impose on public transport in and around the capital was being honed and perfected but was yet far from evident. A new numbering system for all routes, except trams, and based on the old General one but much refined, was introduced in October. 1–199 were for Central Area, red, double-deck routes, 200–290 for Central Area single-deck routes, 291–299 for night routes, 300–399 for Country Area routes north of the Thames and 400–499 for Country Area routes south of the river.

Not all the independents out in the country areas had yet been absorbed and several were taken over at the beginning of the year by Green Line; the last on 22 February. The most important was the fleet belonging to Edward Hillman, who also operated an airline. Based in Romford — the airliners operated

Omnibus Pool since 1914. This tied it in very closely with the LGOC and some of the vehicles it operated were actually owned by the General. This applied to its STLs. However few members of the public would have realised this for they wore Tilling livery and carried Tilling-designed bodies which, beyond being double-deck and totally enclosed, bore scarcely no other resemblance to the LGOC STL. The first Tilling STL predated the first LGOC STL by three months, coming out in autumn 1932, and 17 were in service by the end of that year, leaving the remaining 63 to be produced between January and June 1933.

One of the most curious features of the first months of LT operation was that its buses carried the title 'General'. This was not because they had not got round to painting on the new title but because, for some reason, it was policy to use this title for new vehicles, ex-Thomas Tilling and other independents, even though the legal lettering proclaimed the owner as the LPTB.

Right:
The pioneer Leyland Cub, C1
working the 237 when
new. *Author's collection*

Below:
Bedford BD5 working from WA
garage on the 397. *Pamlin*

from Croydon — 300 employees and 65 Gilford coaches came with the garage.

Production of STLs continued apace throughout 1934 as it would until September 1939. The earlier ones were virtually identical to those of the previous year, although there were some variations within the group, notably in the fitting of preselector gearboxes to many. They had more powerful, secondhand petrol engines, removed from 1931 era LTs. These were replaced on the LTs by diesel engines, but 11 of the next run of STLs had diesel engines (of a smaller size than those on the LTs).

The first of what we can reasonably define as the standard STL, No 609, took up work from Hanwell garage in November, 1934. Not only was the diesel engine now standard but the body was extensively redesigned. Gone was the previous flat front and in its stead was a most elegant, gently sloping, totally modern one. Internally the design was equally well thought out and lightweight, tubular aluminium framed seats, scarcely different to those still familiar in Routemasters, were introduced on some later buses of this batch. An anachronism was the absence of a cab door, insisted upon by the Metropolitan Police, and a generally pretty primitive set up inside the cab with no instruments and a bulb horn.

A very different batch of STLs, Nos 1044–55, entered service in April and May, 1934. Although only 12 in number they became quite celebrated and lasted with LT for almost 20 years. They were front entrance, lowbridge buses with all-metal bodies of MCW provincial type design built at Weymann's Addlestone factory — in their final years some would operate from Addlestone garage. However they were

intended to work from Godstone on the 410, Reigate
to Bromley route and this they did until 1950.
Handsomely appointed inside, with a sliding door,
they were popular with both passengers and
enthusiasts. Like many other country buses at the time
they were at first known only by the registration
numbers.

Four buses which AEC hoped would revolutionise
LT's attitude to the double-decker, but didn't,
entered service in 1934. These were Q2-5, Q1 being
a single-decker which had been operating since
1932. The Q, with its side-mounted engine, full
front, entrance ahead of the front wheels and
smooth, streamlined appearance, was indeed a bus
for the future and when compared with the NS,
several hundred of which were still at work in
London, it showed what enormous strides had been
made in bus design in 11 years. Indeed one cannot
think of any comparable period in the history of the
motorbus where there had been such obvious
progress. Q2/3 had front entrance 56 seat Metro-
Cammell bodies which, except for minor features
bore little resemblance to the STL, while Q4/5 had
similar looking Weymann bodies, but with the
important difference of a central entrance and
staircase and power operated sliding doors. The first
two were painted red and soon became a familiar

Above:
The lower deck interior of Country Area Q double-
decker, looking towards the rear. *Topical*

Right:
Fleet Street in 1934. An LNER N1 tank is crossing the
bridge below St Pauls whilst there are at least 11
buses in the picture, NSs, STs, LTs and STLs. *LT*

sight in central London, taking up work, after a brief
period in the suburbs, on the 52 Victoria to Mill Hill.
Q4/5 were painted green and were sent to work the
406 between Kingston and Redhill. In the summer of
1937 Q2/3 were repainted green and were banished to
the country and with the outbreak of war all four were
taken out of service, there being no resources to keep
such experimental vehicles on the road. LT does not
in any case seem to have had much enthusiasm for the
double-deck Q, although, as we shall see, it
successfully operated the single-deck version in both
Central and Country Areas and as a Green Line
coach. Many of the double-deck Qs features were to
be eventually taken up by the bus industry but the
vehicles themselves were sold after the war (except
for Q3 damaged in an air raid and broken up) and
worked for a little longer with their new owners.

Only one new single-decker entered London's vast fleet in 1934. This was a Leyland Cub, a forward control design and the smallest in that firm's vast range of passenger vehicles. Numbered C1 it seated 20 passengers and was painted red and sent to work from Hornchurch garage, being transferred to the Country Area in 1935 and painted green. Originally fitted with a petrol engine, it was given a Perkins diesel one the following year. The neat, well proportioned body was designed and built at Chiswick, being instantly recognisable as such, a miniature version of standard London practice of the time.

The Underground, like other areas of the LT empire, was biding its time in 1934, waiting for what was shortly to come. On the District Line a new station was opened at Upminster Bridge in December.

1935

In 1935 LT unveiled its New Works Programme. Britain was still deep in the Depression which followed the 1929 Wall Street crash and although the British government was nothing like as courageous or enterprising as the Roosevelt administration in the USA in attempting to alleviate unemployment and re-start the economy, it did provide a modest amount of investment for public works and it guaranteed the £40 million loan which LT and the main line railway companies needed. The latter were involved for part of what was planned was the extension of the underground system out into the suburbs to the east and west either parallel to or over the tracks of the GWR and the LNER. We will look at each of these schemes as they were completed.

Equally important, and perhaps of more immediate general impact, was the announcement of the end of London's tramway network. With hindsight it may seem that this was inevitable, for the tram had reached its heyday around the time of World War 1 and with the great increase in speed and, above all, reliability and flexibility of the motorbus, many systems had already closed. These, however, were relatively small and many of those serving the great cities, Glasgow, Liverpool, Leeds and Sheffield in particular, were being re-equipped with fast, comfortable, streamlined cars and sometimes allowed to operate, in the suburbs, over reserved tracks. They seemed to have a future

and it is possible that if the Felthams and LCC No 1 had been given a chance to prove their worth, that the tram's extinction in London would have at least been postponed. To have expected the reprieve to have lasted until the 1980s and the revival of Light Rail is clearly a pipe dream for only Blackpool kept its trams operating through the 1960s and 1970s, but I am suggesting that the demise of the London tram might not have happened as early as it did.

Nevertheless LT considered that the trams had sufficient time left for 1,000 of them, the entire former LCC E1 class in fact, to be rebuilt, although by August 1935 when the official announcement was made, this had been reduced to 250. In the event even this proved too optimistic, only 154 being rebuilt, including four of the relatively modern HR2 cars and four equally modern ex-Croydon Corporation ones, these being virtually identical to the LCC E1. They were given new roller blind route and number indicators recessed into the panelling, flush fitting sides, windscreens, while internally, and most important of all, for the passenger, there were new ceiling panels, neat little bell pushes instead of the old ones which one struck with one's fist rather like attempting to wallop the bell on a fairground try-your-strength machine, chromium-plated hand and grab rails, linoleum instead of wooden slatted floors, and new upholstered seats upstairs. The result was a very neat looking car and it was only a pity that more could not have been so treated.

It was not the motorbus which replaced the tram throughout the 1930s, but the trolleybus. It might well have been that LT, if it had been starting from scratch, would have gone straight over to the diesel bus and there is evidence to suggest that it regarded the trolleybus only as an intermediate stage. However it wasn't starting from scratch, and although many of the tramcars and their tracks were worn out, the electrical equipment and infrastructure wasn't and could be used by the trolleys.

The first tram replacement scheme took place on 27 October 1935 when further former London United routes (many had already gone in 1931) in west London were replaced by trolleybus routes 657 Hounslow — Shepherd's Bush, and 667 Hampton Court — Hammersmith. Shortly afterwards, across the other side of London, on Sunday 10 November route 698 began operating between Bexleyheath and Woolwich, followed 14 days later by the 696 from Woolwich to Dartford. The vehicles, operating from a brand new depot at Bexleyheath, were chiefly short-wheelbase B2 class 60 seaters, although, as traffic increased, standard 70 seaters became the norm. The standard London trolleybus, closely based on No 62, the prototype of 1934, was a classic design, elegant and comfortable, and ahead of its time in many respects so that it never really looked dated, even when more than 20 years old. It did not, surprisingly, bear much resemblance to the current standard

motorbus, the STL, not even in matters of livery —
beyond a basic red — and route indicators, a
reflection that the trolleybus department of LT was
under the control of ex-tramway men who had their
own ideas and were allowed to pursue them. Trams
continued to operate as far as Abbey Wood and trams
and trolleybuses ran side by side, for part of the way
sharing the same wiring. A unique feature of this
stage was the part replacement of the trams by a
Country Area green bus route, 480.

Before the year was out a third tram replacement
scheme was completed. On 8 December more 60-
seater trolleys began working roughly half way
between the two previous schemes, from West
Croydon to Sutton Green, the 654 replacing South
MET route 7.

Production of new single-deck buses to replace the
motley collection inherited by the Country Area got
under way during 1935. The main batch of Leyland
Cubs, C2-75, began to enter service in the spring. At

the same time 100 full size single-deckers arrived from the AEC works at Southall. This surprised nobody, but much less expected was the fact that they were fitted with bodies by the Birmingham Railway Carriage and Wagon Co: truly remarkable was their layout, for they were side-engined Qs. This was far and away the biggest order AEC had received for the type. The body seated 37 passengers, soon reduced to 35 when the seats beside the driver's cab were removed to aid visibility. Although incorporating many standard LPTB features, there was a slight slope along the roofline from front to back. Designated 4Q4 they served London well and despite being of such an experimental nature, I remember them still working from Reigate and Dorking garages well after the war in the early 1950s.

The half-cab body for a forward control chassis also appeared in 1935, but none of the 43 new Weymann bodies went on new chassis. Twelve went on early AEC Regals, to be used briefly as Green Line coaches, while the remaining 31 went on even older, and outdated, AEC Reliance buses.

The Country Area continued to set the pace as far as innovation was concerned and its first standard STLs, Nos 959–1043 and 1056–9, which went into service from February 1935, had front entrances. In this they were following on from the lowbridge Godstone STLs, and elsewhere, Midland Red for example, front-entrance double-deckers were in production. Nevertheless the open rear platform was vastly more common and would remain so until rear engines and one-man operation came in some 25 years later. The thinking was that the front entrance, with a door, had proved successful in rural areas; unfortunately these standard STLs had no door, the Chiswick engineers claiming that they had nevertheless designed a draught free layout. Experience soon proved they hadn't. The front entrance STLs, coded 10STL6, seated only 48 passengers, the eight missing seats downstairs giving way to racks for luggage and parcels with which it was presumed the country folk of Romford, Slough, Sutton, et al, were usually encumbered, to say nothing of the straws behind their ears. A second batch of front-entrance STLs (1464-1513) began entering service in July 1936. Outwardly similar to the earlier ones, in fact they had Weymann metal-framed bodies. All 139 spent all their lives in the Country Area, working from numerous garages, so that they became a familiar sight on many routes for 15 years or more. Whenever we ventured out into the country from Croydon, I always tried to persuade my father to wait for one of these distinctive vehicles which operated from practically all of the many garages which sent green buses to Croydon. I don't think this included Godstone, which was rather curious given that it was the very first London Country garage to receive front-entrance double-deckers — the lowbridge Weymann version for the 410.

A curious one-off version of the STL appeared in November 1935. This was STL857. At that time, streamlining was all the rage — think of Gresley's 'A4' Pacifics built that year to haul the 'Silver Jubilee' — so STL857 had a full front, an ornamental grille concealing the radiator, and a rakishly inclined profile. It was renumbered into a class of its own, STF, at the end of the year, but remained unique and unloved, and was soon rebuilt, in 1938, with a standard STL half cab and normal radiator. Transferred to the chassis of STL1167 in 1939, the body was scrapped in 1950.

A feature we all take for granted as having been around as long as the bus itself is the fixed stop. In fact before the days of the LPTB a London bus would stop anywhere along its route if requested, just like a taxi. Trams and trolleys had always had fixed stops but the practice was only extended to the buses in 1935, initially between Euston Road and Seven Sisters, Tottenham, and soon to central London; the familiar stop, whether request or compulsory, has scarcely changed since.

On the Underground a series of experimental tube trains were put into service on the Piccadilly Line and extensively tested before orders for the production units were placed. The biggest step forward was in the mounting of all equipment below the floor. Advanced technology made this possible, allowing some 15 per cent increase in passenger capacity. Four six-car trains were built, three of them with streamlined fronts, giving them a startling appearance, which nowadays seems to have a very art deco feel about it. The fourth train had a flat front, with curved roof ends. This proved to be

Left:
Rehabilitated E1R car No 1384 seen in Battersea in postwar days. *LT*

Right:
Boarding short-wheelbase trolleybus No 90 at the Crystal Palace terminus of the 654. *LT*

rather more practical as there was after all little need for streamlining on a train which seldom reached a speed in excess of 35mph and that mostly in a tunnel!

New stock was also built for the surface lines, although this was essentially a repeat of an existing design, the L stock of 1932. Designated M class, there were 14 motor cars and 14 trailers from the Birmingham Railway Carriage & Wagon Co, and 26 trailers from another Birmingham firm, Metro-Cammell. The most remarkable feature of the M stock was that it was fitted with clerestory roofs. In this it may be said to have done no more than followed Underground traditions but for all that this was pretty remarkable. One thinks of the clerestory as being an essentially late Victorian and Edwardian feature and the Underground carriages of 1935 were the very last British standard gauge vehicles to be fitted with them.

The rebuilding of Leicester Square station was completed in 1935 with a circular booking hall and what was claimed to be the longest escalator in the world serving the Piccadilly Line.

1936

The replacement of London's trams proceeded apace in 1936, both north and south of the river, east and west of the City and the West End. First, on 9 February the 654 trolleybus route was extended from Croydon, past Crystal Palace's football ground, through Anerley and up the steep hill to Crystal Palace itself, the fierce 1 in 9 necessitating the fitting of run-back brakes to the B1 trolleys, Nos 64-93,

which operated the route out of Sutton depot. The period when the famous Crystal Palace was served by trolleybuses lasted only a matter of months for, on the night of 30 November 1936, it burned down. Crowds came from all over London to watch the spectacle, although, truth to tell, they hardly needed to for the glow from Norwood Heights was visible for many miles around. Despite the many, many such fires which were to rage during the Blitz, the night the Crystal Palace burned down is still spoken of, not only by those elderly local inhabitants who can remember it, but by later generations to whom the spectacle has been recounted. Indeed when I taught at a secondary school in South Norwood in the late 1960s black pupils who had been born in the Caribbean knew all about the great burning of the Crystal Palace more than 30 years earlier. During the fire, and for some time afterwards, the 654s had to turn round at the bottom of the hill in Penge.

The next tram replacement was the ex-LUT route 89 from Hammersmith to Acton which became the trolleybus route 660 on 5 April. Curiously this lasted only until 5 July when it and former MET tram routes 66 and 68 which linked Acton and Canons Park were replaced by trolleybus route 666 which ran from Hammersmith to Edgware via Acton, Harlesden and Cricklewood. However the 660 reappeared later that summer on 2 August, this time running between Hammersmith and North Finchley. The 645 from Edgware to North Finchley was also introduced, ex-MET tram routes 45 and 60 disappearing. A number of the C class trolleys allocated these routes from Stonebridge depot had distinctive spats fitted over their rear wheels, a unique feature on a London trolleybus. Before August was out yet another section of the one-time MET network serving northwest London had gone, the 62 and 64s being replaced by 662 from Paddington Green to Sudbury and 664 Paddington Green to Edgware.

Next to go was a former LCC route in the northeast suburbs; the 73 which ran from the Royal Albert Docks to Wanstead Park. There was no direct replacement, the 101 bus, which covered most of the route, being strengthened. Staying in that part of London the 23 tram route was replaced on 18 October by the 623 trolleybus which ran from Woodford, Napier Arms to Manor House.

On 15 November the most westerly point in London reached by trams saw them no more when route 7 from Shepherd's Bush Green was replaced by the 607

trolleybus. Finally for 1936 the companion 655 trolleybus route came into operation on 13 December, replacing tram 55 and running between Hammersmith and Hanwell, being extended to Acton during weekday rush hours. The 7 had been worked by London's most modern trams, the Felthams. Unlike the other ex-LUT cars these were far too good to scrap and so they were sent south of the river to Telford Avenue which was the only depot with sufficient clearance to accommodate them.

The loss suffered by the citizens of west London was a gain for southerners. Stanley Collins, a driver at Telford Avenue, in his biography *The Wheels used to talk to us* (Tallis Publishing, 1977) writes: 'We thought they were fine, just loved to get out and drive one of them . . . I can't praise them too much . . . At first the passengers used to let the Standards go by

Above:
Former MET A type bogie tram No 2460 working route 66 shortly before withdrawal. *Author's collection*

Left:
Leaning back STL484 of Chalk Farm garage stands at the terminus of route 3 beside the Crystal Place shortly before it was burnt down.

Right:
Feltham No 2190 in typical southside territory working the 10 from Southwark to Tooting Broadway. *IAL*

just so that they could ride on a Feltham.' They did indeed, for I had the good luck to travel to school every day on Feltham routes 16 or 18, and I would always wait for one if I had the time. I don't think I've ever cared quite as much for any public transport vehicle as I did for the Felthams. They ran beautifully, cruising for long distances with the power off, putting every other type of tram to shame, and never rattled like buses did. Their fame spread far and wide and I once had a discussion on their merits in the Paris Transport Museum with a Frenchman who remembered them with affection. I am sure they will be there in spirit when the trams run once again in Croydon, their ghosts triumphant.

What many consider the truly classic and most handsome version of the STL appeared in October 1936. This was the 'roof number box bus'. All the remaining standard STLs, 360 in all, would be built to this design. Its fame spread far beyond London for Dinky Toys chose it as the basis for the first reasonably accurate mass produced model bus and even today no swap meet or decent model shop is without several, sometimes dozens, on offer. Indeed I bought one of the early postwar ones, in need of repainting but otherwise undamaged, last Saturday, for £9, which is roughly equivalent to what it would have cost when new. The first of the batch finished off the CXX registration numbers, then came DGX and DLU and it is the latter which is perhaps most associated with these buses, for most of the last survivors belonged to this group.

Single-deckers continued to arrive in large numbers during 1936. A most interesting class was the Inter-Station Cubs, strictly speaking one-and-a-half-deckers. Eight were built to work between the main line stations and they were given very large luggage lockers at the rear with a raised seating section above. They were painted in a delightful blue and yellow livery with black roofs and were numbered C106-113. The revolutionary Q class continued to find far more favour in London than elsewhere and two further

Above:
Yours for a penny, Green Line Q195.

versions entered service in 1936. Q106–185, coded 5Q5, were designed as 37-seat buses, 53 for the Central Area, the remaining 27 for the Country Area. They were the only ones to have an entrance forward of the front wheels, level with the driver, and might easily have been used as OMO buses had they been a generation later. Fitted with Park Royal bodies they were probably the best looking of the London Qs, anticipating features perpetuated in the RT, and still looked modern when they were replaced by the RF class in 1952-3.

Q189–238, coded 6Q6, were 32-seat coaches, also with Park Royal bodies. The entrance, with its

sliding door, returned to a position behind the front wheels. Because of the underfloor engine there had to be longitudinal seats over the front wheel arches for six passengers in all, not ideal for a coach, but they nevertheless worked hard. Many went to Hertford and Guildford garages, returning there after the war.

1936 saw the first appearance of a completely new, conventional single-decker. Fifty Regals with Weymann 30-seat bodies, T403-452 went into Green Line service. Coded 9T9 they had a rather curious frontal appearance in that a gaiter, or collar, surrounded the radiator, the nearside headlamp was built into the bonnet and a bumper completed the somewhat clumsy effect. The rear four of the 30 seats were raised as were the two rearmost windows on each side.

1937

1937 saw a new double-deck class enter service, one which was to prove particularly popular with drivers, engineers and passengers. LT put in an order to Leyland for 100 Titan TD4s to be fitted with Leyland bodies. In order to make the bodies resemble the STL, one of this class was lent to the Lancashire firm and the result was a bus which looked very like the standard Chiswick product, although enthusiasts had great fun spotting the differences. The standard Leyland radiator was, of course, fitted and the class was designated STD. A roof number box layout was chosen and the registration numbers were DLU 311–410. The final 10 were originally fitted with torque converters but these reverted to a standard clutch and gearbox in 1939. Sent to Hendon garage

the STDs were a familiar sight on the 13 and the 113 and consequently frequently featured in pictures of Oxford Street in the period 1937–52.

A very different Leyland put into service in December was TF1. This was a 34-seat coach with an underfloor engine and a cab of quite extraordinary aspect. In theory there was no need to retain the half-cab layout — it had been abandoned in the Q class — but as the front wheels were in a conventional position instead of being set back, it was.

In February the last, and least successful, of the Q class, was taken into stock. Q188 looked splendid, being a six-wheel Park Royal-bodied double-deck coach, but it was underpowered and, so it is said, met with trade union opposition. In the event it never ran in Green Line service and did not carry passengers until the following year. It then did a brief, two-year stint as a Country Area bus before being withdrawn at the outbreak of war. It never worked again in LT service, being sold in 1946 for service along the shores of the Clyde west of Glasgow where it seems to have found the climate much to its liking.

In complete contrast was the Underground stock which entered service on the District and Metropolitan lines in 1937. Although now all withdrawn, these trains were for decades, along with the tube stock introduced the following year, the epitome of modern travel below the streets of London and were, like the standard trolleybus, the STL and the 10T10 Green Line coach, a classic design which put LT in the very forefront of urban transport worldwide. They were known as the Metadyne, on account of a new system of control pioneered by Metropolitan Vickers and tried out in 1934, or O and P stock. In all the 573 carriages, which included 205 Q stock, introduced in 1938 to work with older vehicles, had transformed the Underground system by the time the last entered

Above left:
Inter-station Cub C108 and a lady in a hurry meet at Victoria.

Left:
A scene in Chiswick High Road with B3 class trolleybus No 473 on the 655, whilst a shortly-to-be-withdrawn Green Line Leyland Tiger overtakes STL1805 heading for Highgate. *LT*

Right:
One of a fleet of 25 luxury coaches being built at Addlestone . . . when finished these will be the very latest in luxury travel and five of them will be fitted with wireless which will 'pick up the world'. An LTC under construction. *Topical*

Left:
Metropolitan Railway 4-4-4T at Chorley Wood with the down Pullman express for Verney Junction.
Real Photos

Left:
Maunsell-designed former Metropolitan Railway 2-6-4T passing Chorley Wood with a down passenger train. *Real Photos*

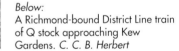

Below:
A Richmond-bound District Line train of Q stock approaching Kew Gardens. *C. C. B. Herbert*

service in 1941. They looked very different to anything which had gone before, being completely flush-sided, the windows using rebated glass. The lower panels were flared outwards, a feature said to have been devised to prevent would-be passengers clinging to the outside after the automatic doors had been closed. It has never been deemed necessary for later stock to be so equipped and one wonders whether it wasn't simply there for stylistic reasons. Whatever, it resulted in a highly distinctive carriage. Tried out between High Street Kensington and Putney Bridge from September 1937, the O stock began work on the Hammersmith and City line in December.

Meanwhile work was proceeding on extending the system and building, or rebuilding, many stations, all showing LT's concern with aesthetics, with the result that a number of them are now listed buildings. In central London, Earls Court was rebuilt to cater for the new exhibition hall; the previous year Eastcote, on the Metropolitan Line, had been given a new station built into an accompanying row of streets, all to the same style. The extensions to the Central, Northern and Bakerloo lines were all going ahead. Acton Central Overhaul Shops was rebuilt, its capacity raised from 3,000 to 5,000 cars. Neasden running sheds were also rebuilt and one spin-off from this was the transfer of LT's largest and most modern steam engines, chiefly used to haul passenger trains beyond Rickmansworth, to the LNER. These included the four G class 0-6-4Ts, the eight H class 4-4-4Ts and the six K class 2-6-4Ts. All inherited from the Metropolitan Railway, they were a particularly fine looking group of locomotives. Their subsequent careers were short and ignominious, ending far away from their old home.

New locomotives which entered service in 1937 were LT's first battery ones. Constructed from redundant tube cars, these service vehicles were 55ft long, weighed 56 tons, had a maximum speed of 30mph and were designed to run off either the live rail or from their banks of accumulators.

Heavy inroads were made into the tram systems of east London and elsewhere in 1937. First to go, in January, was the 85, a former Walthamstow Corporation route, which was replaced by the 685. This trolleybus route was extended over the years and eventually ran from the Crooked Billet in

Walthamstow to Silvertown, with some peak hour journeys even reaching the river at North Woolwich. There was a wait of nearly six months before a whole collection of Docklands trams were replaced in June, the 69, 87, 97, 97A, 99 and 99A, all disappearing, while the 55 and 57 were cut back. Stratford Broadway, one of the busiest tram meeting places, now became equally popular with the trolleybus. The 669 ran to Canning Town, while the 687, 697 and 699 (the highest number of all London's trolleybus routes) all connected Chingford Mount and the Victoria and Albert Docks, by various routes.

Over in West London, in September, the 32 from Clapham Common to Chelsea Bridge was replaced by an existing bus route, the revised 137, while four days later, on 12 September, a much more extensive replacement saw a further Croydon tram route, the 30, disappear, to be replaced by one of London's longest trolleybus routes, the 630, which extended just over 14 miles from West Croydon to the quirkily named 'Near Willesden Junction'. The rest of this stage consisted of cutbacks rather than complete withdrawals. The 12 tram route now operated between Wandsworth and London Bridge; a new trolleybus route, 612, served Battersea and Mitcham; the 6 was cut back from Mitcham to run between Tooting and Southwark; the 14 and 31 ceased to run between Battersea and Wandsworth; and the 26 and 28 were seen no more west of Clapham Junction, safe from Red Indian ambush. New trolleybus routes were the rush-hour-only 626 Clapham Junction-Acton and the 628 Clapham Junction-Harlesden; Craven Park. Wandsworth depot now operated both trolleybus and trams and would continue to do so until October 1950.

On the same day, 12 September, one of the two London No 1 tram routes disappeared, along with 1A, linking Stratford with East Ham and Upton Park respectively. Almost at the other numerical end, routes 95 (Wanstead Flats-Canning Town) and 95A (Wanstead Flats-Upton Park) were also withdrawn, all these being replaced by an extension of the 685 trolleybus route to Canning Town and a new Stratford Circular, 689. After only a few months anti-clockwise, 689s were renumbered 690.

On the single-deck bus (or rather coach) front the year ended with a surprising new class, a petrol-engined six-wheeler. This was the LTC, comprising 24 very imposing looking Weymann-bodied private hire vehicles. Curiously they were slightly shorter than the 9T9s. Both petrol engines, reconditioned Mk 1 Comets removed from LTs, and the four-wheel bogie, virtually identical to that used on the trolleybuses, were said to have been chosen to give the smoothest possible ride.

Below:
The caption for this Keystone picture taken on 5 August 1937 reads 'Poor kiddies left Canning Town this morning for a day's outing in coaches (sic) as the guests of the Transport Workers' Children's Outing Fund.'

Yet another variation of the STL completes our look at 1937. The only Thames road crossings downriver from Tower Bridge, apart from the Woolwich Free Ferry, were the Blackwall and Rotherhithe tunnels. Neither had been designed with the heavy motor traffic of the 1930s in mind and there was limited clearance, particularly at Blackwall. Specially modified NSs, mostly still with solid tyres, operated the tunnel routes, and they were now past their sell-by date. So 40 new STLs, with reinforced tyres, heavily domed roofs and tapered rear ends entered service in March and April. By 1938 all were concentrated at Athol Street garage, Poplar, where they stayed for the rest of their careers. Because of the roof modifications the number indicator at the front reverted to a position between the decks. 1937 was the last year of the NS in passenger service, as it was of the numerically very small LS class of six-wheelers, immediate predecessor of the LT. The last NS, No 1974, came out of service on 30 November. Both NS and LS with their high clearance, squat radiators and various other features, by this date looked archaic. However a number of the NSs survived as staff canteens until the early 1950s. I remember one, No 2295, serving at Chelsham garage alongside brand new RTs; how I wish I had started taking photographs back then. Four LSs became breakdown tenders and these lasted until 1951. One NS, No 1995, was preserved by LT, and I *did* get a picture of this when it first went on display at the Museum of British Transport at Clapham in the late 1960s in exactly the condition it was in when taken out of service on the 29, and before it was spruced up and repainted.

1938

The last full year of peace was perhaps LT's finest, when it was innovating at full throttle, sweeping away trams with smooth, silent trolleybuses, modernising both surface and tube railway lines with fleets of the most up-to-date trains. By this time the hotchpotch of vehicles it had inherited for its Green Line services had almost entirely given way to a series of handsome, comfortable new coaches. Also in 1938, although the STL was still in full production and still being refined, there appeared the first of its successors — a class which would eventually number 4825, with another 2,131 very similar Leyland buses.

The 1938 Tube stock would eventually number no less than 1,221 vehicles. Based on the flat-fronted experimental unit of 1935, the biggest innovation introduced with these trains was that all the electrical equipment and traction motors were beneath the floor,

Below:
Former MET H-class bogie car No 2217 of 1910-2 at the Bruce Grove terminus of route 19.

Left:
A bespatted C class trolleybus does its best to obscure the soon to be redundant tram lines at King's Cross. It is working route 517 North Finchley-Holborn introduced on 6 March 1938. STLs and LTs in the background. *LT*

Above:
1938 Tube stock.

allowing a significant increase in capacity. Like the surface stock of the previous year, the new tube trains presented a very smooth, albeit rather more conventional, outline. Metro-Cammell built 644 DM (Driving motor) cars and 107 NDM (non-driving motors) cars, while BRCW built the remaining 99 NDM cars and 271 trailer cars. They entered service on the Northern and Bakerloo lines, 58 of the 1927 trailers being converted to work with the 1938 stock on the latter. Because the LNER retained ownership of the track over which the Northern Line was extended to High Barnet and Mill Hill, some of the stock actually belonged to the company, although the only indication of this was a plate inscribed 'Property of the LNER' on the underframes. There would seem to be no record of it attempting to attach itself to a Gresley Pacific and hightailing for the Scottish border.

While on matters electrical the demise has to be recorded of 23 more tram routes and their replacement by 20 trolleybus and one motorbus ones. The biggest inroads were into the north London routes and for the first time a number of the LCC's standard tram, the E1, a class which exceeded 1,000, was taken out of service. Between 1926 and 1930, the year the final 50 of the class appeared, they had been modernised with upholstered seating and various other improvements, although the fitting of windscreens was not completed until 1940, many being withdrawn without them.

First to go, on 6 February, were two local Barking routes: 91 and 93, being replaced by the 691 from Barkingside to Barking Broadway and the 693 Chadwell Heath-Barking Broadway. There was also the 692 from Newbury Park to Chadwell Heath which ran on Saturdays, but not for long, disappearing the next year. A minor withdrawal later that month was the 37 from Wood Green to Alexandra Palace, although it was of considerable historical interest in that it marked the end of single-deck tram operation in London — that is until the late 1990s! The 241A motorbus route replaced it at first, then a few months later an extension of the 233. There were plans to incorporate the LNER's Alexandra Palace branch into the Underground network but these never

Left:
Green Line T522.

Below:
Victoria in 1938 with almost as many
STLs, LTs and one STD as people,
with a leavening of taxis, one bicycle
and a Rolls-Royce.

materialised and the line eventually faded away after
the war. Alexandra Palace, in many ways north
London's answer to Crystal Palace, set up on the
heights above Wood Green and the LNER line out of
King's Cross, was at this time home to the world's
first regular TV service and when its 50th anniversary
was celebrated in 1986 in a delightfully nostalgic

Jack Rosenthal documentary drama, the one and only
preserved 10T10 Green Line coach played a starring
role.

1938 saw the introduction of these fine vehicles,
266 of them. A modified version of the 9T9 with a
larger engine, they possessed none of that breed's
slight ungainliness. They became the vehicles which

Above:
The Old Car Body Shop of Acton works with 1927 and 1938 tube stock being attended to.

everyone of my generation associated with the exalted standards of appearance and comfort which epitomised Green Line services in the late 1930s and 1940s. T453-602 originally seated 30 passengers, T603-718 seated 34. The AEC diesel engine was rated at 8.8 litres; the body was built by LT at Chiswick.

Yet another innovative single-decker entered service in January 1938. This was CR1, a Leyland Cub with a rear engine. Painted green it was sent to work at St Albans. In appearance there were similarities with TF1.

STLs, having replaced all the NSs, were now being used to oust the Central Area TD class, Leyland Titans absorbed in 1933 from various sources. By June 1938 production of STLs temporarily ceased, with no more appearing till the following year.

One TD body found further use for a short while, a use which gave it a permanent place in the history of the motorbus. The Dodson body of TD111 was put on to a brand new chassis and on 13 July 1938 the bus was taxed ready for use and given the fleet number ST1140. It was sent to Hanwell garage (later known as Southall) — the traditional home of experimental buses at this time — and took up work there. The

registration number was EYK 396 and it was, of course, the prototype RT.

Now back to the tram replacement programme. In March no less than nine routes disappeared, although one, the Sundays only 11X, was to be revived. Those permanently withdrawn were the 9, 13, 17, 19, 21, 35A, 39A and 51. The new trolleybus routes were the 517/617 and 521/621 North Finchley-Holborn Circus, 609 Barnet-Moorgate and the 651 Barnet-Golders Green and Cricklewood motorbus route 134 was strengthened. The conversion of Finchley depot meant that the MET Felthams were redundant and they travelled south to join their former LUT brothers at Telford Avenue.

May saw the end of tram routes 29, 39, 41 and 41EX, being replaced by the 625 Wood Green-Walthamstow, the 629 Enfield-Tottenham Court Road and the 641 Winchmore Hill-Moorgate. Next, in July, the 3, 5, 7 and 15 disappeared, the 513/613 Hampstead Heath-Holborn Circus, the 615 Parliament Hill Fields-Moorgate and the 639 Hampstead Heath-Moorgate taking over.

In October trams disappeared from their northernmost London outpost, Waltham Cross, the 59 and 79 being replaced by the 659 from Waltham Cross to Holborn Circus and the 679 from Waltham Cross (Sundays only) and Ponders End (weekdays) to Smithfield. The 679 soon saw a good deal more of Waltham Cross, being extended there on Monday to Friday rush hours and all day on Saturdays at the next tram replacement in November. This saw the end of the 27 and the 49A, while the 49 was cut back. New routes were the 627 Tottenham Court Road-Edmonton and the 649 Stamford Hill-Ponders End.

1939

We noted the appearance of the first RT, heavily disguised, in 1938, but it was in April 1939 when the complete bus, with its new body, was eventually finished. As befitted such a landmark it was inspected and modified in several matters, notably livery, before it was officially shown to the press on 13 July. Happily RT1 still exists, at least the body does — the chassis being a postwar one — and is often seen at rallies, so its appearance will be familiar to many and there is no need to describe it in detail. But it must be said that both internally and externally new heights had been reached and there are those who think they have never since been excelled. Here and there one could see a family likeness to the latest STLs, but there was much that was different, the four bay windows, the lower radiator, the superb interior where the minutest attention had been paid to every detail. Probably the feature which most appealed to LPTB drivers was the sliding cab door. In July RT1 was sent to Chelverton Road garage, Putney and on Wednesday 9 August it entered passenger service, on the 22 from Putney Common to Homerton.

The arrival of RT1 did not immediately signal the end of the STL because what was intended to be a final batch, Nos 2516–2647, had been ordered the previous year, STL2647 entering service in September 1939 from Alperton garage. Given FJJ and FXT registration marks, they were instantly recognisable from previous batches by their longer radiators and wheel discs. There were improvements to the chassis and there was a direct injection engine which resulted in improved fuel consumption and easier starting. For the first time standard rear entrance STLs went direct into Country Area service: 39 were painted green and sent southeastwards to Northfleet and Dartford. The

arrival of these STLs meant the end of the oil-engined TD class in both Central and Country areas and, more significantly, the first withdrawals of the Tilling STs. By this date the oldest of these buses was into its 10th year, about the average life of their predecessors, the NS class, and had not the war intervened, many more STs and LTs would no doubt have been earmarked for early withdrawal.

The two unorthodox, experimental single-deckers of 1937-8, the TF and CR, were both considered to have justified production orders from Leyland and so TF2-88 and CR2-49 arrived during 1939. TF2-13 were touring coaches with a generous allocation of curved glass in the canted roof panels and a sliding central section, while the remainder went into Green Line service from Luton, St Albans, Grays and Dorking, enabling the last of the pre-1933 petrol-engined Ts to be demoted to buses. Both had conventional cabs, a design to which TF1 was altered. The CR class, Nos 2–49, were also somewhat different in appearance to the prototype, these having straight sides instead of a stepped waistline. By the time they had arrived so had the war and, although they went into limited service, they were not trouble free and by 1941 all were in store.

Production of trolleybuses by both Leyland and AEC continued apace and was unaffected by the outbreak of war. Three new routes appeared in February, the 643 Wood Green-Holborn Circus, the 647 Stamford Hill-London Docks and the 683 Stamford Hill-Moorgate, while the 649 was extended from Stamford Hill to Liverpool Street. Tram routes 43, 47, 49, 49EX, 71, 75 and 83 disappeared. A month later the 53 was replaced by the 653 which ran in a big loop from Tottenham Court Road to Aldgate via Stamford Hill.

In June most of the tram routes serving Leyton and the approaches to Epping Forest, the 55, 55EX, 57, 57EX, 81 and 81EX disappeared, and the 31 was cut back from the Bakers Arms to Hackney. The trolley replacements were the 555 Bloomsbury-Leyton Green and Downsell Road, the 557 Liverpool Street-Chingford Mount and the 581 Bloomsbury-Woodford (Napier Arms). The 687 was withdrawn between Leyton and Chingford Mount. A week after the outbreak of war the 77 was withdrawn and replaced by the 677 from West India Docks to Smithfield, while on Guy Fawkes' Day, which was certainly not celebrated, the 61 and 63 were replaced by the 661 from Aldgate to the Bakers Arms, Leyton and the 663 from Aldgate to Ilford. Finally on 10 December the 11 and 11EX were replaced by the 611 Highgate Village to Moorgate and the Sundays only 611EX Highgate Village-Islington Green. There was just one more replacement programme to go.

On the Underground the New Works Programme continued unabated. The Bakerloo Line reached

Left:
Former LCC E1 class tram No 1188, dating from 1908-9 and still without windscreens, heading for Smithfield on service 77. Both tram and route were withdrawn on 10 September 1939. *Author's collection*

Right:
Brand new STL2569, delivered to Hanwell Garage in March 1939, at London Bridge. *G. Robbins collection*

Stanmore and on 20 November the revised services, relieving the bottleneck north of Baker Street, began. Surfacing near Finchley Road, the Bakerloo tube trains operated an all-stations service to Wembley Park, while the Metropolitan ones, on separate tracks, ran non-stop to Wembley Park. In July the Northern Line reached East Finchley, taking over former LNER tracks, the 17-mile long tunnel from there to Morden, via the Bank, being at that time the longest in the world. Work was also completed on rebuilding stations in central London on the Piccadilly and Central lines, while the conversion of the Great Northern and City Line from the two current rails being outside the running ones to standard configuration was carried out.

From the foregoing it might seem the outbreak of war had little immediate effect on LT. This is quite untrue. Even before war was declared many buses were on war work carrying service personnel and others to their posts; all Green Line services ceased on Friday 1 September, the Tube lines under the Thames were temporarily closed and bus services substituted, and vast numbers of children were evacuated, taken by bus, tram and trolleybus to the stations where the main line trains were waiting for them.

Left:
Green Line passengers, September 1939.

Below:
RT1, as restored in 1979, its body mounted on a postwar chassis.

Yet normal life continued. Almost my earliest memory is of being taken by my parents on Sunday 3 September 1939, the day war was declared, for an outing by the river at Richmond. I was two years and two months old. We had travelled there by tram and Southern Railway electric train. It was a gloriously sunny day and I can remember waiting for the train home on Richmond station when the air raid sirens sounded. Most people expected instant aerial attack and terrible devastation and something of the panic must have conveyed itself to me, although I doubt if it came from my parents. My father had served throughout World War 1 as a driver in the Middle East; my mother's father had been killed at Gallipoli. Anyhow nothing happened, the train duly appeared and we eventually arrived home safely. Only last year, while visiting the local museum in Richmond the volunteer attendant, a native of the town who remembered the incident well, provided the sequel to the story. The sirens sounded because radar had picked up an aircraft approaching across the English Channel which seemed to be heading straight for the Richmond area. It transpired it was a British aeroplane coming back from France to the Vickers Works at Weybridge but such was the understandable nervousness that the alarm was sounded when it couldn't be identified instantly.

The blackout was imposed immediately, headlamps were masked and interior lights dimmed. This caused many problems and a number of accidents, and one attempt to alleviate some of the dangers was the painting of front mudguard edges in white, with a large white spot on the rear of motorbuses. Trolleybuses did not have the spot so that they could be distinguished and other trolleybus drivers would not attempt to overtake them. Trams had their fenders painted white.

Apart from the withdrawal of Green Line services — there was a temporary, partial restoration a little later — there were many service cuts right across LT and a number of smaller capacity vehicles were withdrawn, ranging from Dennis Darts to STs and front entrance STLs. The entire fleet of Tilling STs was taken out of service.

Left:
10T10 T708c converted to an ambulance; the driver wears a gasmask.

1940

For almost a year after the declaration of war the threatened aerial bombardment of London failed to materialise; the fall of France and the Dunkirk evacuation in June 1940 brought the Phoney War to an end. The first damage inflicted by enemy aircraft was on trolleybus wires at New Malden on 16 August. Initially, and perhaps rather unexpectedly, it was the rural and suburban areas south of the Thames which suffered, chiefly those near strategic targets, such as the Vickers aircraft factory at Weybridge which was badly damaged on 4 September. The first bomb fell on the City of London on 24 August and by the end of the month the Blitz on both suburbs and central London, particularly Docklands and the East End, north and south of the river, was at its height. The disruption and damage was immense. Tram and trolleybus services were particularly vulnerable, their tracks and wires being destroyed; often they could be diverted, but bus services suffered too. Nevertheless temporary tracks and overhead wiring were often set up in a very short time. Many vehicles were destroyed, and although in a number of instances crew and passengers were able to take shelter before a raid began, they weren't always so lucky and there were a number of deaths and a great many injuries. Vehicles were patched up and boarded-up windows became a common sight. Anti-blast netting, first with a small rectangle, later a little diamond left clear in the centre, was stuck on windows. With the perversity typical of people living in extreme conditions who nevertheless try to treat life as normally as possible, I

can remember how we complained about the inconvenience this caused, particularly the nasty yellow colour the glass turned, and we would always try, if possible, to sit beside a window which had not been so treated.

In some respects the damage to buses, trams, trolleys and trains was less than might have been expected, given the overall intensity of the Blitz, and seeing what happened to German cities in the later years of the war. But it has to be remembered that most of the raids took place at night; each evening the sirens would wail, I would be roused from my bed by my mother and we would sit under the stairs — my father would be out performing his warden duties — we would only use the Anderson shelter at the bottom of the garden if the raid seemed to be particularly intense and aimed at us personally. Most public transport had ceased to run and was off the streets and in garages and depots or dispersed in various locations. If bombs fell directly on these locations then of course vehicles were destroyed and it was here that most of the casualties took place.

It would take several pages to list all the damage to parked vehicles, but in the latter part of 1940 mention must be made of 10 Tilling STs written off at Leyton garage, 30 trams at Camberwell depot, four buses at Camberwell garage, eight trams at Abbey Wood, six at New Cross, 16 at Clapham and 53 buses and coaches at the former Thomas Tilling depot at Peckham. No less than 11 of the grand total of 12 of the virtually new TF touring coaches, Nos 2–8 and 10–13, were lost here, leaving TF9 — which was elsewhere — as the sole survivor for the next 12 years. There were many other examples of bodies being damaged beyond repair but the chassis surviving. The one trolleybus depot to suffer serious damage at this time, Bexleyheath, lost four trolleybus bodies but their chassis received new bodies from Weymann. Given that so many trolleybuses operated in East London, it was remarkable that they suffered much less than the motorbus and tram fleets.

Londoners took to tube stations at night to escape the bombing, unofficially and often chaotically at first, but soon on an organised basis. The Central Line tunnels beyond Liverpool Street, completed but not yet operational, were lived in day and night in some cases. However complete safety was not guaranteed even underground. On 14 October a bomb penetrated the Northern Line station at Balham, exploded and 68 people died. The line was not reopened for three months. There were other deaths on the tube but the District, Metropolitan and Circle lines were much more vulnerable, the worst incident being at Sloane Square station on 12 November when there were many deaths. I never used to pass through it, on our way to regular outings at South Kensington, without a shiver of apprehension.

Apart from war damage the fleet underwent a number of changes, not the least being that new vehicles continued to be delivered. The Green Line fleet of modern coaches, some 477 vehicles, had been converted in 1939 into ambulances. However some coaches had been released before the end of 1939 and took up Green Line service again. The Blitz brought about a reorganisation; cross-London services ceased, but nevertheless 33 routes were operating at the end of the year.

The final conversion to trolleybuses took part when the last east London trams disappeared on 9 June. Routes 65, 65EX, 67 and 67EX were replaced by the 565 Holborn Circus-East Ham, the 567, which led a

Below:
A scene at Golders Green in May 1940, a few weeks before the Blitz hit London. A 10T10 Green Line coach with white lines marking its passenger entrance passes two STLs, a former LGOC Central Area T stands in the station forecourt, a train of 1938 Tube stock crosses the bridge while two trolleybuses pass beneath it. *LT*

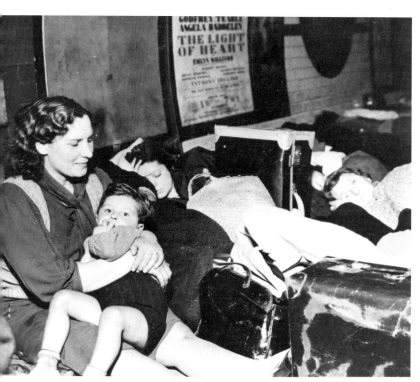

Left:
Sleeping in Piccadilly tube station. *LT*

Below:
The caption of this Fox Photo dated 12 September 1940, reads: 'This omnibus in South London was blown to pieces when hit by a bomb during yesterday evening's raid over London.' Hopefully the passengers and crew had reached the shelter on the opposite pavement in time. The route details of the damaged Tilling STL further up the road have been scratched out by the censor.

Right:
STL1988 negotiates a temporary crossing over a bomb crater, 7 December 1940. *Fox*

very complicated life style, running between Aldgate and West Ham Mondays to Fridays, Aldgate to Barking Broadway on Saturdays, and Smithfield to Poplar on Sundays, and finally the 665 Bloomsbury to Barking Broadway. Even after this new, trolleybuses continued to be delivered well into 1941. The only trams now seen north of the river, other than along the

Embankment, were the three Kingsway Subway routes — 31, 33, 35 — which penetrated some way into the northern suburbs, and the 34 which terminated at the unfashionable end of the King's Road, Chelsea.

Much the brightest spot in this chapter of many horrors was the arrival of the first production RTs, the first seven entering service from Chelverton Road,

Putney, on 2 January. Although generally referred to as the 'prewar RTs', this of course really only applies to RT1, but nevertheless they were built totally to prewar standards. Officially coded RT2, they were superficially very little different to RT1. 338 had been ordered, but clearly this was too optimistic under wartime conditions and production stopped with the delivery of the 150th chassis to Chiswick in May. The building of the bodies took much longer and many RTs were still waiting completion at the end of the year. Some of the later ones went to a new garage, opened on   20 March 1940. This was Gillingham Street (GM), situated just behind Victoria station and close to the elegant squares which typify the area south of Buckingham Palace Road. As the only garage in the West End it inevitably became one of the best known and was home over the years to many vehicles of especial distinction.

Frank Pick retired from LT in 1940. As chief executive from its creation he had headed what was described at the time as 'the world's finest integrated urban transport system' and in an article in the *Independent* newspaper in March 1995, Jonathan Glancey called him 'the greatest patron of the arts in Britain this century.' This remarkable man was well paid for his extraordinary achievements, £10,000 a year, 43 times that of a London bus driver who, as Jonathan Glancey pointed out, was 'among the best-paid workers in Britain'. The latter is a claim no one would make about a London bus driver in 1995.

1941

The Blitz continued unabated through the early months of 1941. Bank station was hit on 11 January and the road above it collapsed, causing traffic chaos for weeks. West Ham depot, newly converted from tram to trolleybus, was damaged in March and L2 class trolleybus No 1492 was destroyed, the only such occurrence during the Blitz. Croydon garage suffered terrible devastation, the worst in the entire LT area. The raid took place on Saturday 10 May and, ironically, it almost marked the end of the Blitz. Four staff were killed and 58 buses destroyed. Croydon, being an ex-Tilling garage, possessed an elderly fleet of petrol-engined vehicles mainly of Tilling and London General origin, but nevertheless LT could ill afford to lose them. I used to be slightly miffed that we had to make do with such antiques and I would have been perfectly happy if something rather more modern had been drafted in. No such luck, there was a whip round and by Monday morning some 50 odd General and Tilling STs from all over London had filled the breach. The former continued to provide the

Below:
A Bluebird LT negotiates the temporary bridge over the emergency staircases being erected at the bombed Bank station, 15 March 1941. *LT*

bulk of Croydon's allocation until the RT era. One particular memory I have of a journey in a 60-seat General STL on the 59B heading home from Coulsdon is of a rumour spreading through the bus as we approached Purley that the police were stopping all traffic to check identity cards; it was obvious from the agitation of my parents and a number of other passengers in the crowded bus that they hadn't got them. I can't recall precisely what happened next but we kept our seats and arrived home safely.

A curious episode occurred during the Blitz when an appeal went out for buses to be sent from the provinces to help out in London. It was curious because, given the size of London's fleet, relatively few vehicles had actually been written off, and service reductions meant that a considerable number of perfectly usable vehicles, both buses and trams, were actually in store. Perhaps it was the crews who were needed, perhaps it was all a publicity stunt to show that Britain was united in the war effort and would not let the capital down. In the event a wonderfully kaleidoscopic variety of liveries brightened up the sombre, war-torn streets. 475 buses, mostly double-deckers but some single, came from all over Scotland, Wales and England, plus 18 bright yellow trolleybuses from Bournemouth. The first, an orange, green and cream Regent from Halifax, arrived on 22 October. Some did not stay long and all had gone home by February 1942, except for two Manchester

Corporation Crossleys destroyed in the Croydon garage bombing.

Towards the end of 1941 the process was reversed when five Tilling STs were sent to help devastated Coventry. These were the first of many, 291 in all, which left London to help out in the provinces. They were all STs of various types. Some stayed much longer than any provincial bus did in London, the very last not returning until 1948 — when they were immediately sent to the scrapyard!

As if to compound the oddness of the influx of buses from far and wide, delivery continued not only of RTs and trolleybuses, but also resumed of STLs and STDs. Production of the standard 'prewar' trolleybus finally ended in October when P1 class No 1721 entered service. From the B1s of 1935 to the final P1s would seem to encompass a great many classes: but this is misleading. Beyond the fact that some were Leylands and others AECs, there was scarcely little more variation than within the STL class. To quote S. L. Poole in the 1949 edition of *abc of London's Trams and Trolleybuses*: 'The London trolleybuses are of three types — (i) the standard vehicle seating 70, with the short wheelbase modification seating the lesser number as noted, (ii) the chassisless pattern introduced immediately prior to the outbreak of war in 1939, and (iii) the 8ft 0in wide vehicles, of which there are two classes, the SA and Q1.'

Left:
The ruins of Croydon Garage on the morning of 13 May 1941. *LT*

Right:
Unfrozen STL2680 with austerity wartime body heads for East Grinstead on the long 409 from West Croydon.

Below:
No 1725, one of the trolleybuses destined for South Africa but diverted to London Transport.

The SAs began to appear in November 1941. They were very different to anything seen on London streets up to now, for these 43 vehicles had been destined for Durban and Johannesburg and had been diverted by the government to London. Of these, 25 were Leylands, the rest AECs. The bodies were by Metro-Cammell and this common combination might have been thought to fit in well with London practice. In reality there were many differences, ranging from the 8ft width to the various features provided on vehicles intended to operate in far hotter climes than the Ilford area, which was where they found themselves.

A return to the STL class might be thought odd now that the RT had established itself but these were standard Regent 0661 chassis which had originally been intended for London but had not been delivered owing to wartime restrictions. The government

Left:
A Manchester Leyland Titan exchanges its home town destination blinds for London ones prior to taking up service from Hendon garage on the 13 in what is thought to be a posed publicity shot.

Right:
A standard former LGOC ST on loan to Trent. The rear of a Midland Red SOS built for Trent can just be seen. *A. D. Packer*

decided to allow manufacturers to finish them and other such vehicles, completion of which had been frozen, and they took charge of allocating them. Chiswick built bodies for their 34 'unfrozen' Regents, which looked very like the standard roof-box product, although internally they were very austere. In addition 14 of them had no roof route number box and nothing at all at the rear. The loss of the roof-box was no great tragedy, although it looked a bit odd, as by this time a restricted display had been brought in for all London buses; all the information had to be contained within the 'via' box and even this space was cut down. Trams and trolleybuses, less generous with their information anyhow, were unaffected.

Of these new STL bodies, 20 were of lowbridge layout — the first, indeed the only, more or less standard lowbridge bodies of its own design LT ever owned. They looked like proper STLs and were among the best proportioned of any lowbridge design, although, like their highbridge brothers, the single-skin roofs, absence of interior panelling and wooden-framed seats were well below the standards Londoners had come to expect. Some of the highbridge bodies, which followed on from 12 similar ones produced a little earlier to replace war-damaged bodies, were put on to the new chassis, the buses being numbered STL2648-81, registrations FXT 371-404; others were fitted to older chassis. Conversely, some of the new chassis gained older STL bodies of various types. Despite being painted red they were all sent to work in the Country Area, not being repainted green until 1944–7.

The 11 new members of the STD class, Nos 101–111, were even less like their predecessors than the new STLs. The Ministry of Supply had specified that bodies built during the war should be as austere as possible in order to conserve materials for the war effort, and STD101 carried the first such body to be produced. Built by Park Royal it bore no resemblance to the high quality standard LT prewar designs. Curves were kept to a minimum, as were opening windows, and there was just one route indicator, which was at the front. Interiors were stark and the rear window upstairs which, according to custom, served as the emergency exit, was unglazed. Side indicators were soon fitted because without them prospective passengers held up the bus by asking the conductor where it was going. The chassis was the Leyland Titan TD7. The unfrozen STDs spent their entire careers at Victoria (GM) garage where they were a familiar sight on the 137.

No new single-deckers appeared during the war years but 253 of various types were converted to 'Standee' layout which meant fitting the seats longitudinally, thus allowing up to 20 standing passengers.

1942

The last 'prewar' RT, No 151, entered service on 1 February 1942. Chelverton Road, Putney, lost many of its services during the war and so a number of the RTs were transferred to Victoria garage where they became most familiar on route 52. Later they worked from other garages but they were always chiefly associated with the two at Putney and when my father and I walked back from Barnes Bridge after watching the 1947 Boat Race, I was amazed at the almost

continuous procession of RT2s which passed us along the Upper Richmond Road.

The lowbridge STL bodies, designed in 1941, did not enter service until 1942. None were fitted to unfrozen chassis, instead they went on to earlier ones whose bodies had been destroyed in the Blitz. All were painted red but they went into both Central and Country Area service, either augmenting routes already worked by lowbridge STs and STLs, or replacing single-deckers.

Although the Blitz was over and relatively few Nazi bombers now attacked London, the war effort still demanded great sacrifice. All Green Line services finished at the end of September. In order to reduce fuel consumption to a minimum, experiments were made with gas produced by burning anthracite in a trailer towed behind the bus. 20 STs from Grays garage in the Country Area were so equipped from June 1942, being the first major conversion.

Only a few months after the arrival of RT151 more new buses began to enter LT service. They were, however, inferior in every respect to the RT. B1-9 were Bristols, prewar K5Gs with Gardner engines, further examples of the unfrozen bus and the very

first Bristols seen in regular London service. They were fitted with Park Royal bodies, pretty well identical to those of the unfrozen STDs. The Bristols were sent to Hanwell garage where they remained throughout their careers and thus were never seen in central London.

The AECs, Leylands and Bristols were the prelude to a fleet of over 700 buses delivered under emergency wartime conditions, a fleet which we might charitably call a hiccup in the continuing development of the London bus, for it fell way below the standards Londoners had come to expect. Its life was short, much shorter than the average achieved by its prewar predecessors, many of whom outlasted it, although a fair proportion of it found employment elsewhere in one form or another after being disposed of by LT.

Both AEC and Leyland, far and away the most popular makes in both London and the provinces, were too occupied with war work to resume bus production, as was LT itself at its Chiswick works, at the new works at Aldenham, which had been built for the never completed Northern Line extension to Bushey, and elsewhere. The 23 was the only other central London Guy route. The G class eventually

Constructed from two old Central Line motor cars, with frames shortened and placed back to back, it was fitted with a Gardner diesel engine and whether working off the live rail or on diesel-electric power it could haul 600 tons on the level or 300 tons on gradients up to 1 in 34.

1943

As the war continued it became obvious that Guy could not supply all the double-deck bus requirements and so a second manufacturer, Daimler, was allowed to resume production. However no Daimler had arrived in London by the end of 1943 and the capital had to make do with more Guys. These had longer bonnets to accommodate the bigger 6LW engine if it was fitted — which it never was in London — a slightly modified Park Royal body and wooden slatted seats. In this they represented a nadir in standards of comfort, but in wartime passengers were prepared to grin and bear it. Like most of their class they were sent to work in the suburbs of east London. After the initial allocation of Guys to Tottenham garage, the next batch was sent to the western suburbs of Hanwell and Alperton. This, however, was to be an exception, for the Guys were very much associated

reached 435. They were fitted with a variety of bodies. The first were Park Royals, exactly the same as those on the STD and B classes, but others were given bodies built by Weymann, Northern Counties, Massey, a slightly altered Park Royal version and one Northern Coachbuilders, the latter being fitted to G30 after its original Park Royal body had been destroyed by enemy action. On the Underground a little-noticed pioneer appeared. This was DEL120, the prototype diesel-electric service locomotive. It is more accurately described as an electro-diesel.

Left:
Former LGOC STL178. *Alan Cross*

Below left:
STL1959, the chassis dating from June 1939, the body a lowbridge one built in 1942. *Author's collection*

Right:
One of the original standard Green Line T class coaches in service as a Country Area bus from Dunton Green Garage on the 454, Sevenoaks, 1943. *Author's collection*

Below:
Another view of Sevenoaks bus station in 1943, taken on 26 June, this time with Q57 working the 454 to Tonbridge. *Topical*

with east London and the great majority was always based there. No G was ever allocated to a garage south of the river, indeed their only regular appearance on the south bank was on the short stretch of route 76 between Waterloo and Westminster bridges.

More Country Area garages and some Central Area ones began to operate gas producer buses in 1943. As gas was seen as an alternative fuel to petrol, rather than diesel, STs were chosen ——as in the Central Area — along with some single-deck Ts. Although Croydon operated some on the 197, like most people the ones I remember best were those which operated out of Camberwell garage on the 36, a route we travelled on between Victoria and Paddington when on our way to stay with my Aunt Agnes near

Shrewsbury. They lasted in this form for less than two years, being both underpowered and unreliable, and were converted back as soon as the fuel situation improved.

A further example of wartime stringency was the appearance of a number of new Guys and some overhauled standard buses, trams and trolleys in a livery of brown and cream. I recall that the brown wasn't so very different to that used on roofs, although more than one shade was used. Roofs had changed from silver when bauxite had been substituted for aluminium as a primer, both because it was cheaper and also made buses less visible from the air. That this was very necessary was tragically illustrated when an ST was machine-gunned in east London and its driver killed.

1944

If Londoners had believed that, with the end of the Blitz, the war turning round in favour of the Allies with the entry of the USA after Pearl Harbor, the defeat of the Germans in North Africa, the USSR standing firm at Leningrad and Stalingrad, and then D-Day, the worst was over, then the sudden onslaught of the pilotless flying bombs (the V1 'Doodlebugs') in June 1944 blew that illusion asunder. It was ironic that the trolleybus fleet, which had suffered so little in the Blitz, should suffer so much from these new weapons. Although V1s could be caught by RAF fighters, if they fired at them at too close a range then the resulting explosion could destroy the fighter too. By the time a doodlebug had reached Croydon it had evaded both anti-aircraft guns and Fighter Command and we would listen with dread for the distinctive note of its engine to cease suddenly. If it did, then we dived for the nearest cover.

Bexleyheath depot was virtually destroyed by a V1 on 29 June, along with 12 of its trolleybuses; the rest being either seriously or slightly damaged. Next month West Ham depot and works was hit twice, no less than 108 vehicles being damaged on the first occasion; even more, 154, on the second, although only one was destroyed.

As in the Blitz of 1940-1 so it was a local bus garage which suffered the most from a V1 attack. Elmers End was hit on 18 July: seven people died, 31 buses and a Green Line Q converted to an ambulance were destroyed, 19 other buses and nine converted coaches had their bodies wiped out. Three trams from Telford Avenue, a Feltham and two ex-Walthamstow cars, were damaged beyond repair at Kennington in August.

Even more terrifying were the V2s, the first guided missiles to be used in war. These were launched on London in September 1944. They flew at heights and speeds way beyond those of any ordinary aircraft and simply dropped out of the sky. There was no defence against them, save that of capturing their launch sites, a task the Allied armies only accomplished some two months before the war ended.

New buses continued to be delivered in 1944. The long awaited Daimlers began to enter service in the late spring of 1944. D1-6 had lowbridge Duple bodies of typical austerity appearance and specification, and were sent to Merton garage to work route 127. Immediately after these the highbridge version of the D, again bodied by Duple, appeared. These too were sent to Merton and this large garage eventually housed all the wartime specification Daimlers.

Guys also continued to arrive in 1944. Although in very small numbers, they were a notable group for they went to Barking garage to work the 23, an east London route which operated from Becontree Heath right through the heart of the City of London and the West End to Oxford Street and Marylebone station. Slatted wooden seats remained the norm on new buses in 1944, although all would be upholstered later on.

The arrival of the austerity buses not only allowed the replacement of vehicles destroyed by enemy action, but occasionally others which were worn out or time-expired could be withdrawn. If an elderly LT or ST was badly damaged it was sometimes written off, whereas similar damage to a much newer STL or RT would be made good. In September 1944 the first withdrawal of an STL took place. This was, however, hardly a reflection on the general standard of the class for the vehicle in question, STL558, was a real oddity, being a former independent with a much-rebuilt outside-staircase body.

Whatever the trials and tribulations of war, most people try to carry on as normally as possible. It is difficult for those who have never lived in such times to understand the seemingly illogical lengths sometimes employed. Why waste effort and money on publicity photographs of new vehicles? Why worry about liveries? Surely it would have made sense to paint all PSVs in dull brown or grey? But it doesn't work like this, indeed making the best of the present

Above left:
The washing bay at Bexley depot on the morning of
27 June 1944 after the V1 hit. *LT*

Left:
The result of the bombing of Elmers End garage, 19 July
1944. *LT*

Above:
Despite the advent of Guys on route 23, LTs, including this
splendid Bluebird example, continued to provide part of
the allocation. *Alan Cross*

Below:
STLs and LTs, their windows fitted with anti-blast netting,
lay over on the Embankment awaiting the evening rush
hour. *Omnibus Soc*

Left:
D94, a Brush-bodied example, working from Merton (AL) garage on the 77 route. *R. E. Vincent*

Below left:
Lowbridge D129 at the South Wimbledon terminus of the 127. *F. G. Reynolds*

and hoping and planning for a peaceful and progressive future becomes enormously important. The Beveridge Report promised a radically fairer Britain and, in its own way, LT responded to the general feeling that after the war better working and living conditions had to come about. Experiments were carried out in 1944 to ease the lot of the conductor by allowing him to sit down while collecting fares. Two trolleybuses, two STLs and RT97 (damaged by bomb blast) were rebuilt with power-operated sliding doors and circulating areas beside the seated conductor. All went into service initially in the Kingston area but proved unsuccessful. Loading took longer, something outside the conductor's control; it was also found that passengers could over-ride their stops and that the conductors could no longer keep an eye on what was going on upstairs.

Of course pay-as-you-enter did come in, decades later and under very different circumstances. Another

experiment of 1944 which would eventually become universal practice was the fitting of a District Line carriage with fluorescent lighting.

Strikes may seem an unlikely occurrence in wartime but there were a number at bus garages and trolleybus depots in the spring of 1944 in protest at working conditions and new, improved schedules. Both the schedules and the strikes were a sign that the end of the war was in sight. The army operated both buses and its own lorries until the dispute came to an end several days later.

1945

New buses of the G and D class continued to be delivered throughout 1945. At the very end of the year a further batch of Bristols joined the fleet. These 20 buses, B10–29, looked quite different to their predecessors in that they had a much lower and very

Below:
STL2482, repainted from red to green in 1944 and retaining full indicator blinds, working from Chelsham garage on the 403D at Tunbridge Wells.
Author's collection

elegant radiator, the standard postwar model which would become so familiar in Tilling fleets throughout the country. They had AEC engines, which were also fitted to most of the Daimlers, and identical Duple bodies — a good deal less spartan than earlier wartime ones, having curved domes, more opening windows and tubular steel seats with cushions covered in moquette instead of drab leathercloth or no cushions at all. B10-29 joined their brothers at Hanwell garage. All the earlier wartime buses had registrations beginning with G, but these later ones, Bristols, Daimlers and Guys, were all HGCs.

The war, of course, continued. Destruction from the air went on until the V2 missile sites were all captured. In March 15 Tilling STs, stored out of use beside Upton Park garage, were so badly damaged by a V2 falling nearby that they had to be written off. For all that, restrictions began to be lifted, beginning with those on headlamps in January 1945; no piloted enemy aircraft now attacked London and neither dark nor light made any difference to the V2s. Curiously the trams kept their masked headlamps, albeit in a modified form, until withdrawal in 1950-2. Just before VE-Day all lighting restrictions, inside and out, were abolished.

Traditionally, summer schedules were introduced early in May each year, one of the features being lots of extra buses on Sundays to places of entertainment and beauty spots. This meant lending red buses to help out in the Country Area and although the traffic levels of 1945 were not yet back to those of peacetime, they were better than anything since 1940.

The war in Europe ended officially on 8 May, but the celebrations began the day before and London and Londoners went mad. Buses, trams and trolleybuses carried vast numbers of revellers, though not at any great pace; schedules were thrown to the winds as the roads in the centre of London, and here and there in the suburbs, became jammed with joyful crowds.

Three months later Japan surrendered; the war was finally over. There were more celebrations and then LT got down to restoring peacetime conditions as quickly as possible. Inevitably this did not happen overnight.

Restrictions on a great variety of materials continued — for many years in some cases — and it took a while for all the soldiers, sailors and airmen to be demobbed. Three ex-servicemen opened an ironmonger's shop beside my local bus and tram stop and I used to peer through the door just to get a glimpse of these heroes. We regarded them as akin to knights returned from the Crusades.

Some 22,500 LT employees had joined the forces; 16,500 women had been recruited to replace them.

Above:
B11, Golders Green. *IAL* .

1946

Although passenger journeys had dropped by nearly 25 per cent at the height of the Blitz, by 1945 they were back to within 3 per cent of the prewar figure. The population of central London had declined by some 16 per cent, some 650,000 people — a trend which has continued to this day — but in the outer suburbs and beyond it had gone up by such an extent that Country Area routes were carrying a staggering increase of 90 per cent more passengers over the 1938-9 figure. To cope with this many single-deckers had been replaced by double-deckers.

426 LT staff were killed either at work or off duty; 2,873 were injured. 166 buses and coaches, 60 trams, 15 trolleybuses and 19 Underground carriages had been destroyed in air raids. Amongst the war work carried out by LT was the manufacture of over 700 Halifax four-engined bombers, the last one being named *London Pride* by Lord Ashfield.

Later, evening services began again on some routes before the summer of 1945 was out, while the winter schedules saw a further improvement. Although other operators resumed some coach services to the seaside, there had been no announcements about the restoration of the Green Line network; this, however, was not far away.

The first two postwar Green Line routes — 715 Hertford-Oxford Circus-Guildford and 720 Aldgate-Bishop's Stortford — began on 6 February 1946, both operated by demobbed 10T10s. The rest of the network, now numbered in the 700 series, was back in operation by late June and with it the familiar Ts, TFs and Qs. Livery was Lincoln green and white, the latter soon giving way to pale green. White and black destinations soon changed to black and yellow, which together with gold on green side boards gave the Green Line an added air of distinction. The network was soon doing as much and more business compared with prewar days, and the particularly heavily patronised routes out of Aldgate restarted with double-deck operation. The vehicles chosen were a curious bunch – 37 austerity Daimlers. Admittedly these D class buses were brand new but they were still built to later wartime specification and were not very comfortable. They were joined after a few months by a few prewar STLs.

A rather more suitable choice might have been yet another variation on the STL theme, if only there had been enough of them. Production of the STL was supposed to have ended in 1939 but in the event the war prolonged it for almost eight years, off and on. The very last went into service at the beginning of 1946. These 20 buses, coded 18STL20, although entering service before the last of the Gs and Ds, had chassis much in common with the unfrozen STLs. Their Weymann bodies showed little sign of wartime skimping — the only note of austerity was the one-piece indicators fitted back and front. Had they been given standard three-piece ones, they would have looked a lot more like a traditional London bus. The late prewar and immediate postwar combination of the AEC Regent and the Weymann body has become a classic: one thinks of the long-lived Brighton examples of 1939, one of which has been preserved. These STLs were fine looking vehicles — but only the livery had much to do with LT traditions. They spent all their short lives in LT ownership working in the Country Area; three were delivered in red livery, but this was changed to green before 1946 was out. Numbered STL2682–2701, HGC 215–234, they were sent to Watford High Street garage. Like many another enthusiast I journeyed all the way to Watford in order to record them in my *abc*.

The arrival of new AECs by no means brought to an end the delivery of Daimlers. Shortly after the last austerity Daimler went into service, D182 was delivered — the first of 100 with similar chassis but with Park Royal bodies and built to more or less peacetime specifications. This body was very similar to that fitted to a batch of Southdown Leyland PD1s. Even though they had full three-piece indicators the Park Royal Daimlers seemed to us bus spotters to be firmly in the austerity camp, not least because of their painted radiators. They were sent to Sutton garage and that meant the Morden area in particular, within cycling distance of home, was awash with Ds from Merton and Sutton garages. My friend Hicks, who lived at Carshalton, copped all 281. D182–281 sported a new livery, basically all red with cream bands above the upper and lower deck windows. It was part of the move away from the magnificent red, white, silver and black of prewar days to the sombre, virtually all red of 1950.

If LT was not yet able to order buses to its own, precise, specific requirements, then at least it could choose from manufacturers' standard provincial peacetime catalogues. So after the Weymann-bodied Regents came 65 all-Leyland PD1 Titans. Another classic design, they were put into the STD class, 112–176, HGF 990–999 and HLW 51–105, following on from the prewar TD4s and the unfrozen TD7s. They had a full set of route indicators at the front — although the actual display was still restricted — including roof number box, which made them instantly look like a London bus. They were painted in yet another livery variation, but one which was

Below:
LT1142 and new TD9, Golders Green. *D. A. Jones*

61

Left:
T733 of the first batch of postwar Ts working from Uxbridge garage. *IAL*

Below:
A well-laden Tilling ST swings round Parliament Square ahead of a spanking new Talbot.

Left:
All-Leyland PD1 STD119 about to set off for Loughton from Victoria.

Above right:
Green Line D161 at Aldgate bus station. *G. F. Ashwell*

Right:
T579 of Reigate enters Regent Street on the 711 in pursuit of two LTs.

standard for the next four years: mostly red, black wings, a cream centre band and cream upper deck window frames except at the back. Some actually worked past the end of our road, from Croydon garage on route 115, alongside Sutton's Park Royal-bodied Ds, but they were soon transferred away and I've never seen a picture of one so employed. In most memories they are associated with Victoria (GM) — on the 77 and 137 — and Loughton (L) and the 38a. The postwar STDs were delivered between August and December 1946.

Yet more new buses delivered in 1946 were the first single-deckers since the CRs of 1939. If it seemed the STL class was destined to go on acquiring new members *ad infinitum*, what of the T? The first member of the class dated back to November 1929; nearly 17 years later production was resumed with a batch of 50 Central Area buses, T719-768 (HGF 809–858), coded 14T12. They had nice looking, if slightly old-fashioned, Weymann 35-seat front-entrance bodies. Slide vent windows gave them a somewhat provincial appearance but there were already so many variations all lumped into the T class that they looked perfectly at home. Because of shortages they did not actually replace any older vehicles, although a number of Ts had already disappeared from the fleet, largely as a consequence of the war.

The final buses of the interim period between austerity types and the postwar standards, began to

arrive in December 1946. These were 31 Leyland (Leylands formed a far higher proportion of the single-deck fleet than the double) PS1 Tigers and were put into a new class (although the classification had been used before), being numbered TD1-31 (HGF 959-989). Their bodies were identical to those fitted to the contemporary 14T12s.

Below ground the wartime brake on expansion was released in December 1946 when the Central Line tunnels, used for war work, were opened and trains began to run as far as Stratford, emerging out into the open just before the station where it was possible to cross the platform to join LNER stopping services.

We cannot end our look at 1946 without reference to the Victory Parades with which London celebrated the return of peace. These took place on 8 June and consisted of a procession of marching men and women and also a mechanised one. My father, despite having been a driver in Allenby's army in World War 1, preferred to watch the march past but we did catch part of the mechanised one, amongst which were four buses, two from the provinces which had helped out in London in 1940, and two RTs, Nos 4 and 39.

Below:
Park Royal-bodied RT214, one of many roof-box RTs allocated to Croydon Garage, sets off from Thornton Heath Pond.

1947

1947 was a year to gladden the heart of LT management, staff and customers. On Saturday 10 May the long awaited first postwar RT entered service. Numbered 402, even though the highest 'prewar' RT number was 151, it established a precedent for the class that meant, for instance, that RT4230 could appear over three years before RT3836. Chiswick was so inundated with overhaul work after the long years of wartime neglect that it would never again take on a production run, and so Park Royal and Weymann had been contracted to build the first postwar bodies for the RT. Park Royals were to run from 152 to 401 and Weymanns from 402 onwards. It so happened that the first Weymann bus was ready before the first Park Royal one — RT152 entered service on 23 May — and thus RT402 became the prototype of what was arguably the largest standardised class of bus to operate in any city, worldwide, although this honour really belongs to prewar RT1. RTs 152 and 402 went to Leyton for route 10, replacing open staircase LTs.

The chassis of the postwar RT was similar to its predecessor, but the engine was a new one, rather more powerful and with a quite different sound, much less of a throbbing roar. Visually the differences between the pioneer members of the class and the postwar ones, the 3RT3s, were not great, chiefly the

level instead of drooping cab window, the front destination indicator below instead of above the 'via', and no roof-box number indicator at the back. It was metal-framed, instead of composite, and its parts were designed to be totally interchangeable. Internally it was superb, absolutely up to date and quite the most luxurious and well-appointed bus on the road. The smell of a brand new or newly overhauled RT was something which one never forgets. Visually John Gillham, the oracle of class 5 in all matters pertaining to LT at Winterbourne Primary School, described it as 'looking like a trolleybus'. And certainly both types shared similar smooth lines and livery.

By the end of 1947 171 new RTs had entered service and I had seen and even travelled on quite a few of them, for many were sent to Croydon and Bromley garages to replace time-expired former Tilling and LGOC STLs and STs. Perhaps surprisingly they weren't all put on the trunk routes to the West End and the City but could be found monopolising such purely local ones as the 197, 130 and 119. They were to stay on the former for more than a quarter of a century. They also saw off the Croydon STDs, the only class of

Leyland buses ever to work from Croydon until the T class Titans of a later generation. The STDs went northeastwards to Loughton and Leyton.

However 171 new buses was nowhere near sufficient to take over from the swathes of LTs, STs and STLs ruthlessly removed from service, sometimes for overhaul but much more often for scrap. In desperation, but with rather more justification, the scenes of 1940 were repeated when, beginning in October, vehicles were hired from many sources to make good the shortages. This time they were coaches, a total of 350, and ranged from the antique to the brand new and appeared on routes normally worked by red double-deckers.

Left:
Aldenham works with four STLs, an ST and a Bluebird LT. *Photo Centre*

Below left:
Central Area Q167, RT274, T16 and an LTC parked outside Wembley Stadium. *IAL*

Right:
The classic RT upper deck, still familiar 56 years after it first appeared.

Below:
A Grey-Green prewar Leyland Tiger coach, one of 350 vehicles hired by London Transport to help out with vehicle shortages, stands alongside an ST at London Bridge, 27 October 1947. In the 1980s and 1990s Grey-Green would become an operator of bus services in London. *Topical*

A startling sight in Katharine Street, Croydon was an ST in blue and yellow. Not even Gillham could explain this apparition. Years later I discovered that this was one of the Inter-Station buses which had been used to replace or augment the one-and-a-half-deck Cubs built for this service. Now the STs could return to ordinary service. Officially they were all modified internally and repainted back into red livery before this happened but the one I saw must have worked briefly in its Inter-Station condition before Chiswick got its hands on it. More STs re-appeared to help out with the chronic shortage of vehicles, a number of the Tilling variety being put back into passenger service.

The final vehicles of the first batch of TDs took up work in June but no single-deckers were withdrawn; they were all needed. Even the private hire LTCs turned up on Green Line relief duties.

Many of the wartime buses still had wooden seats and some, but by no means all, had these replaced by cushioned ones in 1947. Other reminders and relics of wartime days remained — restricted route indicators on all buses, bomb sites which in the summer sprouted luxuriant weeds and wild flowers, while petrol rationing meant there were few private cars to inhibit the progress of buses, trams and trolleybuses.

A sign of better times ahead was the opening on 14

December of the Central Line extension from Leytonstone to Woodford and Newbury Park in place of LNER (in two weeks' time they would have become British Railways) steam trains.

As the year ended so did the 14-year existence of the London Transport Passenger Board. The Transport Act which brought about the Nationalisation of the railways also brought into existence the London Transport Executive, although to the vast majority of its passengers the only difference, if they bothered to look, was a change in the legal lettering on the buses, trams and trolleys.

1948

The London Passenger Transport Board ceased to exist at the end of 1947, becoming, with Nationalisation, the London Transport Executive (LTE). Lord Ashfield was the driving force; with Frank Pick he had raised LT to its pre-eminent position. He had retired as Chairman in October 1947 and died just over a year later.

Production of new buses steadily increased in 1948 as did withdrawal of standard vehicles from the prewar LT, ST and STL classes. Perhaps the most significant new bus was RTL501. Leyland had been contracted at the beginning of 1947 to build its own version of the RT. Like the prewar STD this would closely resemble its AEC counterpart. The Leyland version came in two widths, standard and outsize. Despite the Ministry of Transport having recently sanctioned an increase in width from 7ft 6in to 8ft (the SA class of trolleybuses intended for South Africa were the very first eight-footers to operate in London, but only in the suburbs) it was not considered certain that some of central London's narrowest streets would permit two eight-footers to pass each other without dire results for pedestrians and other traffic. Thus Leyland was asked to build 500 8ft wide buses complete with bodies and 1,000 7ft 6in wide chassis. The first of the latter went into service in June 1948. The resemblance to the RT was so close that it actually carried a Park Royal body intended for RT657. The chassis was a much modified Titan PD2/1 fitted with a radiator, which was instantly recognisable as Leyland, but of similar dimensions to the AEC one on RTs. The Leyland 7ft

Below:
Bristol/ECW lowbridge K5G at Victoria on the 38 alongside an STL on the 16. *IAL*

Above:
Conversation piece at Kingston bus station alongside Mann Egerton TDs 127/118.

Right:
Mann Egerton-bodied T791 representing the final 15T13 version of this class, 10T10 T574 and postwar STL2689. *IAL*

6in chassis was modified to accept the standard RT body, and some other components were identical to those on RT chassis. RTL501 was so numbered because it had originally been intended that the 8ft wide Titans would be RTLs 1-500; in the event they were put into a separate class.

The production Leylands went into service from December 1948, but these were noticeably different in appearance to the prototype, as they had Leyland 8ft wide bodies. We'll return to them but meanwhile we must record the first Country Area RTs. These arrived in July, Nos 597-603, and were sent to Tring. More followed, to a variety of garages north and south of

the river. RTs 152-401 had HLW registration letters, 402 onwards HLX. These ended at RT621, 622 being JXC 430 (RTL501 was JXC 20).

Because so many new buses were needed to replace the virtually defunct LTs, STs and many of the STLs, suffering acutely from the neglect of the war years, Park Royal and Weymann were unable to supply all LT's needs so other builders were contracted to build bodies for RTs: Craven in Yorkshire and Saunders on the Isle of Anglesey.

The first of 120 Craven RTs, No 1402, arrived in September 1948. It looked very different to any other RT, being basically a standard Craven product

modified slightly, fitted with RT seats and roof-box indicator, and adapted to fit the RT chassis. Its shape was different, it had a five-bay window layout, a more curvaceous back and a flatter front. We contemporary bus spotters found the Cravens an interesting variation but I don't think anyone thought them a patch visually on the standard RT. Craven RTs were distributed all over the network, painted both red and green; we had a few of the former delivered new locally to Elmers End and Croydon.

What the 1948 *abc* was pleased to call 'the single-deck version of the RT' entered service in the early part of 1948. These were the very last members of the T class, Nos 769-798, HLX 439-468. Painted in the now outdated green and white, despite the fact that ancient rebuilt Ts and single deck LTs and contemporary RTs had substituted cream for white, these 30 buses, coded 15T13, had 31-seat bodies built by Mann Egerton. They were handsome looking vehicles, but were hardly the single-deck equivalent of the RT, despite their modified Regal III chassis with air-operated pre-selective gearboxes, fluid transmission, 9.6 litre engines, and interior finished in RT style. All were sent north of the river to the garages of Two Waters and Leavesden Road, Watford. At the beginning they were associated with Hertfordshire and later Essex, although many later migrated south of the river, particularly to Sussex at Crawley.

The 1/1TD2s was the second group of 100 Leyland PS1 Tigers which began to arrive in the autumn of 1948. Close relations to the 15T13s, they had Mann Egerton bodies identical to the Ts except that, being in the Central Area, the Metropolitan Police (a body who in PSV matters never seemed to have quite got over the trauma of the replacement of the horse)

refused to allow the fitting of a sliding door. They were painted in the new standard all-red, with a smidgen of cream, and, numbered TD32-131 (JXC 225-324), were sent to a number of garages, allowing the withdrawal of many single-deck LTs and some of the earlier Ts.

The arrival of Ian Allan's *abc of London Transport* in 1948 was a tremendous boon to enthusiasts. Written by S. L. Poole, here for the first time was set out just about all one wished to know about the contemporary London bus scene, with a bit of history thrown in. I still have my original — somewhat less than mint condition copy — second edition, which was a reprint of the first, both appearing in 1948. As with many contemporary railway 'ABCs' its cover featured a woodcut by A. N. Wolstenholme, not quite 100 per cent accurate for RT567 on route 46 seen alongside T637 on route 703 has the drooping window of the 'prewar' RT, but attractive for all that.

One more group of very welcome arrivals on the London scene must be recorded. In January the first of a new class of trolleybus arrived. This was the Q1, 77 of which had been on order since 1946. Described in the 1948 *abc* as 'the ultimate development of the standard trolleybus', they were very much in the LT tradition but improved in various respects, being 8ft wide, of five window-bay construction and more powerful with their MCW bodies mounted on BUT chassis. BUT was a joint selling organisation set up by AEC and Leyland; nevertheless the Q1s were basically of AEC design but assembled at Leyland's Ham factory, near Kingston. All were sent to Fulwell depot where they replaced the original London United Diddlers.

Despite the frustrations of continuing restrictions on new equipment and the need to keep outdated

1949

vehicles and rolling stock serviceable, in one sense 1948 was LT's finest year for it carried more passengers — 4,675 million — than it ever had before or would again. It was a year for optimists. We might have been annihilated by the Australians on Don Bradman's final tour, despite the valiant efforts of Hutton, Washbrook, Edrich, Compton, Evans and Alec Bedser, but we did stage the first postwar Olympics, LT playing its part to the full by providing transport for the competitors in anything from a little CR to an ancient LT double-decker. Unemployment was just a bad memory left over from the 1930s. We had enough money to go out regularly and on holiday, but probably not enough to afford personal transport, nor the petrol coupons even if we did own a car, so we went by bus, motor coach or train. So popular were excursions out of London that red double-deckers on loan to the Country Area became a common sight on Sundays when every available green bus was already out and about — a situation inconceivable today.

If 1948 was a year when production of postwar standard vehicles really began to take off, in 1949 it became a flood ——no less than 1,592 being delivered, a figure almost sufficient to have completely renewed the fleet of Midland Red, that provincial giant which covered a greater area of England than any other company. It gives one some idea of the pre-eminence of LT.

Three more new types appeared, although only one was destined to last long. First came RTC1, a highly glamorous innovation which fired the imaginations of us schoolboys, although I saw it only once, in late May when it worked briefly on the 708 which passed through Croydon. RTC1 was the much-rebuilt RT97 and intended as a prototype for a fleet of double-deck Green Line coaches. Not for the first time such a concept failed, although it would eventually succeed. RTC1 served only nine months in its intended role, being then relegated to country bus duties and sold in 1955.

Another failure, equally interesting but visually of much lower profile, was the SRT. It seemed to LT that production of new bodies was going to outstrip that of chassis and so it was decided that 300 STL

Right:
Metro-Cammell-bodied RTL968
crossing Putney Bridge.

Below:
Moorgate station; two Metropolitan
line trains about to depart, the
nearer, bound for Watford, is made
up of brown-liveried, compartment T
stock dating from the late 1920s,
whilst alongside is a P stock train for
Uxbridge. *R. E. Vincent*

chassis would be rebuilt to take RT-type bodies. The final, FJJ/FXT-registered batch dating from 1939 was chosen, their bodies being transferred to the STL2014-2188 group which had been given all-metal bodies; these were now in an advanced state of decay. The first SRTs entered service in April 1949. They met with a frosty reception from the crews who found the STL engines, perfectly adequate for the lighter original vehicle, lacking in power for the more than half a ton heavier SRT, while the brakes also gave trouble. Put to work on such trunk routes as the 35 from Camberwell garage, the 16 from Victoria and the 24 from Chalk Farm, as well as less demanding suburban ones, their lives were short and they were withdrawn in 1953-4, although, of course, their bodies lasted for decades longer, being transferred to new RT chassis. Production was cut short to end at 160.

The third new type was the long awaited 8ft wide Leyland. Classified RTW: the first, registered KGK 501, took up work from Tottenham garage in June 1949. The RTW was the truest descendant of the prewar STD for it too carried a Leyland body skilfully disguised to look like its AEC counterpart but giving its origins away in certain details. It has to be said it was a pretty convincing copy of what an 8ft wide RT would have been like if there had ever been one and you had to look hard to detect the tell-tale differences. Chief was the rear-end upper deck where some of the earlier RTWs had the standard and distinctive

Leyland guttering above the emergency window, curving upwards on the nearside, downwards on the off. Rubber stops either side of the indicator to cushion the emergency window should it be opened meant that the rear adverts had to be moved outwards and this, as well as the extra 6in width, instantly distinguished an RTW from an RT or an RTL. These are not matters of any great significance perhaps, but the spice of life to ardent bus spotters.

Among the many withdrawals were the last Tilling STs, although several were converted to mobile canteens, and one miraculously returned to passenger service in central London many years later, as we shall see. The last open staircase buses in normal service, the first group of LTs, were withdrawn in April although they and some Tillings lasted a little longer in the special events fleet.

One July afternoon, heading for Paddington aboard an STL on the 36, I was not a little surprised to see approaching as we turned out of the Edgware Road into Praed Street a shiny green RT on route 7 heading towards London Bridge. LT seemingly deemed the Central Area's need the greater and thus allocated a batch of new green RTs to Middle Row and also Mortlake garages, although only for a few weeks until sufficient new red buses became available.

Yet another supplier of RT-type bodies appeared on the scene in August when the first of 450 built by Metro-Cammell and fitted to RTLs 551-1000 started

Above left:
RTW116 of West Green Garage and
D2 class trolleybus No 489 in Forest
Road, Woodford. *R. E. Vincent*

Above:
SRT15 on the 24 approaching
Parliament Square whilst a former
West Ham car on the 36 rounds the
curve from the Embankment to
Westminster Bridge, pursued by a
Feltham on the 18. *IAL*

Right:
SRT43 from Cricklewood Garage
and RTL793 from Old Kent Road at
Victoria. *Author's collection*

work. Although visually the only external difference from the Park Royal and Weymann version was a thicker moulding above the central cream band, variations in construction meant that these bodies always stayed on this batch of buses. Despite all these new buses, London was still desperately short of serviceable vehicles, and was able to secure the loan of new ECW-bodied Bristol double-deckers intended for various Tilling bus companies. The Tilling group, like LT, was now part of the British Transport Commission. The first of some 190 had arrived before the end of 1948. LT also managed to secure further hired coaches from independent operators.

On the Underground the first of the 143 new R47 stock cars entered service on the District Line. All were motor cars. There were 91 new Tube cars, the

Above:
RTC1 at Grosvenor Bridge atop Victoria station.

Right:
An ST heads a long line of STs, LTs and a Tilling STL at
Epsom Downs, performing some of their last duties.

1949 stock, built to the last prewar design; 21 of them
were trailers, the rest UNDMs — which being
translated means uncoupling non-driving motor car.
This meant that you could actually drive them for
short distances to enable uncoupling and shunting, not
from a proper cab but from a control cabinet by the
door and the guard's controls, thus saving space.
These all went to work with the 1938 stock on the
Northern and Bakerloo lines.

1950

Enter a new decade and, in several senses, a new era.
Two of the three modern standard classes of double-
deck bus inherited by LT from the General
disappeared in January 1950. These were the ST and
the LT. I think just about all enthusiasts had a special
affection for the LTs in particular. The big six-
wheelers, whether the pioneer open staircase version,
the later ones with camel type front indicators, or the
stylish Bluebirds, simply exuded personality. They
had disappeared from Croydon in the autumn of 1948.
On starting my new school, Whitgift Middle, in

September that year, one of the Elmers End contingent would convey me each Wednesday and Saturday afternoon from the centre of Croydon to the playing fields at Sandilands, Addiscombe, where I was initiated, with no great enthusiasm, into the mysteries of scrums, line outs and fatal injuries — or so I expected — but within a couple of weeks they were all gone, replaced by RTs even newer than my sparkling, mitre-embossed black blazer.

Petrol rationing also disappeared in 1950 and from now on private motoring would steadily take away many of its passengers from all forms of public transport.

1950 was especially significant in LT's history for it marked the final beginning of the end of its huge tram fleet. The outbreak of war had prolonged the life of the south London routes, but with the production of the RT family now in full flood, there were sufficient new buses to resume the tram replacement programme. For various reasons it had been decided that the trolleybus also had a limited lifespan and in the autumn of 1950 Wandsworth depot lost both its trams and trolleybuses, 75 RTs taking over, while Clapham had some of its trams replaced by 54 RTLs.

Not all the trams were scrapped, for Wandsworth had been home to the relatively modern E3 class and these went off to New Cross and Telford Avenue. However for the older E1s the end had arrived and these were driven to Penhall Road, Charlton, where a large yard had been made ready to receive them. Many buses also met their end there. Saturday 30

September was the day chosen for the tramway replacement programme to begin and on the following Monday, 2 October, E1 No 1656 was toppled over and set alight. It was all over in about an hour.

A route operated by Wandsworth depot was the 31, one of the three surviving North London ones, which ran through Kingsway Subway. It had originally terminated at Hackney but the prewar trolleybus programme had seen it diverted to Islington. Now its replacement bus service, the 170, resumed working to Hackney but not through the Subway where there was insufficient clearance. Buses did appear on the Embankment for the first time, southbound they ran over the tram lines, which were still used by many services, and there was at least one accident where a tram and bus collided. In all, six tram routes disappeared, the 12, 26, 28, 31, 34 and the all night 3, along with the 612 trolleybus. The 44 bus route replaced both 12 and 612, restoring a state which had existed before the trolleybuses had arrived, the others being the 45, 168, 169, 170 and 288.

Wandsworth's RTs and Clapham's RTLs all entered service displaying full indicator blinds. The first full blinds had appeared in country buses in May and were the first such since the early war years. There was also a livery change around this time but far less welcome.

Above:
GS23, RTs 2504, 3669 and 971 and a second GS inside Dunton Green Garage.

Left:
The 'Meccano Set' STL2477. IAL

Cream upper-deck window frames disappeared leaving just a thin cream band between the upper and lower decks to relieve the vast expanse of red. The shock of seeing the first vehicle so painted, Catford's RT1679, which worked into Croydon on the 54, was considerable and although a brand new RT always looked splendid, from now on we had to rely on the acreage of adverts, front, sides and back, to brighten up the otherwise almost unrelieved red or green livery of the vast London fleet. Croydon also saw the first Country Area buses to have full indicator blinds when all Godstone's RTs, which worked the 409 and the 411, were so equipped. We also got our first RTWs, a batch being sent in June to Bromley garage to work the 119.

However, much more excitement awaited the RTW class when a series of tests took place that summer in central London. Temporarily allocated to garages which worked into the West End and the City, they appeared for the first time on a number of the routes with which they would later be associated. No fearful

consequences for either traffic or pedestrians resulted from the extra 12in which two passing RTWs occupied and the ban on them appearing in Oxford Street, Shaftesbury Avenue, Threadneedle Street, etc was lifted. However they could not run alongside trams.

The curious situation where wartime Daimlers operated Green Line services was brought to an end in August 1950 when they were replaced by 36 RTs. These Romford buses, despite being identical inside to the standard vehicle, always looked particularly distinguished for they carried no external adverts, had a pale green central band and a raised Green Line motif between the decks. The displaced Ds went to join their brothers at Merton and I saw several of them still operating from there in green livery before they were repainted.

The last petrol-engined STL had gone in 1949 and vast inroads into the oil-engined fleet were made in 1950. At the beginning of the year there were 2,110 licensed for service but by the end this had shrunk to 903, the biggest drop ever and a drastic decline from the maximum of 2,620 at the end of 1946. Remarkably a brand new STL body was under construction at Chiswick Works. The foreman of the experimental shop, Arthur Sainsbury, jointly with LT had patented a system using prefabricated units and this was used to provide a new body, albeit in pre-1946 red and white livery, for STL2477, ELP 154. Nicknamed the 'Meccano Set' it bore some resemblance to a standard STL and ran for four years in London before being sold. It, and its method of construction, remained unique.

Two further classes were on the way out by the end of 1950. LT's last petrol-engined buses, the little Inter-Station yellow and blue Leyland Cubs,

Above:
An extremely down at heel former General STL39 ending its days on learner duty. *IAL*

Right:
RLH17 climbing past the Pilgrims Way north of Westerham.

C106-113, were withdrawn, although they came back in the following March to operate a BEA service between Waterloo and Heathrow, while the first wartime buses, members of the G class, were also delicensed. Although only a stop-gap measure, one somehow hadn't expected any of the austerity classes to go just yet. Both types were replaced by members of the RT family, although STLs were also used to displace Gs. Amongst the first routes to lose its Guys was the 76 — one of only two West End routes operated by Tottenham garage. Yet a new Guy entered the fleet in 1950. This was G436, KGK 981, an Arab with a standard Park Royal-designed provincial body and a big Meadows 10.35 litre engine. Like the 'Meccano set' STL, it seems to have been a unique experiment which had no influence on future vehicle policy.

By the end of 1950 the RT fleet number had reached as high as 4264 (to Croydon, of course!), although there were many gaps yet to be filled and the quite extraordinary, and to this day unique, total of 1,828 new buses (if one counts the final 18 SRTs) had been delivered.

Left:
Green Line RT3243 and 4507 and
trolleybuses at Aldgate.

Below:
RTW406 takes up work on London's
most famous route.

Above:
An immaculate Feltham, No 2156, heads through Streatham with an early STL following respectfully behind. *Alan Cross*

Right:
A wooden-bodied rake of District Hurst Nelson pre-1914 stock passing a semaphore signal on the East London Line. *IAL*

1951

The beginning of 1951 saw two endings. The very last roof number box bus, Saunders RT4267, was delivered to Streatham garage in February. On the night of 6-7 January the second stage of the tram replacement programme took place when all of Clapham's remaining trams and many of Telford Avenue's were replaced by RTLs and RTs

respectively. A third tram depot, Brixton, also began operating buses — RTs. Mention of Telford Avenue immediately brings the Felthams to mind. Despite being in their 20th year these magnificent vehicles were still in excellent condition and it seemed inconceivable that they could meet a fiery end in downtown Charlton. Leeds agreed and bought the lot. They were already being withdrawn from service in London, older cars filling in for them for the last few months of the routes on which they were normally

employed: the 8, 10, 16, 18 and 20. Of these the 8, 10 and 20 disappeared on 6-7 January, along with the 2, 4, 6, 22 and 24. Trams had now disappeared from Wimbledon and the last bit of LUT track, while the Tooting route had been the very first to be electrified by the LCC in 1903. Some E3s were sent to Norwood depot to work the 16 and 18 and to allow room at Telford Avenue for conversion to a bus garage; some E1s were broken up, while others took over from the Felthams on Telford Avenue's remaining routes. I was very indignant at the loss of my beloved Felthams, especially as their substitutes were run down ex-LCC E1s, the oldest cars in London.

Replacement bus routes were the 50, 57, 57A, 95, 104, 155B/W, 189, 189A and 287. The curious suffixes to the 155 indicated whether they preceded around the Embankment inwards by way of Blackfriars or Westminster (replacing the 2 and 4 trams), but they caused only confusion and were soon dropped.

In February RTWs first began to operate regularly through central London, Clayhall and Willesden garages putting them on the 8 and 8A. More Guys and STLs were withdrawn as new RTs and RTLs arrived and an interesting development saw the 'Tunnel' STLs begin to give way to ordinary buses, consequent upon the lowering of the roadway through the Blackwall Tunnel.

I was suffering from a bad cold on the weekend of 7-8 April and thus wasn't able to witness the end of the trams which had been so much part of my life. My parents went and reported on the large crowds, a feature of every tram abandonment. Not only did the 16 and 18 routes — which at peak periods needed no less than 80 cars — disappear, but also our local 42 which ran between Thornton Heath High Street and Coombe Road, Croydon. Thornton Heath depot, from which I could hear the trams setting off each morning, had been closed for several months, demolished and a new bus garage erected on the site. The old Purley depot, where one could catch glimpses of non-windscreen-fitted E1s (I had at first thought them war casualties) in store for many years after such trams had last carried passengers, was cleared out and Thornton Heath's allocation moved in. Now that had gone too, although the building was to remain, the new home for Bedford lorries belonging to Schweppes. The very last tram was No 839, a rehabilitated E1, chartered by the Croydon and Purley Chambers of Commerce, suitably decorated, which ran from Purley to Thornton Heath, completing its journey sometime after midnight.

The new Thornton Heath bus garage had its entrance round the back in Whitehall Road, the road next to ours, where my friend John lived; his father was a policeman who had been on the roof of the sweet factory in Croydon on the night of the notorious Derek Bentley and Christopher Craig fatal shooting. The trams had made their entry straight out into the main London Road, the new arrangement avoided possible traffic congestion.

So on Monday 9 April I waited for a 109 or 190 bus to take me to school and when one appeared I was doubly disappointed for not only was it secondhand, being a hand-me-down RT from Wandsworth which had converted to RTLs, it was also full up. I can't recall any occasion when I hadn't managed to squeeze on to a tram; now it was quite common to have two buses pass by full up. Also it cost me more money; on a Feltham if one was quick and lacked scruples, one could nip down the front staircase when one heard the footsteps of the conductor ascending the rear one and alight without paying.

The next abandonment took place on 10 July, a Tuesday, when two termini, Waterloo and Tooley Street near London Bridge, each lost their sole routes, the 68 and 70 respectively, both of which served Greenwich. Although the trams lived at New Cross the replacement bus routes, the 70 (one of only two bus routes which took the same number as the tram route it replaced), 70A and the 188, operated temporarily out of a new garage at Peckham. Tram route 72, briefly extended during stage 1 to Borough, now went back to its Savoy Street terminus.

Stage 5 arrived on the night of 6-7 October when 99 trams from Camberwell depot were replaced by 109 buses. Routes 36, 56, 58, 60, 62, 66, 84 and the all night 7 disappeared. Most of these were operated by the HR(hilly route)2 class trams designed to cope with the steep gradients, the climb through the sylvan surroundings up to exclusive Dulwich culminating in

the four-track Dog Kennel and a swoop down past the exotica contained within the Horniman Museum. The HR2s were amongst the most modern London trams and too good to burn, even at this late stage, and were sent for service elsewhere, including the 35 Kingsway Subway route. It was about this time I had my one and only ride through the Subway, a unique tram experience, to dive from the bright sun of the Embankment into the gloom beneath Waterloo Bridge, curving round before the long straight stretch beneath Kingsway itself and to alight at the intermediate Aldwych, just as though it was an underground railway station. In its new guise Camberwell depot became known as Walworth bus garage, because there was already an existing Camberwell bus garage.

On the opposite side of the river the South bank of the Thames was occupied that summer by the Festival of Britain. A marvellous extravaganza, marking the centenary of the Great Exhibition held in the Crystal Palace, but also a final turning back on the years of austerity. Shiny RTs seemed part of the brave new world the Festival promised, trams did not. Elderly STLs didn't either really, but nevertheless no fewer than 183 of the class had been overhauled and were put to work on eight of the nine special services in connection with the Festival.

Although not as old as the STLs, nor for that matter the prewar TD4 STDs, the 11 unfrozen TD7 STDs, very unpopular with crews, were all taken out of service by March, 1951 and subsequently sold.

1951 was the year when the true single-deck version of the RT, the RF, entered service. Destined to be almost as long lived, this was based on the AEC Regal IV underfloor-engined chassis and had a body designed, of course, by LT, and built by Metro-Cammell. The first 25 were only 27ft 6in long (the remainder were 30ft), and like all the class, 7ft 6in wide. RF1-25, LUC201-225, were 35-seat private hire

coaches, fitted with glass cant panels and painted in an attractive Lincoln green and grey livery with red lettering and lining out. Immediately after them the production Green Line coaches began entering service. These were destined to replace all prewar coaches and initially numbered 263 vehicles, although there were subsequent transfers to and from the Central and Country Area fleets. They seated 39 passengers.

Concurrently with the first RFs an 8ft-wide version entered service. This was the RFW. It was quite unlike any other London single-decker, having an ECW body of unique design with 39 proper coach seats — Green Line coaches were really only glorified buses. There were 15 of them and they joined the private hire fleet.

At the other extreme a couple of Country Area lowbridge STs were transferred to the Central Area to work the 230.

On the Underground the first five car trains of modern P stock had begun operating on the Circle Line in 1947, replacing older stock, including that with hand worked doors. One of the reasons I found travelling on the Underground scary as a small child was rattling through tunnels with the sliding doors partly open; I had nightmares about falling out. By the

beginning of 1951 the last rake of these ancient, wooden-bodied cars dating back to the 1920s and beyond had finally been withdrawn.

1952

1952 opened with the largest number of trams taken out of service in one fell swoop so far; before the summer was out they would all be gone. Stage 6 on 5 January saw 88 trams withdrawn from New Cross depot and 21 from Norwood. Routes 48, 52, 54, 74, 78 and all night 5 were replaced by bus routes 48, 149, 69, 179, 178 and all night 285. The West End terminus of Victoria saw trams no more. Vauxhall Bridge Road here was so wide that the replacement buses were able to turn round in the middle of the road.

A new garage, Rye Lane, in Peckham, opened with tram replacement stage 6. Although it was not on the site of a former tram depot, a permanent way store had previously been there.

Leyland was in the news at the beginning of the year when a handful of new RTLs, in red livery, was sent to the Country Area; they quickly came back to

the Central Area. Other RTLs went to Hendon, home of the prewar STDs which had worked the 13 ever since their introduction in 1937. These were still in good condition and took up work at Enfield, displacing Gs, a class which was disappearing rapidly.

The Green Line fleet was seeing its biggest transformation since the late 1930s. Production of the RF was proceeding apace and many of the prewar coaches which were being displaced — 10T10s, Qs and TFs — were demoted to bus work, sometimes in the Central Area, although only the Ts were repainted red. These in turn replaced older Ts and LT

single-deckers, although some of the latter survived into 1953. As well as wartime Guys being taken out of service, the two other classes of double-decker introduced during the war, the Bristols and the Daimlers, were also being withdrawn. A few were broken up but the great majority found homes elsewhere and often served their new owners longer than they had LT, either with their original bodies, or with new ones.

It was a curious thing that some undertakings managed to make these much maligned and allegedly ramshackle bodies last as long as the most cared for

Above left:
No 1849 of the last Q1 series of London trolleybuses heads for Twickenham. *Author's collection*

Left:
A District Line train of R silver stock emerges from the depths at Ravenscourt Park on its way to Richmond.

Above:
Former Green Line 10T10 No 598 repainted red and working route 200 from AL (Merton) Garage. *D. A. Jones*

prewar and postwar vehicles. Burton-on-Trent Corporation, for instance, bought five ex-London Gs from the Leeds dealer, W. North in November 1953 and kept the former G351 running until January 1967, 20 years and 11 months after it had first entered service from Upton Park garage. After that it was bought for preservation by John Lines. It was seen a number of times on the HCVC London to Brighton run, and is presently living happily, the only survivor of London's wartime utilities, in running order, at Cobham Museum. Not bad for a wartime reject. Other utility buses went off to the Celtic fringe, Guys to Edinburgh, Daimlers to Belfast, where both were rebodied. Some of the Daimlers came to sad endings, destroyed in the Troubles which erupted in 1968.

Three new buses, RTs 2775/6 and RTL1307, took themselves off on an 8,000-mile goodwill tour of the USA in March, returning without one mechanical

failure and to an official welcome from the Minster of Transport in August. Perhaps it was they who put the idea into the heads of American entrepreneurs to import London buses and employ them on sightseeing work, a practice which continues to this day.

The night of 5-6 April saw the last trams operating though Kingsway Subway and consequently the last North London trams. Not surprisingly there were many special runs in the final days, the very last passenger carrying service being conducted, fittingly, by E3 No 185, this class having been associated with the Subway since their building 20 years earlier. The 33 was replaced by bus route 171 and the 35 by 172. The two depots concerned suffered quite different fates, Norwood being closed, while Highgate continued to provide a home for its large trolleybus fleet; indeed, it held the largest number of all, 127.

A remarkable new garage was opened and allocated about a dozen RTLs to operate route 178 (although it would eventually house over 200 vehicles). This was Stockwell. Bus garages don't usually feature in anyone's list of great architecture but Stockwell is the exception. Designed by Adie, Button and Partners, it boasted the largest expanse of roof without intermediate support anywhere in Europe. The great, sweeping reinforced concrete arches matched the great railway stations of the 19th century, and even now, more than 40 years on, Stockwell is still a beacon for the future.

The big story of 1952 was the end of the trams. This came on 5-6 July. The final six routes were the

36, 38, 40, 44, 46 and 72, all but the 46, which terminated at Southwark Bridge, negotiating that celebrated Mecca of tram enthusiasts, the Embankment. Not many of the LCC standard E1 cars were left, most of the services which Abbey Wood and New Cross depots operated being worked by the later corporation version of the E1 and the E3s and HR2s. One E1 which would live on was No 1025. This dated back to 1908 and it had been set aside for preservation in the LT collection. A unique feature of the final conversion was the use of 50-odd elderly buses — STLs. They were joined by some 'prewar' RTs, numerous RTLs which had been used to train tram drivers to drive buses, and just 15 brand new RTs.

Saturday 5 July dawned sunny and warm and the crowds were out and about everywhere between Abbey Wood, Woolwich, Eltham, Charlton, Greenwich and central London, not forgetting the Elephant and Castle. A delightful film, *No Trams to the Elephant* was in the process of recording the London tram and those who regularly rode it. There were many specials that day, the last ordinary service car being E3 No 1951 due to leave Savoy Street, Embankment on route 40 at 11.38pm and arrive at New Cross at 00.29am. In the meantime LT Chairman Lord Latham, together with nine London mayors, had left Charlton works in the appropriately numbered E3 No 1952 to greet No 1951 at New Cross depot. Not surprisingly the vast crowds threw these schedules to the winds, and in fact one more car, E3 No 187 from Eltham, was the very last London tram. Later all those cars still in New Cross depot left for the final, short journey to Penhall tramatorium, the motors finally falling silent around 03.00.

The crowds who attended were in a festive mood and while there was a nostalgic regret that something familiar had gone — Paul Jennings wrote a particularly elegant farewell in the *Observer* — most looked forward to a new era of reduced traffic congestion, safer road conditions and up-to-date, rubber-tyred comfort. For a little while all this came about, but soon the congestion was back too, and then exceeded anything the trams had caused. The absence of trams lines certainly made life easier for cyclists, but other traffic conditions conspired against them: few then worried overmuch about pollution from petrol and diesel fumes, and who would have thought that in the mid-1990s there would be hundreds of double-deck buses operating in central London, older by 10 years and more, than the HR2 and the E3 cars when they were withdrawn and broken up?

An ironic coda to all this is that London's very last electric-powered road vehicles — trolleybuses which once would have been intended to replace the trams — were delivered in 1952. These were further Q1s, identical to the earlier ones, numbered 1842-1891, LYH 842-891. Allocated to Isleworth and Fulwell depots they allowed a number of the oldest standard,

Above left:
HR2 No 1896 at Victoria. *IAL*

Below left:
Former West Ham car No 337 at Beresford Square, Woolwich. *IAL*

Above:
RT3414 and RTL1275, two 1952 deliveries, alongside RT422 of 1947 at Thornton Heath. Taken nine years later, all are changed: RT422, by then the oldest bus in LT passenger service, has a later body, RT3414 has the type of body which originally graced RT422, whilst the RTL is in green livery, having just been dispatched from Hatfield.

as well as some experimental trolleys, to be withdrawn.

On the Underground a new design of car for the Circle Line entered service. This was the R49. Most looked very like their predecessors but the 90 carriages were significantly different in that their bodies were built of aluminium alloy. This allowed a significant weight saving of over five tons for each vehicle. Built by MCCW they took up work in 1952-3. Amongst them were eight cars which looked quite different to anything previously seen and would set the pattern for the future. These were left unpainted. Remarkably no less than two tons was thus saved over a similar, painted, eight-car train, so that although the aluminium cars were more expensive to build than steel ones, they were cheaper to run.

The new towns, planned to create homes out in the country for Londoners displaced by bombing and slum clearance, were growing rapidly by the mid-1950s. The vast Harold Hill estate led to a new garage being opened at North Street, Romford while many Country Area routes were being re-organised and expanded to cope with the new business. In those days few of the houses were built with garages, storing up complications for the future when cars would line both sides of the not-very-wide residential roads, impeding the progress of buses.

Delivery of new RFs to the Central Area was completed in 1953 and large numbers then went to the Country Area. Virtually all prewar single-deckers were eliminated, including the veteran LT six-wheelers, the last of which were withdrawn from Dalston garage at the end of January 1953. They disappeared at the same time as the last 1T1s and thus no buses inherited from London General remained in service any longer. Only the 10T10s remained at the end of the year, some 30 odd at work in the Country Area and on staff duties.

A new class of single-decker entered service in 1953. This was the GS. Looking back it may seem rather extraordinary that LT had need for normal control buses as late as the mid-1950s, but 84 of these little Guy 26-seaters were thought necessary to replace the prewar C and CR classes and work the lanes and more sparsely populated regions at the outer

Above:
GS42 in suitably rural surroundings at the Plough, Coldharbour in the Surrey hills. *Mark Chadwick*

Left:
STL1716 working a Coronation route tour. *Alan Cross*

limits of 55 Broadway's vast empire. The family likeness with the RF was plain enough, as was their ECW origin. Their bonnet design was based on that used on contemporary Fordson lorries, which had slightly down market connotations; if one could overlook this they were rather handsome little vehicles.

Many familiar classes were seen no more in LT by the end of the year. Apart from the Ts and LTs already mentioned, other single-deck/coach classes to disappear were the TFs, the Qs, the 9T9s, the 11T11s (thus severing the link with the old Reliance, upon whose chassis the bodies had begun their careers), the Cs and CRs. Of the double-deck fleet, the last of the austerity Gs and the Bs were withdrawn, the Ds reached near extinction and the prewar STDs were fading away rapidly, as was the short-lived SRT class.

The STL class, after the onslaught of 1950 when over half the class had disappeared, had subsequently been making something of a fight back, often replacing withdrawn austerity double-deckers. In 1952 no less than 48 had been used in the final tram replacement programme, including several of the old sit-up-and-beg variety, scarcely

Above:
TF40 now in the ownership of the London School of Economics and with its rear indicator removed at Waterloo.

Right:
C31 of Hertford (HG) garage, 28 February 1953, with some choice prewar hardware in the background, amongst which is a fabric-roofed Riley and a Morris 8. *Alan Cross*

Below:
Dunton Green garage with RTs 4525, 3496 and 3869, RF587 and 568.

newer than many of the trams and, some opined, rather less comfortable. However with the austerity classes virtually extinct and no let up in the delivery of new RTs and RTLs, 1953 saw STL numbers decline from 508 to 223. The last overhauls and repaintings of the class, into the dreary overall red, were completed in April. By the end of the year all the lowbridge varieties of STL had gone, as had the last red and white one, the livery which best suited the class. However there was one more significant chapter to be written in their history.

1953 was Coronation year and, just as with the Festival of Britain two years earlier, a fleet of STLs was got together to operate tours of the route and cope with the huge influx of visitors to the capital for the great event. 160 members of the class, of many varieties, were used on these duties.

An innovation which greatly pleased us Croydonians was the first orbital Green Line route. This was the 725. It linked the outer Thames-side Country Area towns of Gravesend and Windsor by way of Dartford, Bromley, Croydon, Kingston, and Staines. The entire journey took 3hr 22min, but no one except a rabid enthusiast patronised the complete half circle. The value of the 725 was that it provided direct links between places which had hitherto only been connected by several changes of bus or by train journeys into and out of central London. Croydon and Kingston, for example, were now only 45min apart, Croydon to Dartford was just 4min over the hour. The 725 was deservedly popular and the following year the service frequency over most of the route was increased from one coach an hour to two. It was the first Green Line route to avoid central London.

Left:
The former D119, rebodied by Harkness and operated by Belfast Corporation, seen in Donegall Square alongside a Gux BTX trolleybus, also with a Harkness body.

Below left:
STLs and Gs on the scrap line at Charlton. *IAL*

1954

1954 saw a number of lasts — and a first of great import. Most significantly it saw the delivery — although not entry — into service of the last RTs and RTLs. However, before we reach those momentous events, Merton and Sutton garages, long the homes, or so it seemed to us bus spotters, of the D class, said goodbye to their last Daimlers. The older, prewar STD class continued to operate out of Hendon garage until June, while the very much newer SRT class operated its last journeys, from Cricklewood garage, during July.

Throughout the early part of 1954 the numbers of the prewar STL class had been steadily declining until by mid-June they were operating just one Central Area route, the 101 out of Upton Park, although there were still a number spread about the Country Area. At peak times the 101 was London's most frequent route with 64 buses working through east London from Wanstead to the Thames at North Woolwich, a terminus it shared with several trolleybus routes. RTs had begun to oust the STLs in February and on 30 June they saw off the final 14. At the same time there was a slight decrease in frequency and the tram replacement 109 became London's busiest bus route.

A month later, on 1 September, the only STLs left at work in the Country Area were the 20 postwar vehicles. Thus London's standard double-decker of the immediate prewar years, a familiar sight in West End, City, suburbs and the Home Counties for 21 years, would carry passengers no more. They were not yet quite gone from the streets of London for they were still of use as trainers and as staff transport, at least for a few months longer.

Below:
Morden station forecourt with STL1813 of Sutton (A) garage, a wartime D from Merton (AL) and a postwar Park Royal-bodied D182-281 series Daimler from Sutton garage. *D. A. Jones*

Left:
The former Country Area front-entrance STL1494 was converted to a tree lopper; here it's parked on the forecourt of Thornton Heath Garage.

Below:
A pair of RTs, 2063 leading, enjoying a day out at the the seaside beside Ramsgate Harbour, and a selection of pre and postwar East Kent Leyland Tiger coaches with bodies, like RT2063, by Park Royal. *Author's collection*

Right:
Shiny new RT4763 of 1954 vintage based at Godstone garage, turns beneath the trolleybus wires at West Croydon and sets off on its long journey southwards to Sussex and the Ashdown Forest.

At the same time as the end of the prewar STL the last prewar single-decker, the 10T10, ended its passenger service in London, the final Country Area examples being withdrawn. Again it would last a little longer as staff transport. No sooner had the 10T10s gone than they were followed by the first postwar Ts, some of the 14T12s based at Norbiton. Only eight years old and far from worn out, although they looked no more modern than the prewar ex-coaches, they went because they were victims of a changing world. Car ownership was increasing, television was becoming a real factor in keeping people at home in the evenings, LT in an era of full employment was finding it increasingly difficult in recruiting and holding on to staff: all of which meant fewer buses were needed.

Another result of this decline was that many new RTs and RTLs found they were not needed and went straight into store. At this late stage the first Park Royal RTs in green livery and the first batch of Weymann-bodied RTLs appeared. The RTs had bodies which had originally been fitted to SRTs (the last of this markedly unsuccessful experiment went at the end of July) while the Weymann-bodied RTLs started at 1601 and continued to 1631 — the very last of its class. It was delivered on 10 November and like its 29 predecessors it went into store. The final RT was 4794, also with a Weymann body, which arrived a day later. However the float body, from Park Royal, did not arrive until 19 November. The highest number RT was 4825. This had a Park Royal body and it entered service from Cricklewood garage on 29 March.

Thus construction of the RT family, the most standardised example of bus production ever seen or likely to be seen in this country, was over. Its grand total, AEC and Leyland, was 6,805. Sadly, and ominously, no fewer than 144 of the newest example were not immediately needed. They were expected to be required for future growth and were hidden away, chiefly at Garston and Loughton garages, although I also came across a batch of RTLs, mounted on wooden blocks and without tyres, at Reigate.

In April LT announced that its trolleybus fleet, the largest in the world, was doomed and that replacement by diesel buses would start in four years time. The large majority of its vehicles were of prewar or early wartime origin and had outlived their motorbus contemporaries. Nevertheless they seemed in perfectly sound condition and did not look dated. The main problem was that new trolleybuses were vastly more expensive than diesel buses and, environmental concerns being of much lower priority to most people than they are today, the decision was generally seen as inevitable.

The last relic from a long vanished time, an NS canteen, was withdrawn in 1954. One which survived into the 1950s was 2295 which sat beside Chelsham garage. I knew it well but somehow took it for granted. Looking back it seems extraordinary that I should have done so, for the contrast between it and the shiny green RTs which had just been delivered was as great as that between, say, the first underfloor-engined coaches and canvas-roofed charabancs.

In the mid-1950s no great fuss was made of old buses as they disappeared and complete classes could vanish without ceremony, witness the end of the celebrated STLs and the 10T10s, but there was no shortage of publicity for *the* event of 1954. This was the appearance at the Commercial Motor Show of the

first Routemaster. Hundreds of RMs are still with us, millions of words have been written about this celebrated vehicle, and it has exceeded both the length of service and the fame of the RT, so there is no need for a description of it here. But it's worth commenting that the RM was rather less favourably received than its predecessor, that many modifications were made before it entered production and that while it contained a number of advanced features, it was also in some respects old-fashioned in 1954, and even more so when it did finally enter production.

1955

1955 was a gloomy year for LT. Passenger numbers were declining and cuts in double and single-deck motorbus and trolleybus routes were made in February. The summer programme in the Central Area brought about more cuts at the beginning of May, and although there was still plenty of extra recreational business on Sundays, this also was substantially down on the previous year. Less than a month later more reductions meant that overall scheduled Central Area bus and trolley services were down 5.25 per cent on those of six months earlier.

A number of strikes resulted, the men worried that their earnings, and even possibly their livelihoods, were under threat; at this stage they didn't last long but they were a warning of what was to come.

Inevitably these cuts meant many buses were withdrawn, permanently, from service. A number of the older trolleybuses, the experimental ones and all the surviving non-standard postwar double-decker motorbuses — G436, the all-Leyland PD1 STDs and the 18STL20s — had gone by the beginning of the summer. Not only this but the 'prewar' RTs now

began to be taken out of service. For some time it had been the practice to place a number of them in the training fleet halfway through their overhaul cycle; now many more were to serve permanently in this capacity, often for a number of years. Some were sold to other operators, while RT59 became the very first of its class to be scrapped. The very last to operate in the Central Area, appropriately from Chelverton Road, Putney, came off the road on 25 May. However seven of the class rather unexpectedly reappeared in the Country Area. A bridge at Broxbourne on the 327 route was unable to bear the weight of the postwar RT — up to then the postwar STLs had worked over it — so a batch of 2RTs, each one 15cwt lighter than its postwar brethren, was repainted green and sent to Hertford garage.

The postwar STLs and STDs not surprisingly soon found buyers and all worked for their new owners for many years. The demotion of the 2RTs to the training fleet meant that they could replace the fleet's mainstay — prewar STLs, which could now be disposed of. Most garages usually had at least one, sometimes more, STLs on its books and I used to cycle around the local ones in the evenings or at weekends ferreting them out. Most were roof number box types with DGX or DLU registrations, although there were a number of slightly earlier CXXs as well as the occasional sit-up-and-beg veteran. June saw the last of them withdrawn.

I had not expected to see a 10T10 again but one April evening I was greatly surprised when T631 went bustling up Purley Way with a load of homeward-bound LTE employees on its way from Chiswick Works to Reigate. By this time I had acquired an unreliable BSA Bantam and a couple of weeks later I managed to pursue it as far as Reigate where I was able to photograph T613 and a brother

parked outside the garage. Very soon both these and all other remaining 10T10s had gone.

So heavy were the three lots of service cuts in 1955 that, following on the withdrawal of the 'prewar' 2RTs, the very first postwar ones went. The ones chosen were the least standard, the Cravens. Fifty were delicensed on 1 June, although a number reappeared briefly during the two-week rail strike which began over the Whitsun Bank Holiday weekend. I had been staying in the Isle of Wight and had to make my way home by service bus from Portsmouth. Southdown PD2s got me as far as Horsham but the traffic jams were monumental. I just managed to catch the last 414, a standard green RT from Dorking garage. This was going no further than its home but a red RT on the 93 got me to Morden where another on the 118 took me as far as Mitcham Common, leaving me to walk the last three miles. Country Area service cuts were less severe than in the Central Area and 13 of the stored RTs, delivered in 1954, were put into service.

One other new bus appeared in 1955. This was the second Routemaster, RM2. Similar in appearance to RM1, it had a redesigned and rather clumsy looking front end, and the same inadequate route indicators as originally fitted to RM1. It appeared in March, and spent the rest of the year undergoing a variety of tests.

Aldenham works, originally intended to deal with Tube trains, began to operate its celebrated flow-line overhaul system, taking over work on RT-type chassis and bodies from Chiswick during 1955.

New Addington, known locally as Little Siberia, was a huge council estate on the windy slopes of the North Downs south of Croydon. It was begun just before World War 2 but was greatly expanded afterwards. One of the chief complaints of the local inhabitants — chief of all was that they didn't want to be there — was that public transport out of the place was expensive and slow. In an effort to alleviate the latter condition, though it could do nothing about the former, LT introduced its first express bus service in August. A proportion of the 130 service was given new white on blue route blinds and boards indicating the various stopping places within the estate, whence it ran non-stop to East Croydon station. Later in 1955 Croydon also saw the introduction of the first Country Area express service when certain peak hour services on the 403 between West Croydon and Chelsham were so designated.

Above left:
The 2RTs finished passenger service in the Central Area in 1955. Some spent all their lives at Putney (AF) garage and here two in all-red livery work the special service from Southfields station to the Wimbledon tennis championships. *Alan Cross*

Left:
Former Green Line T613 and 631 used as staff transports at Reigate garage, May 1955.

Above right:
RT492, newly fitted with a non-roof-box body, at Addiscombe, September 1955.

Right:
RT3142 ready to work a 403 express service, alongside RT2504 at Chelsham garage.

1956

Probably the most interesting event of 1956 was the entry into passenger service of RM1. It was sent to Cricklewood garage in January and began work on route 2 on 8 February. The most noticeable visual difference was that it now had a standard three-piece destination display, like the RTs, except the number was on the left, rather than the right of the via display — in other words identical to STLs of the 1933-7 period. Roof number boxes were gone for good.

RM1 worked until August, the reactions of both passengers and crews being carefully noted. The seats were not as comfortable as the RT pattern: personally I found neither these nor the interior decor as pleasing as the RT design, while drivers and engineers realised there were severe front end problems. Chiswick quickly got to work and RM1 reappeared at the Lord Mayor's Show in November with a very different, and much less attractive looking front. However behind this was a more advanced engine, power steering and a much better flow of air. The Lord Mayor's Show over, RM1 went back to Chiswick for more modifications. Those unfamiliar with the parade

which London's new Lord Mayor makes each year through the City may think of it as purely a civic occasion but it's much more than this, rather more of a carnival, even if the weather can be pretty discouraging. Among the many aspects of London life which it features, transport is often prominent. In 1950, for instance, a very authentic mock up of the then new Western Region Gas Turbine locomotive appeared and LT, naturally enough, regularly takes part — as do medical and other students who can be less than totally respectful to their elders, though possibly not their betters, on parade.

The Monocoach, an experimental AEC underfloor-engined bus with a Park Royal body, which had previously done a stint with LT, reappeared from Reigate garage. Both its appearance and its registration number, NLP 635, were reminiscent of LT practice.

One-man-operation had always been a feature of the smallest buses in the fleet — the Dennis Darts, the Cubs and the GSs — but experiments had begun with RFs in 1954 and these continued with many more Country Area vehicles being added to the original four. Musical chairs proved a popular pastime within the RF fleet in 1956 with others being converted to

Left:
The experimental AEC/Park Royal Monocoach at St Albans. *IAL*

Right:
RT149 on learner duty in Piccadilly with an RT opposite and an RTW coming up behind the Morris Oxford taxi.

Below:
RM1 speeds across Waterloo Bridge whilst working from Cricklewood garage (W) on the 260.

Green Line coaches. These included the final 10 private-hire RFs, 16-25, now in a very sombre livery of green all over, six red ones and four Country Area green ones.

Very few new buses arrived, just a handful of green RTs from store; rather more disappeared. The last of the Craven RTs went in October, all but one of them quickly finding new owners; two of the first batch of TDs were sold and 41 trolleybuses went, five travelling to the other side of the world to take up work in Penang in Malaya. A seemingly insignificant event in the service fleet which decades later would have great significance for the preservation movement was the transfer of the body of RT1 to the chassis of the one Craven not to be sold, RT1420. The body had

been written off after it had been badly damaged in trying to pass under a low bridge at Norbiton. As mobile training unit 1037J and running on trade plates it remained with LT until 1978.

Two other events of great import concerned with preservation — a topic we have barely touched upon until now because, apart from the admirable LT collection, the concept barely existed — took place in 1956. The first was the celebration of the centenary of the LGOC. Nowadays we seem able to find a virtually limitless supply of anniversaries to celebrate but then such jollifications were most unusual. LT cranked up some horse-buses, some motor ones including B43, K424, NS1995 and STL445, and some current types, and drove them around Regents

Above:
The preserved T31, restored to its original 1929 condition, at Brighton after taking part in the 1977 Commercial Vehicle run.

Left:
Craven RT1513 alongside three standard members of the class shortly before withdrawal from Catford garage.

Park on 16 July; five days later it displayed them on Horse Guard's Parade. In October one of the earliest of the T class, No 31, which had entered service with the LGOC early in 1930, was sold into private preservation, the very first time this had happened to a London bus.

On the Underground plans were being laid for developments on both the tube and the surface lines. On the former, design work was beginning on new rolling stock while on the latter the decision was made to institute new works and extend the electrification of the Metropolitan Line to Amersham and Chesham.

In December the Suez Crisis, brought about by the Egyptians deciding to nationalise the canal which ran through their country, and the UK and France deciding to send forces to prevent this, erupted and brought about petrol rationing. I was very aware of this for I was serving Her Majesty at the time, or rather the Adjutant of RAF Abingdon, as his typist. We, he and I that is, with the help of a few others, trained the Parachute Regiment how to fall out of aeroplanes without hurting themselves. It looked like a good many of them might be falling on top of the Egyptians and some of us clerks might have to follow in order to record the number of fezs damaged in the process, etc. However it all ground to a halt after a few days, but the petrol rationing continued and London's buses suddenly found they could get around a great deal quicker with far fewer private cars cluttering up the streets.

Above:
Former GWR '57xx' class pannier tank at Neasden depot.

1957

The dearth of new deliveries — after the extraordinary period from 1947 to 1954 when the vast RT family had been in production — continued through 1957. Just two new buses arrived, the third and fourth Routemaster prototypes. RML3 had Leyland mechanical units, hence the 'L', and a body built by Weymann at Addlestone. It was the closest yet to what the production buses would look like, although the front end was not yet finalised. RML3 arrived in July but spent the rest of the year undergoing various tests at the Leyland works and at Chiswick. For this reason it attracted little publicity.

Quite different was the reception given Routemaster No 4. This was the most distinctive of all the prototypes, being a double-deck coach. One might have thought that given the lack of success of their previous attempts at this concept — the much heralded RTC1 after its brief days of glory had ended its London career and had been sold — LT would have ceased heading up this particular avenue. However Green Line travel was increasing and they

Above:
'Prewar' RT65 on learner duties approaching Holborn.

obviously thought third time lucky; up to a point, they were right.

CRL4 had, like RML3, Leyland mechanical units, but what attracted all the publicity was its handsome 55-seat body. While it followed basic Routemaster proportions and general design, it was rather more refined with nicely padded seats (although, like all Green Line ones they were still basically glorified bus ones with low backs rather than proper coach seats), luggage racks, pale green window surrounds, platform doors, polished lamp surrounds and front wheel trims, and full independent front suspension. The steering was not, however, power-assisted. The builders of the body were ECW, the nationalised Lowestoft firm which had built the GSs and the distinctive RFWs, but were otherwise chiefly associated with putting bodies on top of Bristol chassis.

Unlike the other prototypes, CRL4 went into passenger service relatively soon upon delivery. It arrived from Suffolk on 14 June and took up work from Romford garage on route 721 on 9 October. Here it ran alongside the RTs which were normally used and continued to the end of 1957. We will pick up CRL4's career subsequently; suffice to say at this stage that it saw vastly more passenger service than all the other three prototype RMs put together. Meanwhile RM2 had been repainted green and at long last went into service. It was sent in May to Reigate to work the 406; but not for long. By August it was back in red livery, despite which it was sent to Turnham Green (turn 'em green, get it?) and the following month started working the 91. RM1 began work from Cricklewood garage on the 260 on 1 March.

The petrol rationing brought about by the Suez

Crisis ended and LT produced figures showing how much faster its buses had travelled, carrying more passengers, while the roads were uncongested. The arguments about restricting the private car and its selfish use of valuable road space were hotting up.

The famous Red Rover ticket made its appearance on 12 October 1957. It cost 5s (25p) and was available on Saturdays and Sundays.

The same month the Cromwell Road air terminal opened. It was built over the District Line tracks and was a replacement for the vastly more convenient one at Waterloo which had to close because its lease ran out. LT's particular interest was that it provided the 65 coaches which linked the terminal with Heathrow airport. Although they didn't actually own them, these Park Royal-bodied 1½-deck coaches were classified 4RF4 and lived at Shepherd's Bush garage, having been transferred from the basement of Victoria. Initially each service was supposed to run in connection with a particular flight and thus all sorts of exotic destinations featured, Bulawayo or Reykjavik for example, providing an interesting contrast to Camden Town and Putney Heath, which was where the 74s, the only LT route to pass the Cromwell Road terminal, were bound. Before long, with the increase in both the size of airliners and the frequency of their departures, these destinations became meaningless and the only time I can remember travelling on this service I was assured I would not be forced to travel to Singapore, which was where the RF claimed it was headed, rather than exotic Manchester, my destination; phew, what a relief!

The 17 years of the 'prewar' RTs' passenger service came to an end in August when route 327 was diverted away from the weak bridge which

Above:
RML3 at the Bank.

Below:
Clapham Common station on the Northern Line. Although this picture was taken decades after 1957 nothing much has changed since then, when it was already something of a period piece.

necessitated their use and the final seven 2RTs entered the training fleet.

One of the worst rail accidents ever, at Lewisham on 5 December, resulted in substitute bus services for six days. The accident occured in thick fog, a phenomenon still common in London then. I was hitch-hiking home from RAF West Malling in a lorry that evening and about the same time, not far away at Sidcup, I had to get out and walk ahead of the lorry at a roundabout until I could find the turn we needed. Such conditions made it almost impossible to run public transport services. Whatever present day pollution hazards we may face, that is one which thankfully has been banished.

The first of the three experimental tube trains known as the 1956 stock, appeared in 1957 (LT always gave the number of the year when they had thought up the idea of a new train rather than when it appeared). One seven-car train was built by Metro-Cammell, one by the BRCW and one by the Gloucester RCW Co. Fluorescent lighting was standard, the car bogies had rubber suspension and livery was the now standard unpainted aluminium. Visually they were not very different, inside and out, to the 1938 stock, although the front end, which incorporated a roller destination blind, was less well proportioned. They were put to work on the Piccadilly Line and, proving successful, led to production orders for sufficient units to replace the pre-1938 stock in use on that line.

Above:
RT2119 of Reigate garage passing South Croydon. This was one of a number of not quite standard RTs, the chassis having been delivered at the beginning of 1950, whilst the body was some two years older. It was the first RT body to be repainted from red to green. RTs 2116–21 were the only ones in the 2000 series to enter service new with roof-box bodies.

1958

1958 was a very unhappy year for LT (it was all right for me, I got demobbed on 16 January). By the end of the first quarter, passenger journeys throughout the system were down by 7 per cent. Much worse was to follow. On Sunday 4 May the Transport and General Worker's Union (TGWU) called out its members and for seven weeks, until 21 June, Londoners had to make do without motorbuses, trolleybuses and Green Line coaches, the only exceptions being a motley collection of vehicles operated by an extreme political set-up calling itself the 'People's League for the Defence of Freedom'.

The industrial dispute had been rumbling on for months. After going to arbitration in February an award was proposed only to drivers and conductors in the Central Services Department, and although LT said it would consider the position of the Green Line staff this left plenty of men and women with nothing.

Above:
A former Lytham St Anne's Leyland Cheetah operated by the People's League for Freedom during the bus strike.

Right:
Stockwell's RTL1610, newly into service after four years in store is most unusually devoid of adverts and has shiny wheel discs; seen here motoring majestically over Lambeth Bridge.

At the beginning of April the TGWU gave a month's strike notice and although there were further talks the two sides could not agree and the strike began. Although there were calls by some railmen to join in, the Underground was not affected, except that demand upon its services was so great that at times it could barely cope. Most road passengers made use of British Rail trains, others came in by hired coaches and, inevitably, private car use increased dramatically.

Eventually concessions were made to the staff who had not been included in the earlier proposed deals and the strike ended on 21 June.

The aftermath of the strike was almost as dramatic as the dispute itself, if not in every respect immediately so. Many staff had left, either because they couldn't exist on strike pay or because they saw no future with a contracting LT — and remember this was the days of full employment so switching jobs was easy enough. My fellow students and I never had problems in the late 1950s and early 1960s finding vacation work, often in the transport industry. I worked at King's Cross, Victoria, Gatwick Airport and Haywards Heath stations. A friend got a job as a conductor on route 93. One morning some joker amongst the passengers rang the bell at the bottom of Wimbledon Hill while he was standing behind the bus; fortunately he was a champion miler and managed to catch it up before it reached the top of the hill!

Many passengers never returned, services were cut and fares rose. By the end of the year there were 546 fewer buses on the streets and roads of London and its suburbs. A rather extraordinary process had already started in January 1958. This was the withdrawal of the standard postwar RT. LT had simply overestimated the number of vehicles it would

Above left:
Chelsham garage with Country Area RT2256 and 2510 of 1949 and 1950 vintage respectively and RT4760 and 4741 newly into service.

Left:
RT1619 dwarfed by a Boeing Stratocruiser, Heathrow airport. *LT*

Above:
Dunton Green garage with five GSs and six RTs.

Below:
Central Area red RF335 pressed into Green Line service rounds Hyde Park Corner accompanied by a Vauxhall Wyvern of similar vintage.

need in the mid-1950s. The last built RTs and RTLs had gone straight into store, and the Craven RTs — good, modern buses with many years of service left in them — had been sold. Now it was the turn, less than four years after production of the RT ended, for it to begin the long — very long as it turned out — process of withdrawal. The logical decision — or what seemed to be the logical decision — was taken to remove the lowest numbered RTs and RTLs. Thus RT402, and RTLs 501 and 502 had all been taken out of service before the winter was out. However, because of London's unique overhaul system, there was no guarantee that a bus which emerged from Aldenham possessed either the same chassis or body that it had gone in with. In other words it was a totally different vehicle. This sounds pretty loopy but the explanation was that LT would be losing large sums of money on the road tax with vehicles off the road for many weeks being overhauled. Thus as, say, RT624 entered the works, another RT just emerging would assume RT624's identity. Perfectly sensible, although it was something we bus spotters knew nothing about in our early days and would have been very nonplussed if we had, and it has caused all sorts of fierce arguments in the preservation era as to just which chassis, bodies and complete vehicles are still with us.

What all this meant was that selling off the nominally oldest RTs and RTLs was not as logical as it first appeared. Body changes at overhaul could

Above:
Green RT4764 of Reigate garage, RT1042 from Leatherhead, red RT3330 from Norbiton and TD128 of Kingston all on Kingston station forecourt.

mean that a chassis dating from 1947-8 might carry a body dating from 1954. The HLW and HLX-registered batches were going for overhaul at the same time as those registered OLD and so this did happen. Clearly it didn't make sense to sell off the best and keep the worst and so after a time it was decided that those buses with the oldest bodies would go. This meant that the roof-box versions were the first to disappear from the fleet. Ceylon purchased vast numbers of RTs, RTLs and RTWs, but many also stayed in Britain, a good number going to Scotland while Bradford Corporation built up a sizeable fleet to run alongside its trolleybuses. The withdrawals did at last allow nearly all the stored OLD-registered RTs and RTLs to come out of hiding and take up work. Unlike most of their class they entered service without adverts and so were instantly recognisable — especially as they also retained their polished wheel hubs and discs, features painted over on the rest of the fleet, which made it look very sombre. Some remained in this state for several months, although their appearance was marred by their paintwork — already slightly less than pristine after four years in store — growing steadily less bright in service. In Croydon we had such RTLs from Chalk Farm on route 68 and green RTs from a number of garages, notably Chelsham, Reigate and East Grinstead.

The first batch of TDs had all gone before the strike, while their AEC equivalents, the 14T12s,

disappeared afterwards, all having gone by the end of November. By the end of the year the T class, dating back to 1929, had almost vanished, just eight of the final batch of 15T13s still being at work. Even the GS class suffered, its operational numbers being down from 63 to 57.

1959

The year will be remembered chiefly for the start of the dismantling of London's trolleybus system, the largest in the world. The trolleybus never quite caught the imagination in the way that the tram did, perhaps because it was never quite sure of its own identity — it was a tram without wires, or a bus without independent propulsion. This is not to say it didn't — it doesn't — have its own enthusiasts and proponents. The trolleybus can still be found abroad and is still in production, but it can only dream of the remarkable reversal of fortunes of the tram. Once doomed to extinction both in England and overseas, tramways are now fortune's favourite with a proliferation of new systems and extensions to existing ones.

The principal *raison d'être* of the Routemaster was to replace the trolleybus. However, although RM1 appeared in 1954, the type was still not in production by early 1959. By this date the wisdom of such a long period of gestation was being questioned: in a number of respects the Routemaster seemed to be out of date, compared, for example, with the Bristol Lodekka and the Leyland Atlantean. The subsequent history of the Routemaster has more than vindicated all the care put into it; in the meantime LT had far more RTs than it knew what to do with and so the first three trolleybus replacement stages utilised members of the RT family.

First to go were three routes south of the river, the Bexleyheath-based 696 and 698 — isolated from the rest of the system, if only by the Woolwich Free Ferry — and Carshalton's 654. The 654 operated the oldest vehicles in the fleet, the short-wheelbase B1s, the most elderly of which dated from 1935. The changeover date was the night of 3-4 March. Many of the 23 newly overhauled RTs which were allocated to Carshalton had roof-box bodies; I never discovered if there was any particular reason for this interesting quirk.

Little over a month later, on 14-15 April, Clapton and Lea Bridge in northeast London lost their trolleybuses although most of the actual vehicles were

Above:
RT422 with a chassis dating from 1947 but a much newer body, operating in Bradford.
Author's collection

Right:
A cyclist attempts to outpace a B1 short-wheelbase trolleybus near Selhurst station.

relatively modern and lasted a little longer, migrating to other depots. Three routes, the 555, 581 and 677, were replaced by RTL-operated ones.

Stage 3, on 18-19 August, saw taken out of service London's most unusual trolleybuses, those destined for South Africa but diverted during the war to Ilford depot. Bow depot also closed, but nearly all its vehicles — mainly the N1 class dating from 1939-40 — migrated westwards to Colindale and Stonebridge. The routes which disappeared were the 661, 663, 691 and 693. RTLs and RTs were used as replacement vehicles.

The Routemaster was now at last in production. One-off RM8 had been shown at the September 1958 Commercial Motor Show. This introduced the standard front end, a most handsome design which was not only vastly better than that of the prototypes but also looked as if it might well be an AEC; this

Left:
Contrast in learners; 'prewar' RT115 and RM44 at Waterloo.

Below:
Dartford trolleybuses in the Charlton scrapyard. Prominent are D2s 407 and 480. *Central Press Photos*

was confirmed when the famous blue triangle reappeared later in the production run and was applied retrospectively to many earlier vehicles. The first production RMs were not used initially for trolleybus replacement but appeared mainly on central London routes and as trainers. The 8 was the very first route to receive them, from Cricklewood garage on 4 June.

They took up the work for which they had been originally designed on the night of 10-11 November when 61 went to Poplar and 16 to West Ham to replace the 567, 569 and 665 trolleybus routes. Among the trolleybus types operated by these depots was the L3. This was a chassisless design with Metro-Cammell Weymann bodies and AEC running units. Despite being 20 years old the L3s were still in fine condition and were moved several times as the system contracted, many ending up at Fulwell where they worked until the very last day of London trolleybus operation. Inevitably there were teething problems with the new RMs and many had to be taken out for short periods in order to rectify them. Nevertheless they settled down relatively quickly and rapidly became a familiar sight along the cobbled streets and amongst the cranes and lifting bridges of the London docks.

The four stages so far completed not only resulted in various replacement routes but many other motorbus routes were altered. The opportunity was taken to extend the sphere of influence formerly enjoyed by the trolleybus, essentially a suburbanite, into the heart of the West End and the City.

From time to time LT had closed garages and opened new ones: on 14 April one of the best known Country Area ones, Watford High Street, was replaced by Garston. It was possible, if eccentric, to hold a somewhat romantic image of the Country Area's vast empire and equate it with that once ruled by the Roman Empire where Croydon was the southern hub, just as Rome was the western one, and Watford in the north could be likened to Constantinople in the east. Anyone familiar with Croydon and Watford will know precisely what I mean.

One-man operation continued to spread in the Country Area, all its RFs being converted by the spring, and in the Central Area several Uxbridge and Norbiton routes went over to OMO, bringing about the withdrawal of many TDs. Some of these went abroad while I came across a number of others at Heathrow, where they carried passengers to and from the terminals to the aircraft; the first instance of an occupation which several generations of single-deckers would take up after being retired by LT. Their AEC counterpart, the 15T13, had all but disappeared, just one being scheduled for service, from Tring garage, at the end of the year.

A long way away, but of perhaps even greater significance, the last London trams were taken out of

service when the Leeds system closed down on 7 November and the Felthams — sold to Leeds some nine years earlier — were withdrawn.

At the end of 1959, because of the first three trolleybus replacement stages, there were actually more RTs and RTLs scheduled for service than there had been a year earlier: 3,388 of the former against 3,266, and 1,235 of the latter against 998. The last green RTs had been taken out of store, while the RTW class was still intact.

A small, unique section of the Underground system closed in 1959 when the South Acton branch, which was worked by a single car between Acton Town and South Acton, went out of business on 2 March.

1960

1960 saw the culmination of an ambitious scheme which would extend the electrification of the Metropolitan Line beyond its Rickmansworth frontier deep into Hertfordshire and Buckinghamshire to Amersham and the Chesham branch. Beyond Rickmansworth trains to Chesham, and to Amersham and Aylesbury, had been steam-hauled, originally by the Metropolitan's own locomotives, later by LNER ones, notably the 'L1' 2-6-4Ts, and latterly by LMS 2-6-4Ts.

A few years later Poet Laureate John Betjeman made his never to be forgotten documentary *Metroland*. The door plates of Metropolitan Railway carriages were engraved with the slogan 'Live in Metroland' and the film is a wonderful evocation of a journey over the Metropolitan. It starts at the palatial refreshment rooms above Baker Street station, stops off to view 'sin and mystery' in the prototype garden suburb of St John's Wood and takes a stroll through Neasden to an excruciating ditty sung by, I think, Peter Cook, with Eric Hoskins who informs us that 92 species of birds live in the vicinity. Then it's on to the site of what was intended to be Wembley's answer to the Eiffel Tower and where many years later — yesterday afternoon to be exact — Everton beat Manchester United 1-0. After that viewers drop in on a

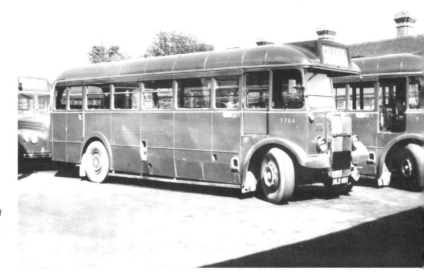

meeting of the finest collection of Tory ladies' hats ever seen, a snatch from the mighty Wurlitzer which once graced the Empire, Leicester Square and is now installed in the lounge of a semi-detached in Chorley Wood; then finally to the rural idyll of Quainton Road, where Metroland never quite managed to penetrate.

Until 1960 the trains operating to Rickmansworth and beyond were quite unlike any others found on the Underground system. They were a direct link with the days when the Metropolitan had ambitions to become a main line railway, linking the north of England with London, the southeast and even the Continent by way of the Channel Tunnel, for they were compartment stock, identical in layout and general appearance to those produced by the main line companies. They wore a brown livery as opposed to red or silver. The oldest dated back to Edwardian times, the most modern from the early 1930s. There were, however, some even older carriages. These were six, low-roofed vehicles, known as the Ashburys, dating from 1898-1900. They had originally been steam-hauled, had later been converted into electric multiple-units, and had then reverted to steam haulage in 1941 as push-pull units working between Chalfont, on the main line, and Chesham. The more modern, elliptical-roofed carriages either worked as multiple-units, the .T stock, or were hauled by a class of Bo-Bo locomotives, dating from 1921-3.

Craven was the firm chosen to build the replacement A stock, 248 carriages being ordered in 1959, a further 216 following for the Uxbridge services. They have lasted rather longer than the Craven RTs, and are today the oldest surface stock still at work. They bore some resemblance to previous Underground cars but were of less distinctive outline, without the turned out body sides or the elaborate valences over the windows. Designed to operate as four-car units, either singly or in pairs, internally they were a compromise between traditional Underground stock which always allowed plenty of room for standing passengers, and the needs of the longer distance passenger so all the seats, bar a few tip-up ones, were higher backed than usual and arranged transversely in threes and twos.

Concurrent with the electrification extension, four-tracking was extended as far out as Watford South Junction.

The scheme was inaugurated on the night of 11-12 September, when steam working ceased on the Chesham branch and A stock also began public working to Amersham. It would be another year before steam working ceased between Rickmansworth and Aylesbury. Steam would survive for a while longer on engineering duties, the motive power being former Great Western pannier tanks, the first of which, No 7711 (L90), was transferred from British Railways in October 1956. Five of the six ancient Ashbury carriages, the oldest in ordinary regular service in the United Kingdom, went for preservation on the Bluebell Railway.

In another part of the LT empire electric power was out of favour and the removal of the trolleybus continued throughout the year. On the night of 2-3 February further inroads were made into the east London network when 34 trolleybuses were taken out of service from Walthamstow depot and no less than 80 from West Ham. The 557, 669, 685, 689 and 690

routes disappeared. Woolwich had lost its trolleybuses with the stage 1 replacement, now they were gone from the opposite bank at North Woolwich. Eleven weeks later the remaining West Ham and Walthamstow trolleys disappeared. If you wanted to sample electric traction at Stratford Broadway, once one of the busiest centres on the network, from now on you had to make do with the Central Line and the Eastern Region of British Railways, and the reminder of Tramway Avenue. Routemasters took up residence at Walthamstow and West Ham. More and more of the earlier classes of trolleybus were being wiped out, all of the Es for example. E2 No 622, had inaugurated trolleybus operation at West Ham and it performed the last journey there, almost 24 years later.

With trolleybuses gone from most of the docks area and Essex, abandonment now moved westwards. A one-off removal was that of route 611, which ran from Moorgate to the heights of Highgate Village. Special vehicles, AEC J3s with run-back brakes, were provided by Holloway depot. As with the RTs, which had replaced the similar-equipped B1s for climbing up to Crystal Palace, technology had moved on and standard motorbuses were deemed perfectly capable of dealing with the severest gradients. Route 611 had its terminus in the heart of Highgate Village, and a real village it was, and is, even if one can stand in its centre and look down the hill to the towering heights of the City offices. The replacement bus route, the 271, is today unique in that it is the only one which still repeats exactly the trolley route it took over with no diversions, extensions or reductions. What was utterly different was that it was worked in the mid-1990s by London Suburban, a later subsidiary of MTL in Merseyside, which often transferred vehicles between its London and Liverpool fleets.

The loss of route 611 made only a small dent in Holloway's allocation of 127 vehicles, more than any other London trolleybus depot. However the greatest impact of stage 7 was felt to the southwest where Hammersmith depot closed along with the three routes it operated, the 626, 628 and 630. These routes should have lasted longer but the celebrated Hammersmith Flyover, then under construction, would have necessitated quite a lot of alteration to the wiring and the trolleybus depot was also needed to house the fleet of BEA RF coaches. The 630 was my

local route and its disappearance meant no more trolleybuses in Croydon, the southernmost outpost of the network and the end of London's longest trolley ride — 77 minutes from West Croydon to 'near Willesden Junction', or 'Harlesden' as it was more prosaically known in its last days. It also meant the withdrawal of No 1721, the last prewar-designed trolleybus. This, one of the numerically small P1 class of 25 vehicles, had entered service in October 1941. That it and large numbers of the K1 and K2 classes were also now being broken up for scrap was an ominous sign of how far down the road to oblivion the London trolleybus had gone. The Routemasters which took over were provided by Shepherd's Bush garage.

The final abandonment of 1960, stage 8 in November, saw trolleybuses disappear from their westernmost terminus, Uxbridge, when the 607, worked by Hanwell depot, was replaced by the 207. Hanwell's other route, the 655, was also withdrawn. Hanwell had always been associated with the F1 class, by now the oldest vehicles in the fleet — all-Leylands delivered between March and December 1937. Route 607 had also been worked by some of the newest vehicles, the LYH-registered Q1s, which would last a little longer.

Perhaps not surprisingly the motorbus fleet experienced no great traumas during 1960, apart, of course, from the expansion of the RM class to around 500. The TD class continued to dwindle but

surprisingly there was still work for the last T. There were just three new single-deckers. They were a portent of things to come — eventually — in that they owed nothing to current LT practice being off-the-peg AEC Reliances with provincial Willowbrook bodies. They had separate entrances and exits and were bought so that this concept could be tested. Numbered RW1-3, they were the first London buses to have reversed registration numbers, 495-7 ALH. Painted in Country Area livery they entered service on route 322 from Hemel Hempstead garage in late September.

1961

1961 took the London trolleybus perilously close to extinction; although it has to be said that, small though their numbers were by December 1961, the fleet was still big by any other operator's standards. The intention had once been to keep the oldest section of the network, that operated from Fulwell and Isleworth depots, in place after all the rest had gone, because it was worked by the newest vehicles — the postwar Q1 class. However, before long it was decided to make a clean break, perhaps because they had managed to sell their postwar trolleys, and so as the new year came in the Q1 class began to be withdrawn. In batches they were sent to Poplar depot, handy for the docks, and then shipped out to Spain. One was reminded of the

Left:
Edgware's TD105.
Author's collection

Below:
Short wheelbase B2 class trolleybus
No 101 at the Hampstead Heath
terminus of route 513. *G. G. Gillham*

Right:
L3 trolleybuses Nos 1496 and 1448
peer out of Finchley depot. Lurking in
the gloom behind is an RT2 used for
driver training on conversion to
motorbuses.

last months of the trams when the most modern cars, the Felthams, were sold to Leeds, leaving older ones to take over their duties until the end came. All the Q1s, bar two, had gone by the end of the year. No 1841 donated its chassis to Imperial College Museum and its body to the scrapyard, while No 1768 joined the collection of preserved LT vehicles. K1s and K2s were drafted in to Isleworth and L3s to Fulwell; these classes were thus destined to be the last operational ones in London. Isleworth was quite a small depot with just one route to take care of, the 657, which needed 25 vehicles but Fulwell was very much bigger and a number of trolleys, other than the L3s, could be found there during 1961-2. Certainly I came across a least two L1s there which had officially been withdrawn months before.

Highgate depot, one which had always housed an unusually mixed bag of vehicles, lost most of them on 31 January-1 February when routes 513/613, 517/617, 615, 639 and 653 all disappeared, leaving just 22 vehicles to work route 627. The 653 was one of London's longest and most interesting routes, working its way northwards from Tottenham Court Road to Camden Town, then northeastwards past the Nags Head, Holloway — the busiest place in the entire network with around 4,500 trolleybus movements each weekday — and the almost as busy Manor House to Stamford Hill, where it then headed south through Clapton, Hackney and Bethnal Green to Aldgate. It was virtually the last east London route and the last to use Aldgate bus station. Two of the pleasantest parts

of London, Hampstead and Parliament Hill Fields, saw the last of the trolleybus, and two of the five routes which served the rather less sylvan North Finchley, the 517 and 617, also disappeared. The 111 Routemasters took over and a number of existing RT and RTW-operated routes were also affected, resulting in various reallocations. Individual to the last, no less than eight different classes of trolley suffered withdrawals, although not all had been allocated to Highgate.

Stage 10, on 25 March-6 April saw the last remnants of Highgate's trolleybus fleet vanish with the withdrawal of route 627. Edmonton and Wood Green also lost trolleybuses for the first time. Wood Green's route 629, which ran from Tottenham Court Road to Enfield, was replaced by the 269, operated by 39 RMs, while the Edmonton routes which were lost were the 659 and 679. Their outer terminus was Waltham Cross, the northernmost point reached by London's trolleybuses. 50 RMs from both Wood Green and Edmonton took over, although, as with practically all conversions, a number of diesel bus routes were also modified. Many K1s and K2s and the last P1s were withdrawn.

Stage 11 on 18-19 July removed the last routes from Waltham Cross, and trolleybuses disappeared from Edmonton and Stamford Hill depots with the replacement of routes 543/643, 647 and 649a. Yet more K1s and K2s and all the newer K3s were taken out of service.

Stage 12 on 7-8 November was particularly interesting for it introduced a new type of bus, one which is still almost complete and a familiar sight in central London 35 years later — an extraordinary record. This was the RML. For a long time there had been little logic in persisting with the production of a bus which was shorter than the permitted length, particularly when it was replacing vehicles of a greater capacity. So the lengthened Routemaster came into existence. An extra bay was inserted, allowing four more seats on each deck, a total of 72 in all. The windows in the new bay were shorter than those on either side, which ought to have given the RML, as it was coded (ER initially but never carried in service), a somewhat peculiar look. I can't say I ever thought it did and the RML has been around for so long now that we all take this slightly odd feature for granted. Finchley was the lucky depot (garage) to receive most of the trial batch of 24 to work route 104, which replaced the 609. The 521 (the last 500 series route), the 621 and the 641 also disappeared. The 521/621 were replaced by standard Routemaster-worked route 221 (Dinky Toys produced an RM in kit form with transfers for this route), and the 641 by the 141. Wood Green had trolleys no more but Finchley still needed nine L3s for the 645.

A second innovation at the time of stage 12 was that of lower case lettering in via blinds. A number of routes, not all ex-trolleybus ones, were so equipped and the practice gradually spread throughout the system. Although extensive tests had been carried out by LT on the legibility of upper versus lower case, the case (whoops!) for the change seems to have been more whim than practicality.

Unlike the situation 10 years earlier when the trams were on their way out, no grandiose claims were being made that the removal of trolleybuses would do wonders for traffic congestion. An ever growing problem, the introduction of one way schemes provided some relief, although it did nothing to speed up bus services, while the insistence of developers that car parks were provided underneath or alongside the tower blocks sprouting all over London simply

Below:
It had originally been intended that the RMLs would be classified as ERs but it wasn't until the 1990s that one actually appeared so styled. ER880 of London United in red and white livery with silver roof working route 9 pulls ahead of East London's RMC1456 on the 15.

Right:
The driver of Bromley's RT811 waits patiently in a traffic jam.

encouraged more and more private motorists to take up precious road space. These office blocks were to be found not only in central London, but out in the suburbs too. Croydon, for instance, became a veritable Manhattan (although it had no Woody Allen). Bus and rail services between suburbs orbitally had never been as well developed as those in and out of the City and the West End, and so more and more commuters took to their cars. This was the era of Harold Macmillan, the Swinging Sixties when we 'had never had it so good'. It was indeed a time of great optimism, tolerance and style but not one when investment in public transport was a priority, if this restricted individual freedom. Fares were increased twice and passenger numbers continued to fall.

The motorbus fleet remained, as in 1960, virtually unchanged — apart from the steady increase in the Routemaster fleet. Now over 1,000 units, it included one, RM664, turned out, like Underground and tube trains in experimental unpainted aluminium: the idea did not catch on. No more TDs disappeared and even the sole T kept working.

On 9 September passenger steam working on the Underground finished with the extension of electrification to Amersham. From then on Amersham was the terminus for LT trains, Aylesbury now being the exclusive preserve of British Railways reached from Marylebone either by way of the joint line with the Metropolitan or High Wycombe and Princes Risborough.

1962

I can scarcely recall more Arctic conditions in London than those on 2 January 1962 when I struggled through slush and snow to record the passing of four trolleybus routes operated by Finchley, Stonebridge and Colindale depots. The bulk of the snow had fallen on the previous Sunday, 31 December, and settled, but there were further flurries on Tuesday 2 January and practically every bus, Green Line and trolleybus service in and around London was affected. Paddington looked positively romantic as I watched the N1s and N2s on the 662 ease their way under the snow-clad branches of the trees surrounding the green which had served as their terminus for over 25 years. This was the last trolleybus terminus close to central London. The forecourt of Stonebridge depot, overlooked by the London Midland Region main line out of Euston, was a solid blanket of frozen snow despite the numerous trolley and motorbus services which terminated there. Stonebridge and Colindale, once the home of bespatted C class vehicles, had played host to the more modern AEC N1s and N2s, transferred from east London when their depots closed. All were withdrawn by 3 January. Along with the 662, 645, 662 and 666 all disappeared. Finchley was now an all motorbus garage; Stonebridge became one, while Colindale closed — its duties now performed by motorbuses from Edgware and Cricklewood garages. Colindale was where the trolleys met their end and so many of Stonebridge's and Finchley's vehicles made a final journey there, although others went into store for a while at Fulwell before eventually being towed to the graveyard behind Colindale depot.

Now there was just one more stage to go. The remaining routes were the 657 from Hounslow to Shepherd's Bush, worked by Isleworth depot, and six worked by Fulwell. These were the routes in Kingston area: 601 Tolworth-Twickenham, 602 The Dittons-Kingston Hill-Dittons circular, 603 Tolworth-Kingston Hill-Tolworth circular, 604 Wimbledon-Hampton Court, 605 Wimbledon-Twickenham and, finally, 667 Hampton Court-Hammersmith. Parts of the 657 and 667 covered London's first tram route

which had opened in 1901 and had been worked by electric traction longer than any other.

The evening of 8-9 May was scheduled to bring it all to an end and as the day approached more and more enthusiasts, and members of the general public, turned out to take a last ride on a London trolleybus. If many of the previous abandonments had attracted little attention, the build-up to the finale rivalled that of the trams approaching their end 10 years earlier. A nice touch saw the preserved pioneer London trolleybus, Diddler No 1, brought out some days before the end. It was posed alongside L3s and Routemasters in the forecourt of Fulwell depot, where the tram tracks, disused for the past 31 years, were still *in situ.* They became redundant when No 1 and its companions entered service.

The end was fittingly marked. No 1 did a ceremonial tour over the 657 and the 601, London's very first trolleybus route, and large crowds stood and watched all day long, the numbers increasing as night fell until the very last ceremonial runs took place. The last 657 from Isleworth was decorated with streamers, balloons and flags while, to quote the *Wimbledon Borough News*, 'London's last trolleybus was given a magnificent send off by hundreds of people. Dozens had waited for hours for the honour of a seat.' The vehicle in question was Fulwell's L3 No 1521. Although the souvenir hunters had left it less than complete, nothing irreplaceable had gone and Cohen's, who had the contract to break up it and its companions, presented it to the Historic Commercial Vehicle Club for

Right:
Green Line RMC1505 passes a Ford Prefect from the Isle of Wight on Eccleston Bridge.

preservation. It eventually found a home at Carlton
Colville, near Lowestoft, where it was restored and
can now regularly be seen at work.

In all nine London trolleybuses have survived; their
details will be found elsewhere. Of the rest the last
were rapidly broken up at Colindale, all having gone
by the end of July 1962. The final section of wiring
disappeared some two months later: the 28,000
traction poles were no longer needed, although a few
still survive today, supporting lamps or in some cases
seemingly just forgotten and left. Many of the
motorbus routes which replaced them can still be
traced, although hardly any remain unaltered and
often they have been broken into sections and are now
worked by single-deckers.

Another notable disappearance at this time was that
of the last of the Metropolitan Railway T stock trains,
the final one being taken out of service on 5 October.
Again something was left for posterity. Apart from
the five Ashbury carriages on the Bluebell Railway,
two later motor coaches were converted to double unit
sleet locomotives, while three trailer carriages, a
brake 3rd, a 3rd and a 1st moved far away to
Yorkshire where they took up work on the Keighley
and Worth Valley Railway. Two of the Bo-Bo electric
locomotives were also preserved. No 5
John Hampden is in the LT Museum at Covent
Garden while probably even better known is No 12

Sarah Siddons for she is kept in running order and
hauls specials from time to time.

Routemasters had replaced the last of the
trolleybuses but this did not bring production to an
end. By the end of the year virtually 1,300 had been
built, but new deliveries were all being stored
because of union opposition to proposals to replace
10 RTs by nine RMs on individual routes. Eventually,
LT changed its plans and went for one-for-one
substitution on central London routes. An
unspectacular start was made on 5 December when
Hounslow — not a garage one nowadays associates
with a central London route — sent out six RMs on
route 73. However a week later the entire allocation
of RTLs from Mortlake and Tottenham, which also
worked the 73, gave way. Suddenly Thames-side
West London had become RM homeland for,
alongside the Fulwell former trolleybus routes and
the 73, Putney and Stockwell received them for route
37. Next Rye Lane and Hendon replaced its RT
allocation on route 13 with RMs and finally, on
Christmas Eve, Cricklewood began putting them out
on the 16. At the weekends RMs could be seen on
several other routes. By the end of 1962 the
scheduled RT fleet had dropped by 59, and the RTL,
which was to have received the brunt of the
dismissals, by 141.

Two classes, long under threat, finally disappeared
from schedule service in 1962. First Kingston,
traditional home of the single-decker then and now,
lost its last TD, and then on 9 October the final
operational vehicle, TD124, came off route 240A and
disappeared into Edgware garage. Meanwhile in the
Country Area the single allocation of a T at Crawley
ended on 13 August when T787 was delicensed. A
class which had first appeared in 1929 had finally
gone. In actual fact 13 TDs and one T were still
owned by LT at the end of 1962 but were soon sold.
The little GSs were also finding they were no longer
in such demand and with the inauguration of the
winter programme in October, RFs took over a

number of their duties in the Country Area; Chelsham garage lost its entire allocation.

One of the reasons there were RFs to spare was yet another development in the RM story. LT decided that, despite previous failures, the prototype Routemaster coach had been a success and ordered a production batch of 68, RMC1453-1520. On 29 August the first of these went into service from Hertford and Guildford garages on routes 715 and 715A. Virtually identical in appearance to CRL4 but with double headlights and the standard production RM front end, they were splendid looking vehicles and deservedly attracted much publicity.

One further variation on the RM theme must be recorded. This is RMF1254. The front-entrance double-decker was becoming the norm throughout Britain and so a front-entrance RM made its debut at the 1962 Commercial Motor Show. Containing a high proportion of standard RM parts, it had electrically operated jack-knife doors and seated 69 passengers. After the show it took up work, not in London but, to my utter amazement, on the 27 Shiel Road circular in Liverpool. I was a student there at the time and the 27 was one of my local routes. One evening I was waiting for the usual green PD2 when round the corner appeared this gleaming red, familiar yet utterly unfamiliar apparition. It was hoped that the RM, in one form or another, would appeal to provincial operator hence RMF1254's migration to Merseyside. It returned to London before the year was out and we will pick up its subsequent career later.

London Transport Since 1933

Part Two
1963-1999

London Transport Since 1933

Part Two
1963-1999

Contents

Foreword

Within these pages we record the types, the changes, the liveries, the contractions and expansions, some of the people and a few personal reminiscences of the last 30 years of London Transport. With its companion volume *London Transport 1933–1962* it completes the 60-year old history of the largest urban transport undertaking in the world.

1963

For the first time since the turn of the century a new year began in London with no electrically powered passenger vehicles on the streets – unless one counted the odd milk boy getting a lift on his float. Would they ever return? Read on. A change which few members of the public noticed was the disappearance of the London Transport Executive and its replacement by the London Transport Board (LTB). If you looked closely, the legal lettering on the lower nearside panels of buses altered but nothing much else on the surface did.

If the weather had been seasonal 12 months earlier, it was even more so at the beginning of 1963. Snow was heavy enough in London but out on the North Downs and elsewhere in the Country Area roads were blocked and buses were abandoned. I watched 403s struggling up Sanderstead Hill and they could get no further south than Chelsham. Dunton Green garage was snowbound, its fleet immobile, as was Crawley. To the north, Hertford and Stevenage garages were also out of action. For weeks there was no sign of a thaw and snow remained piled by the roadsides into March. It is hard to imagine such conditions in the London area in the 1990s.

Apart from the weather, on the whole 1963 was a less dramatic year than many. Routemasters continued to be delivered, replacing RTs and RTLs, although there were still so many of the former, and the onslaught on the latter seemed to have eased, so that, other than in central London where they were significant, the changes were not particularly noticeable.

The 'prewar' RTs, withdrawn from passenger service in 1957, had seemed to be a permanent fixture

Below:
The very last 'Prewar' RT – RT79 at Dunton Green garage shortly before withdrawal. *All pictures by the author or from the Ian Allan Library unless credited otherwise*

in the trainer fleet, so long had they served in this role, but with so many postwar RTs and RTLs now surplus their time had come and the last, green RT79, was delicensed, appropriately at a Country Area garage, Dunton Green, on 13 February.

Another standard class to have its ranks reduced was the RF. One, RF464, was burnt out at Fulwell garage while 10 of the one-time private hire coaches, 16-25, converted to Green Line use, were sold. The GS class, already reduced in numbers, also began to find new owners. GS3 and GS4 were pioneers in a process which would become commonplace in future decades, that of remaining within LT territory with their new owners. They went to Tillingbourne Valley, which operated, jointly with LT, route 448 from Guildford to Peaslake and they actually found themselves working alongside GSs from Guildford garage.

Croydon had long been promised a bus station and at last, in July, it opened at West Croydon, alongside

the back end of the railway station and on the site where the route 630 trolleybuses used to turn. It was a handy spot for photographers, having plenty of fresh air and daylight, but by the same token was not over-endowed with creature comforts for the customers, who were, after all, the first priority. It would be several decades before the situation improved. Nearly 1,000 buses used it each Monday to Friday.

Returning to central London a curious contrivance, something like a giant molehill, appeared at Oxford Circus over the August Bank Holiday. London's newest tube railway, the Victoria line, of which more anon, passed under it and to enable the new interchange station to be constructed the road had to be removed and an umbrella of steel girders erected in its place. This hump was tarmacked over and was ready for traffic within three days, although only southbound and westbound vehicles were allowed to use it.

Production of Routemasters continued throughout the year. A small, but pleasing, visual variation which took place in 1963 was the fitting of the traditional AEC triangle to the radiator, both to new buses and to many earlier ones as well. Once conversion to Routemasters of route 16 was completed early in January, the 36A and 36B, which kept the 16 company from Victoria, along Park Lane and up the Edgware Road as far as Praed Street, followed. Next came route 9, then 43, then 63, followed by the suburban route 85 and 85A, then back to central London for the 14. Until now the 8ft wide RTWs had been, to all intents and purposes, unaffected but route 14, worked by Putney garage, had been one of their strongholds – they had taken it over from the 'prewar' 2RTs. Most of the RTWs displaced went to Brixton garage, joining some newly arrived RTLs, but four were downgraded to learners. Many more RTWs went into the training fleet when RMs moved on to that interesting route, the 24, which was to see so many different, and often unusual, types in the years to come. The last conversion of all was route 7 in December, when Middle Row garage began to move out its RTLs.

The Leylands were generally regarded with less favour than the AECs both by drivers because of the heavier steering and by the engineers on account of problems with engine changes; because of this the RTs would outlive both RTLs and RTWs in passenger service in London by some 11 years.

In November a new crossing of the Thames, much nearer the sea than any other, opened in November when the Dartford Tunnel came into use. A new Country Area route, 300, made use of it, running between Grays and Dartford; an existing Green Line route was extended through it, while five curious looking Strachan-bodied, Thames Trader double-deckers operated a service for cyclists and pedestrians. They were owned by the Tunnel Authority and crewed by LT. None of the services were very well patronised and all have long since gone.

Apart from the Green Line Routemasters no RMs had yet appeared in the Country Area. However withdrawal of green-liveried roof-box RTs began in the summer and to replace them red RTs were repainted and overhauled. Various refinements had been fitted to RTs over the years, notably trafficators and heaters, although the latter only to Country Area vehicles, the thinking being presumably that the rural parts were colder than the suburban and central London ones. There were several flaws in this, not the least being that many Country Area routes were actually far more suburban than rural in character. Tacit recognition of this was given in 1963 with the announcement that, with the completion of the programme in the Country Area – apart from the roof-box RTs scheduled for early withdrawal – red RTs with an expected lifespan of eight or more years would also have heaters. No RTLs or RTWs ever had them. A Chelsham conductor told me that he thought an RT fitted with heaters was the acme of double-deck bus comfort and in all respects superior to an RM; he was not alone in holding this opinion.

Below:
RT1079 battles through the snow in Oxford Street.

Above:
Country Area roof-box RT992 and RT3617 at Kingston.

1964

1964 saw the decline in the RT family fleet continue.
One of the sub-groups which disappeared was the
Country Area roof-box RT, the last of which ended its
passenger duties 10 days into 1964. This distinctive
and virtually unique feature would last some time
longer in the Central Area and an interesting variation
appeared when RTLs began to appear from overhaul
with this type of body. Previously the prototype
RTL501 had been unique in this respect but 21 RTLs
were fitted with roof-box bodies in 1964. The thinking
behind this was that both the RTL and this type of
body had not long to go in LT ownership and so they
might as well be paired. In March the very last
'prewar' RTs still owned by LT, Nos 88 and 118,
were sold and broken up by Cohen's.

One of our local garages, Carshalton, best known as
home of route 654 trolleybuses, went out of business
at the end of January, most of its RTs moving to the
former Daimler strongholds of Sutton and Merton.
One route linking Croydon with central London no
longer did so after the end of January when route 133
was cut back from South Croydon garage to Thornton
Heath high street. This was part of a trend becoming
common with many of the longer LT trunk routes.
Increasing congestion, chiefly caused by private cars,
meant the longer a route the greater the opportunity
for delays, and so they were gradually being broken
into more manageable, shorter sections. Thus new
route 133A was inaugurated between South Croydon
and Kennington, being extended at peak times to
Victoria Embankment.

Another local event which typified what was
happening throughout the system was the appearance
of RTWs at the top of our road in Thornton Heath.
Displaced from their familiar haunts by Routemasters
they had been sent to Brixton to work the tram
replacement route 109. Apart from the brand-new
batch which worked out of Bromley for a short time
on route 119, this was the first, and last, time RTWs
were seen regularly in Croydon, and Purley was the
furthest south they were ever to reach.

It would be tedious to list all the routes which were
taken over by Routemasters as the year progressed but
some are certainly worth recording. In April Upton
Park garage began to receive the type for the 15; 31
years later Upton Park still operates Routemasters, of

several varieties, on the 15. Later they took up work
on the 3 and the 137, both of which routes still see
regular Routemaster workings.

No London bus type has ever remained completely
standard and inevitably there were changes, some
minor, some more radical, to the Routemaster as its
numbers grew. RM1923 appeared with an illuminated
advert on its offside and was sent to Putney to work
route 30. Many more such RMs appeared in 1964.
Naturally enough this group of buses was restricted to
routes which worked through central London thus
ensuring the maximum exposure and, it was hoped,
making the exercise a profitable one.

Many people had wondered for some years what
would happen when the last Y prefix registrations –
there would be no 'Zs' – were used up. 1963 proved
to be the crunch year and all was revealed when
vehicles began to appear with an 'A' suffix. LT had
still plenty of CLTs and DYEs to use up and it wasn't
until the spring of 1964 that the first suffixes appeared
on Routemasters with Upton Park's new buses
starting with RM1866, ALD 866B. RM2000 arrived
in September and was given the registration ALM
200B while the 'B' series ended on 31 December with
RM2105, ALM 105B.

In the 1960s unemployment was virtually unknown,
certainly in the London area, and the unsocial hours

and declining pay in comparison to other jobs of busmen meant staff shortages. Recruiting was actively carried out in the Caribbean and this helped but did not totally overcome the problem. Private hire and tours were let go to other operators and thus the RFW coaches, which had spent their entire careers in this employment, were all taken out of service and sold.

Tackling the problem from another angle, and also cutting costs, one-man operation (OMO) at last began in the Central Area. The date was 18 November and was one of great significance: getting rid of the conductor was seen as the panacea for the ills of the bus industry and would become virtually universal outside the capital. Central London, late to embrace it, would by the 1990s be the only part of the kingdom where two-person buses were still to be seen in large numbers; where there were others these would almost always be operated by ex-LT Routemasters.

It is worth recording the routes which became one-man (women drivers had not yet arrived on the scene) operated. They were all worked by RFs: three from Kingston garage, the 201, 206, and 216, and the 250 worked by Hornchurch.

Left:
RM2179 with illuminated offside advertisement panel passing Battersea Park station whilst working the 137.

Below left:
RF369 in Kingston bus station.

Right:
Godstone RT986 working route 410.

Below:
The Shuttle from Acton Town at South Acton. *Dr H. Zinram*

By the end of 1964 the fleet had declined by some 250 vehicles, most of those withdrawn being RTs and RTLs, although some RFs, GSs, RLHs (the first two) all but two of the 15 RFWs and one TD (leaving just one in the fleet) had also been sold. What was probably the best known London lowbridge route, the 410, was diverted to avoid the reason for its existence in November; RTs replaced the RLHs and it was a lowbridge route no longer. As someone who a little later went to live in Oxted, I could only wonder why the diversion hadn't been made decades earlier and thus the inconvenience of producing several one-off designs avoided.

On the Underground the section of District Line between Acton Town and Hounslow West closed, it being covered by the Piccadilly Line.

The London bus (and tram, train and trolleybus) had always had a considerable following amongst small boys, big boys and grown men, although, sadly, rather less so with the female sex. The Ian Allan *abcs* and associated publications beginning in the 1940s had, for the first time, provided really comprehensive information and pictures and in 1964 another dimension was added to the steadily growing hobby observing and recording in the minutest detail London's vast public transport network when the London Omnibus Traction Society (LOTS) was founded.

A year earlier enthusiasts had hardly been able to contain themselves when, at long last after years of illicit sneaking into Reigate garage, the collection of preserved London vehicles had gone on display at the Museum of British Transport in Clapham, alongside *Mallard*, carriages from the royal train, a Brighton trolleybus and many other treasures, large and small. The premises had been a bus garage, a relatively new one built on the site of Clapham tram depot. It was not destined to be permanent and the LT section would eventually be separated from the railway exhibits which would go to York, but it was a wonderful display.

1965

The dawn of what we might call the modern age of bus travel in London, which had peeped over the horizon in a cold late autumn morning in 1964 when OMO began on four red single-deck routes, tiptoed a little further into the daylight on 15 September. Eight rear-engined Daimler Fleetline double-deckers with Park Royal bodies began work from East Grinstead garage. This was, admittedly, about as far as you could get from central London and still come across a LT bus – Southdown and Maidstone & District (M&D) also had garages in the town – but it was the start for all that, and in the autumn the rear-engined bus finally arrived in central London.

LT had already announced plans for trials of a new generation of double and single-deckers and on

7 November the XA class – which would eventually number 50 – entered service from Chalk Farm garage on route 24 from Hampstead Heath to Pimlico. The X stood for experimental, the A stood for Atlantean; if you were prepared to stand for these monsters you were prepared to stand for anything, ho, ho! A bit harsh perhaps, but they were crude vehicles, with standard provincial Park Royal bodies, not very well proportioned externally, and internally very basic, far below the standards which the RT and RM provided. They had sliding vents, unlike the more sophisticated winding windows hitherto standard, and they also introduced a new livery variation in that the pale cream band became pale grey – which sometimes was quite noticeable, and sometimes wasn't. There was no reason why the first generation of rear-engined double-deckers had to be ugly – they just were. The Atlantean was not very reliable either, although this may partly have been because LT engineers found it so unfamiliar. Having front-entrance power-operated doors Londoners could no longer hop on and off whenever they felt like it and this, too, contributed to their unpopularity. For all that the Routemaster suddenly looked rather old-fashioned beside them; the RT more so.

However the RM was still in full production, or rather the RML for the last of the shorter vehicles was delivered in May. The next batch consisted of 43 coaches, similar to the RMCs, but seating an extra row of passengers on each deck, 65 in all. The front

Above left:
XF8 newly in service working out of East Grinstead (EG) garage on route 424.

Above:
XA10 in Trafalgar Square following an RM on route 15 with an RTW on the 11 alongside.

Below:
RTLs from Victoria (GM) could be seen working on route 11 until November 1965. Newly overhauled RTL1519 is seen inside its home garage.

end, still with twin headlights, was slightly modified, as was the route indicator, while the livery was a little different. All of this produced what many considered the most handsome of all the Routemaster variations. Numbered RCL2218-2260 (CUV 218C-260C), they were sent to Romford, Grays and Hertford.

More new coaches arrived in the Green Line fleet at the end of the year. As handsome as the RCLs, these were 14 AEC Reliance single-deckers with Willowbrook bodies. These were to the BET pattern, found in great numbers at that time in such fleets as Southdown, M&D and East Kent and wore a striking new livery of pale grey with a green waist band. Measuring 36ft long and 8ft 2.5in wide, they were fitted for the first time in LT history with proper coach seats. They went to Windsor and Dunton Green garages to operate route 705.

Immediately following the RCLs, delivery of red-liveried RMLs commenced. They were virtually

identical to the pioneer batch of 1961, RML880-903. Starting with RML2261 they had CUV xxxC registrations, like the RCLs and the majority of the XAs, and some were put to work in direct comparison with the latter. The RML achieved a fuel consumption of 7.8mpg, making it a most economical bus, and over a mile a gallon better than the heavier XA; fleet-wide this amounted to a considerable saving for LT.

Comparison between front and rear-engined buses was not immediately possible as the XAs were not yet ready so some new RMLs were sent, somewhat surprisingly, to the Country Area at Godstone. Brand new red RTs had appeared in the Country Area and new green ones in central London but until now the only Routemasters seen in the outer reaches of Chiswick's empire had been Green Line ones. It was intended that the 409, 410 and 411 routes should all go over to RML operations so they were sent to East Grinstead, Godstone and Reigate garages too. Yet another first for the Croydon area! Their stay was short for green RMLs were also being delivered and soon there were enough to allow the red ones to return to the Central Area where they went to Tottenham to work the 76 alongside other newly delivered members of the class, while XAs took up work from Chalk Farm on the 24. More red RMLs went to Stamford Hill for the 67. Either directly or indirectly they replaced many RTWs and this class was now well on the way out.

Meanwhile more new green RMLs arrived at Northfleet where their principal duties were on route 480. A minor, but noticeable, variation, which would become standard, on the constantly fascinating topic of destination blinds first appeared at Godstone when the rear via box was given over to nothing but a large route number.

By the end of 1965 only 144 RTWs were scheduled for operation Monday to Friday. Interestingly they still clung on to route 11, London's most famous route. Sixteen years earlier I had my last glimpse of a Bluebird LT also at work on the 11. However there the comparison ends, for although the LTs, having exceeded their intended lifespan and suffered the neglect of the war years, really were worn out, while to the passenger the RTWs seemed almost as good as new. In fact they were getting on for 16 years old and although many found new owners, they were never very popular with crews being the heaviest of all the RT variants to steer. After a shift on route 11 one certainly knew one had done a day's work.

The RTL fleet declined by over a hundred during 1965, although proportionally this was much less than their fatter Leyland brothers, while there was actually an increase in scheduled RT numbers. The very last TD, No 118, had been sold.

A change, which could have had a huge effect on the public transport scene in London if it had been allowed, took place in April 1965 when the Greater London Council (GLC) came into being. It planned, as we shall see, to make London a more egalitarian place to live and visit, where subsidised public transport would be so cheap and convenient that there would be little need for the private car. Entrenched vested interests and a pretty peculiar reading of the word freedom eventually won the day – but it was a brave try.

One attempt, or rather many on the same theme, tried throughout the year to improve traffic flow was the introduction of one way schemes, the most grandiose being that around Victoria. One traditional feature no longer encountered was the meeting of the many Green Line services on Eccleston Bridge above the long extended platforms of Victoria station, for this now became one way. However Victoria remained, and indeed remains, very much Green Line territory.

1966

On 31 July 1966 Bobby Moore climbed to the royal box at Wembley Stadium to collect the World Cup . If that was the high point of English football, a few weeks later an announcement heralded an equally momentous event in LT's history. The one-man bus would become standard. Elsewhere rear and underfloor engines enabling the entrance to be beside the driver at the front of the bus were becoming almost universal, facilitating the demise of the conductor, which reduced costs. This was the primary objective of nearly all bus companies, desperate to fight the motor car which was taking away their passengers throughout England, Wales and Scotland, whether out in the villages and the country towns or in the cities and conurbations.

High capacity single-deckers were already on order and the first of these arrived in February. They were AEC Merlins with rear engines and a Strachan body which seated 25 with standing room for no less than 48. Londoners weren't at all used to this, although commuters in many other European cities were. Designated the XMS they began work on the first Red Arrow service, route 500 Victoria-Marble Arch, on 18 April. They stopped only at Hyde Park Corner during the rush hours, and ran for shoppers outside these periods. The journey cost 4d instead of 6d on the ordinary routes; it was certainly faster and was rather popular, although not because of the automatic ticket machines, which proved very unreliable.

There were six of these XMSs. Nine similar XMBs in green livery with 46 seats were also delivered but only one actually worked in the Country Area. The

Above:
XMS6 in Park Lane. *IAL*

Below:
XMS4 in later years working for London Country from Leatherhead garage.

Right:
Brixton (BN) was the last garage to operate RTWs. One stands here beside an RT at Thornton Heath.

Below:
RMF1254 after being sold to Northern General at Newcastle in 1978.

rest were converted to XMS standard and repainted red.

Meanwhile the passenger carrying days of the RTW were drawing to an end. In February they at last relinquished their hold on route 11; in April they disappeared from the 22, and in May from the 95 and 109. The very last, RTW467, ran in to Brixton garage off the 95 at 00.30 on 15 May. For a while, as with the 'prewar' RTs with which they seemed to have an affinity working as they did from the same garages, they continued in learner service.

No amount of one way schemes, fine new Routemasters, or avant garde rear-engined double-deckers and high capacity single-deckers could defeat

the private car and yet more service cuts in both May and June saw many RTLs delicensed.

Two more variations on the Routemaster theme appeared in 1966. In October the first of 65 front-entrance buses for BEA took up work. They replaced the one and a half deck RFs and were basically to the design of the RMF, but shorter so they could legally tow luggage trailers. RMF1254 left London in November. It was sold to Northern General which already had a fleet of front entrance RMs. In its four years with LT it never entered ordinary passenger service and was the first Routemaster to be sold by LT. My experience of seeing this bus of pure LT design on ordinary stage carriage work but twice, once in Liverpool and once in Newcastle, can hardly have been unique.

Above:
A group of BEA Routemasters, some repainted into British Airways livery.

Below:
FRM1 at Roundshaw whilst working from Croydon (TC) garage on route 233.

There was another variation on the Routemaster theme, which I saw many times working in the LT area and which was completed in 1966; this was FRM1. One of the great might-have-beens of British bus history, this was a belated attempt by AEC to enter the rear-engined double-deck market. It contained 60 per cent standard Routemaster parts and was unmistakably one of the family. Far handsomer than the XAs and XFs, although perhaps rather staid compared to some later stylish rear-engined body designs, it did not enter passenger service until 1967.

OMO continued to spread and now reached the Green Line network. A new route covering some 70 miles in the far northern reaches was the 724, which ran from High Wycombe by way of Watford, St Albans, Welwyn Garden City, Hertford and Epping to Romford and was worked by OMO RFs from the garages at the extremities of its route. It was a bold venture, very much the northern version of the 725, and very nearly as successful.

Crew-operated operation of RFs had almost come to an end in the Country Area by the end of 1966 and although many of the Green Line vehicles were being refurbished with a two-tone livery, twin headlights and fluorescent lighting, passengers were deserting the Green Line network with considerable enthusiasm, either heading for their cars or the ever-growing electrified British Rail network.

The bus industry has always involved working unsocial hours and on the very last day of 1966 a five-day week was introduced in order to bring about better conditions. Sunday bus operation was declining rapidly; no more were red buses needed to help with the crowds heading for the country and a sign of the times was that there were actually more RMs scheduled for operation in the Central Area on

Sundays than RTs, while the number of RTLs at work on that day was now less than 100. Only 261 buses in total worked in the Country Area on Sundays, compared with 893 Monday to Friday. Both the RLH and the GS were well on the way to extinction.

1967

1967 was a less dramatic year than many in that only one new type of bus entered service, and this was destined to remain a one-off. On 26 June FRM1 took up work from Tottenham garage on route 76, working alongside the XAs. It had a forced air ventilation system, which looked a little odd in that there were no opening windows of any description, except beside the driver. No doubt we should have got used to this but the system was not a success. Leaking flywheel oil resulted in FRM1 burning its rear end quite severely in the last day of August, the damage added to by London's brave fire brigade, Matilda style, bashing away at its engine compartment. However a period of convalescence and some nice new opening windows saw it back at work from Tottenham before the year was out.

RMLs continued to come off the production line, but not for much longer. The nine years of standard

Below:
RTLs at Victoria in 1967, alongside an RM on the 16 and an RT on the 38. On the far right is RTL458 while next to it is RTL384, which was one of 23 members of the class fitted with roof-box bodies in 1964.

Left:
RTW28 on learner duty at Morden.

Below:
Modernised Green Line RF66 of St Albans Garage working route 727. *G. Mead*

Bottom:
RF313 was one of the precursors of the modernised RFs; along with others working route 711, it was repainted at the beginning of the 1960s in a lighter shade of green.

Above:
RML2563 of Putney (AF) garage at Isleworth.

RM building exceeded that of the postwar RT by one year, although there had been more than double the number of the earlier bus, to say nothing of the RTL and the RTW. The final Routemaster registration appeared in August, SMK xxxF, with RML2658. However we have not quite reached the end so let us not anticipate.

The other great stalwart of the early postwar years, the RF, still had plenty of life in it and the programme of modernising the Green Line version, mentioned earlier with twin headlights, a new livery with a broad, pale green waistband, and an improved interior, was completed by the spring of 1967 More one-man Green Line RFs went into service in April on the longest Green Line route yet, the 727 operating between Luton and Crawley. The principal feature of the limited stop 727 was that it linked Gatwick, Heathrow and Luton airports, a pointer to the future and to a network of routes which would eventually be hived off to become a separate entity. RFs with extra luggage space were provided. The service proved so popular that later the larger RCs took over. These handsome looking but mechanically unreliable vehicles were not one of LT's better buys. However this was true of a whole generation of single-deckers about to appear on the streets of London and its suburbs and the RCs' contribution to the 727 story was fairly minimal.

RTLs continued to be withdrawn as RMLs continued to be delivered. The last Metro-Cammell members of the class had gone by the end of May and in September the last garage to operate nothing but RTLs – Clapton – received a batch of RTs to begin their replacement. By the end of the year only 216

RTLs were scheduled for operation Monday to Friday, while the Sunday total was down to a paltry 28. Many RTs withdrawn from the Country Area, whether on account of being replaced by RMLs, single-deckers or service cuts, were repainted red and helped bring about the end of their Leyland brothers.

The autumn saw the RMLs enter the 27xx series, and just as the final standard FXT-registered STLs had gone to Hanwell when new, so some of the 27xx RMLs also entered service there. Many also came to Croydon garage from November where they were put to work on the 130 group of routes. Here their extra capacity proved useful for there were always plenty of clients anxious to quit its windy slopes on Monday to Friday mornings though they mostly had to return each evening.

In December details of the revolution which was about to engulf LT were announced. The Country Area would be taken out of LT control and given to the new National Bus Company (NBC). It was ironic that it was a Conservative government which set up the GLC, to whom LT would be handed over, for the GLC under Ken Livingston (Red Ken as the *Evening Standard* liked to call him) became a fierce thorn in the side of Maggie Thatcher, to the extent that she eventually managed to wipe it out – which benefited no-one except 'she who must be obeyed'. If Ken Livingston had been rather more subtle and Margaret Thatcher less vindictive, London might today have a

for the Post Office each year from 1958 to 1963; the former was the last time there had been a delivery on Christmas Day. Bus services had not yet gone the same way but they were headed in that direction and were cut by half compared with 1966.

1968

1968 was one of the most eventful years in LT's history, though no doubt there were some pretty big events in many of our personal lives that year. But I digress. We'll begin with the opening of the Victoria Line. A serious gap in the Underground/tube network was the lack of a direct link between Victoria and Piccadilly, Euston, St Pancras and King's Cross. The Victoria Line was designed to fill this and the government had sanctioned it on 20 August 1962, although plans had existed, in embryo form, since the 1940s. It was quite the most ambitious Underground

better integrated and cheaper public transport network, with fewer motor cars clogging up the works; but such is the vanity of politicians. The Ted Heath government put forward proposals which today sound like pure socialism. Grants of up to 75 per cent would be available for capital investment in facilities such as bus stations and interchanges, and new one-man buses attracted a 25 per cent grant. Further money was available for research, while local authorities could subsidise rural bus services, to which the government would contribute 50 per cent.

With the inexorable advance of the private car and television there was less and less demand for public transport on Christmas Day. The five-day week also complicated the situation. As a student I had worked

or tube scheme for decades and the first service trains began to run on 1 September on the northernmost section from Walthamstow Central to Blackhorse Road, Tottenham Hale, Seven Sisters, Finsbury Park and Highbury and Islington. Three months later the section on to King's Cross and St Pancras, Euston and Warren Street opened. The most needed section, on to Victoria, would have to wait until the next year, while the final extension, to Brixton, would not be ready until 1971.

The Victoria Line was revolutionary in a number of respects. In the late 1930s LT had taken industrial design and its associated arts, such as poster design, to new heights but it had seemed to lose its way by the 1950s. The Victoria Line was a reassuring re-affirmation of this fine tradition. Each station was instantly recognisable from its brothers by its own motif, picked out in tiled panels and designed by highly respected artists. Edward Bawden, for instance, provided Highbury and Islington with a high bury, or castle or manor, the original having been destroyed during the Peasants' Revolt, while Crosby, Fletcher and Forbes produced a complex maze, or warren for Warren Street.

Automatic fare collection, now the norm on the Underground system, was installed for the opening of the Victoria Line. Most important of all, the trains were controlled automatically, from a central control

room near Euston. This wasn't immediately obvious for there was a driver in the front cab of each train. In reality it would have been more accurate to call him a guard for his chief function was to open and close the doors. When the train was ready to start he merely pressed a button and the automatic control system then took over. He could, in an emergency, over-ride this and he was also in telephone communication with the control room. Fitted with wrap around windscreens, an improvement over the rather bland visages of their predecessors, the 1967 Victoria Line cars originally consisted of 122 driving cars and 122 trailers, others being added later. They had rheostatic brakes, a combined traction/brake controller, powerful headlights and a public address system. For the first time they carried the legend 'Underground' instead of the hitherto universal 'London Transport'.

As big a milestone was the delivery of the last Routemaster. Only nine were still to come when 1968 opened. All but one went to Croydon garage. The odd one out was the last of all. This, RML2760, together with Croydon's 2754/6, started work on 1 March. No 2760 went to Upton Park. It has been a celebrity all its life, often appearing at rallies and various special events but it still lives at Upton Park and its regular beat, as from its first day in service, is route 15, which now operates between Canning Town and Paddington. 27 years on the same route from the same garage must be some sort of record in the annals of public transport. Two RMLs, which had been on an overseas

Left:
The interior of a Central Area MB.

Below:
The last RTLs were withdrawn from passenger service in 1968 but a few remained a little longer in the training fleet. RTL1223 was one of 18 which had been painted green and sent to work from Hatfield garage in July 1960, lasting less than a year in this role. It stands alongside RT3274 and RT422, the latter by this date nominally the oldest bus in LT passenger service, having been delivered with a body identical to that borne by RT3274, to Leyton garage in September 1947.

tour, entered service a little later, at the end of May, and over the years, as we shall see, other Routemasters have taken up passenger work with LT after various careers elsewhere. But construction had ended.

At this time it was thought that the RM, an outdated design by 1968, might well not last very much longer and that the later ones would be lucky to live out their full lifespan with LT. Unlike the RT family, which had swept away all its predecessors, the RM had certainly not done for the RT, nor even quite the RTL, a few members of which lingered on. Nevertheless front engines, half cabs and open rear platforms were rapidly becoming anachronisms in 1968 and the rear-engined Atlantean and Fleetline were the choice of most bus companies, unless you happened to be a member of the Tilling family, when you were wedded to the front-entrance Lodekka, although not for much longer. But the future is notoriously unpredictable, perhaps fortunately, and the Routemaster has proved to be astonishingly long-lived – and not just in London.

The new era, which – it was confidently assumed – would sweep away RTs, RMs and all such ancient concepts, dawned on 7 September. On that day Red Arrow routes 501 to 507 started operation, along with a complete reshaping of routes in the Walthamstow and Wood Green areas, 22 OMO services in all. The revolutionary buses provided were 36ft long, 8ft 2.5in wide AEC Merlin single-deckers, fitted with MCW bodies. Although the chassis was basically of standard provincial design there were certain modifications. The body was similar to that of the experimental Merlins but rather neater, particularly at the front end. For the first time slide vents were provided in the windows on a standard body for London requirements, a retrograde step in the author's opinion.

There were three variations. The MBA worked the Red Arrow routes. There were 44 of these little beauties. They seated 25, with additional room for 48 standing passengers. You entered at the front; if you didn't have the exact money, 6d to be exact, a machine might give you change, although it might not. You left by centre doors.

The MBS class for use in the suburbs was virtually identical to the Red Arrows, with the same layout and capacity. They also had MCW bodies. The Merlins flooded into London throughout 1968 (though many did not enter service for months). By November they had appeared in green livery in the Country Area, at Reigate, Amersham and High Wycombe.

The third version was the MB which had seats for all its passengers. The Central Area version had doors only at the front and had seats for 50 passengers; the green version retained the centre exit and had 45 seats. One MBA, six MBSs and 13 MBs were licensed early enough in 1968 to receive F suffixes to their registrations; the rest were Gs.

The Merlin was bad news for the RT and the RTL for it was designed to replace these veterans. The new buses were not necessarily any more comfortable but with mounting losses LT had little option but to go over to OMO and the 36ft long single-deckers could equal the RT's capacity. The new Red Arrow services saw an extensive revision of many long-established central London routes, while there were many other changes elsewhere on the network. Buses ceased to run through Rotherhithe Tunnel while MBs took over from RTs on route 108 through the Blackwall Tunnel.

The final RTL routes, the 176 and the 226 worked by Cricklewood, succumbed to MBSs on 29 November; RTL543 was the very last to go, although the type lasted a little longer in learner service and as Aldenham staff buses. Many of the displaced Country Area RTs were repainted red so that they could take over from roof-box versions. Some Routemasters also found themselves displaced. They were not, of course, withdrawn but moved on to remove RTs from passenger service.

And so by the end of December 1968 the London bus fleet was looking markedly different to that of a year earlier. It would change very much more in 1969, although it would quickly become clear that the Merlin was falling far short of its expectations.

1969

To start on a cheerful note and record an innovation which was to prove durable, the extension of the Victoria Line to Victoria itself took place on 7 March 1969. It was a great occasion. HM the Queen performed the opening ceremony. Royalty is not often found beneath the streets of London and no reigning monarch had ever taken part in such a ceremony before. The Victoria Line proved even more popular than had been predicted. The journey time between Victoria and King's Cross was reduced from 24 minutes to ten and by the summer the line was carrying passengers at the rate of 58 million a year.

Up above it wasn't the new generation of single-deckers which provided the first Central Area OMO conversions of the year, rather the RF which replaced Sutton's RTs on the 80A. However the Merlin onslaught resumed with a vengeance in May and continued through to October at Bromley, Muswell Hill, Enfield, Loughton, Alperton, Hounslow, Potters Bar and Plumstead garages.

The reason the Merlins did not appear earlier was that they were fully occupied in the Country Area. In February they arrived at Hatfield, Windsor, St Albans, Garston and Hemel Hempstead garages, while RFs followed the examples of their brethren at Sutton and ousted RTs at Dunton Green and Dartford. Next month more Merlins went to Windsor.

There were many who felt that the building of a large fleet of Green Line double-deckers was flying in

Left:
RF431 of Sutton at Morden station.

Left:
MBS407 of Crawley works a local service in the town centre.

Left:
RMC4 was among the Routemaster coaches which were sent to work as buses from Hatfield garage. This far outlived its prototype brethren in ordinary passenger service; it is seen here inside the garage.

the face of experience and common sense, and within four years of the last RCL entering service the first RMC was demoted to bus service. On 15 February route 708 was reconverted to RFs and the RMCs which had worked this service from East Grinstead and Hemel Hempstead garages could find no employment elsewhere on the contracting Green Line network. So they went to Hatfield, and later in the year Addlestone – briefly – and Grays, where they took up bus work, replacing RTs.

October saw the last Merlin deliveries. Excluding the 15 experimental vehicles of 1966, 650 had been put into service in the extraordinarily short time of 13 months, between September 1968 and October 1969. It was an unlucky 13 with a vengeance, for the type was nothing short of a disaster. When one considers

how thoroughly the prototype RTs and RMs had been tested before going into production, one can only wonder what on earth possessed LT to invest so much in an unproved design. It is true that one-man services needed to be introduced quickly in order to cut costs, but the Merlins saved little and the RTs soldiered on for another 11 years after the Merlin's introduction, outlasting them all – except for the Red Arrow vehicles, which outdid the RTs by one year, while the Routemaster is, of course, still with us. The last non-Red Arrow Merlins were taken out of traffic by the end of 1976.

One of their principal liabilities was their length. Looking back it seems somewhat naive that it was felt that their troubles would be over merely by shortening them and fitting a smaller engine. Nevertheless this

Above:
Seen between the Gasworks and Copenhagen tunnels outside King's Cross BR station, an LT battery locomotive has charge of a train of Northern Line tube stock. A Class 47 is waiting to back down to the terminus whilst a Class 40 has just emerged in the right background.

was what happened. A 33ft 5in long version, the Swift, was ordered, again in very large numbers. The first, SM1, appeared in late 1969 and was sent to Catford garage. It had the same neat looks of the Merlin although the body was actually built by Marshall. This was the first time the Cambridge firm had built new bodies for LT, although it had taken part in the rebuilding programme immediately after the war.

RTs continued to be taken out of service as the big one-man single-deckers became a familiar sight throughout the LT empire, in both Central and Country areas. They in turn replaced many of the RTLs and RTWs in the training fleets although both types managed to last into 1970.

1970

If we continue to describe each year as 'particularly significant' or even 'traumatic' then you, dear reader, may well feel we are suffering from adjectival overkill. However we must take the risk and note that 1970 can lay claim to being perhaps the most traumatic of all years since LT came into being. For on 1 January the Country Area passed out of 55 Broadway's control and became part of the newly set up NBC while LT itself passed from state control to that of the GLC.

1,267 buses and coaches were handed over to London Country, as the former Country Area was now to be known. The first obvious sign of these changes was the new wording appearing in gold Johnson face capitals on green buses. The livery, for the moment, was otherwise unchanged. The new Swift single-decker had been ordered for both Country and Central Area services and, although they probably wouldn't have been London Country's choice, it was too late to do anything about this and anyhow the new concern was desperate to go OMO just as quickly as possible. The first green ones took up work in June 1970 from Leatherhead on routes 418/418A, followed in August by deliveries to Addlestone, Crawley and Guildford. Not only were RTs replaced but also the last of the green RLHs. One might have thought that these 53-seat double-deckers with their inconvenient lowbridge layout would have been replaced by the very first batch of high capacity single-deckers but they had managed to last into the new decade.

London Country's new symbol appeared in the early summer of 1970. It lacked the classic simplicity of the

traditional LT logo, being a solid circle, surrounded by an open one with what was assumed to be wings surrounding this. Some wit remarked that it looked like a flying polo and, not surprisingly, the name stuck; this was particularly appropriate for London Country was a peculiar animal having a vast hole in the middle of its territory, ie the red bus area. There were those who reckoned that such a geographical oddity was destined for a short and not particularly merry existence.

Croydon, always at the forefront of new initiatives of course, found itself host to the XAs which inaugurated flat fare C1-4 routes between New Addington and Croydon, C1 being the express service, except on Saturdays when it became the C3 for the benefit of shoppers and ran along North End, the principal shopping street. FRM1 also arrived at Croydon and worked route 233 which served Roundshaw, a new housing estate with a spectacular see-through power station, built on part of Croydon Aerodrome. Croydon had been London's airport before World War 2 but afterwards, there being no room to extend the runways for the much bigger

Above:
The birth of London Country. The interestingly numbered RT4444 still carries its old insignia but the RT behind at West Croydon bus station has just received its London Country fleetname.

Right:
London Country's first Swift, SM101, in Reigate garage. Just visible behind it is a former M&D Harrington-bodied Reliance coach which London Country used as a trainer.

airliners coming into service, its importance declined and it was eventually closed. The 233 was London's very first OMO double-deck route, inaugurated by XA22 on 22 November 1969.

As host to some of the final batch of RMLs, the XAs and the FRM Croydon was the proud possessor of the most up-to-date fleet of double-deckers in London, although not all were equally appreciated. The RMLs and the FRM were fine buses but the XAs, despite being overhauled before being sent to Croydon, soon became know as 'rattle-boxes'. Worse was to follow.

The first Central Area Swifts, SM1-10/12, took up work from Catford garage on routes 160 and 160A on 24 January as part of yet another reorganisation of routes and cuts in services. Although shorter than the Merlins they were still longer than the RTs they replaced and this immediately caused problems, the drivers deciding to take a different route on the Middle Park Estate to that announced. In April the nearby Bexleyheath garage received Swifts, as did the west London garages of Fulwell and Hounslow, while the final batch of SMs arrived at Cricklewood in June. All the SMs seated 42.

Before this the first SMSs had entered service. The SMS was a two-door version of the Swift. It had 33 seats, mostly in the raised, rear portion and room for 34 standing passengers. The entrance on the left was for passengers who preferred the human touch and wished to pay the driver; that on the right was for the technologically minded with the correct fare who pushed it into a slot which they were misled into

believing would then instantly send a message to a turnstile to let them enter the magnificent interior. It mostly did, but sometimes it didn't and of course even a few failures got the apparatus a bad name. Most passengers preferred to pay the driver which did nothing to speed things up.

The London Country Swifts, although dual-door, did not suffer these problems as all passengers had to pay the driver. The SMSs introduced a third body builder of the large capacity OMO single-deckers, although one more familiar to London than any other, Park Royal. Marshall, MCW and Park Royal bodies were built to very close specifications as regards appearance and, whatever the failings of the actual vehicles, they were neat and well proportioned.

Route 70, previously operated by RTs from New Cross, was the first SMS route, the conversion taking place on 18 April. Next they went to Edgware, taking over on 13 June, a day long-remembered for the utter chaos they caused; passengers and staff seemed quite unprepared for their arrival to the extent that someone had forgotten to order paper rolls for the automatic ticket machines. In September SMSs and new route 82 were introduced between Hounslow bus station and London airport, although it would be some years yet before RTs disappeared from Heathrow routes. On the last day of October SMSs replaced their longer brothers at Enfield.

The conversion I best remember also took place that day, when Croydon, Thornton Heath and Elmers End garages received the type. At that time I was regularly travelling on route 194 and one could hardly say the new single-deckers were received with unalloyed joy. Apart from sentimentalists like me who were simply fond of the RT for its own sake, the general public liked neither having to queue up to pay the driver before they could board the bus nor then finding they had to stand when they were properly inside. Many decided it was more comfortable to wait for a 54 or 119, both routes still worked by RTs, and often quicker as the double-decker would catch up and overtake the SMS laboriously loading up at a stop down the road.

The last Swift conversion of 1970 was the 226 when seven were sent to Willesden garage and took up work on 7 November.

The huge RT fleet, numbering 2,775 scheduled for service in January 1970, was in rapid decline now and by the end of June all those without heaters had been withdrawn from passenger service. None had been built with these comforts and when they began to be fitted it was decided that no roof-box bodies, these generally being the oldest, would have them. One did, the Saunders body on RT1903, by mistake so it is said. This lasted out 1970, but otherwise the roof-box body, so distinctive a feature of the London bus, was now gone for ever from passenger service. Some remained a little longer in the training fleet, but the last of the Leylands used in this capacity and as staff buses, RTLs and RTWs, were all withdrawn in 1970, although some stayed delicensed with LT until the very last was sold in April 1971.

No RTs received complete Aldenham overhauls after the beginning of 1970 and even standard RTs with heaters were now being sold, but repainting went on and some RTs received the now standard RM fleetname with all the letters of equal size and no underlining.

In September 1970, a new design of surface car, the C69, began to enter Underground service. A total of 212 vehicles were built by Metro-Cammell, sufficient for 35 six-car trains with one spare two-car unit. It was now possible to use identical types of vehicle on both the Circle and the Hammersmith and City lines; 14 trains took up work on the former line, 17 on the latter. Each six-car train consisted of three two-car units, with a driving cab at one end of one of the cars. One of the curious problems which has always affected Circle Line trains is that, apart from giddy drivers, the wheels wear unevenly. So, every so often one is sent to Whitechapel which ensures that when it returns to the Circle Line it is facing the opposite direction: devilishly clever.

By 1970 the dangers of smoking were becoming apparent – we shall arrive at the horrors of the King's Cross fire later – and instead of 50 per cent of the cars allowing this, only two in each six-car train were so designated. This rather complicated matters as no three units stayed together for very long, so the no smoking signs had to be moveable. The C69 stock – so designated because it entered service in 1970 –

looked rather like its immediate predecessors, the A stock. However there were many differences, notably the provision of four doors in each carriage instead of the three used on the essentially outer suburban As; all measurements were in metric although this hasn't as yet seen any units transferred to the Paris Metro. The arrival of the C69s saw the end of those antiques dating from the 1920s, the Q stock. I used to travel regularly in these on the East London line at that time and marvelled, as we rattled past what remained of the London docks, at the plethora of swaying leather straps hanging from the clerestory roofs. It was 1971 before the very last was taken out of service. Several were preserved, notably driving motor car No 4248 which can be seen in the LT Museum at Covent Garden.

1971

The inexorable, although far from all-conquering, march of the one-man single-decker continued through most of 1971. However its replacement had already appeared at the 1970 Commercial Motor Show and it began work in London on 2 January 1971. Keith Hamer wrote a piece for the *London Bus Magazine* entitled, 'The Good, the Bad and the Dodgy', which precisely encapsulated the career of the DMS. In 1970-1 I had a part-time job teaching photography at Tower Hamlets College of Further Education, and one evening, after slaving away over a hot enlarger and talking to the rather engaging daughter of a dock engineer and the son of an Afghan chief, on my way home to sylvan Oxted I bought a copy at London Bridge of the *London Transport Magazine*. In its pages I learned all about its wonderful new bus, the DMS or Londoner, as it wished to be called. No one had ever thought of giving such a grandiose title to the original B, the STL nor even the RT. A little later I took my students for a ride in one on route 5 down Commercial Road and we got roared at by the driver for over-riding our stop, which taught me that one-man drivers took the conducting side of their two-man duties seriously.

Anyway, the *London Transport Magazine* was fulsome in its praise of 'London's Bus of the Future', as one would naturally expect and I must say it looked rather nice, though not everyone thought – or thinks – so. It was much better than the XAs and the XFs, which were its ancestors. The Daimler XF Fleetline, having performed better than the Leyland XA Atlantean, was chosen as the basis for London's next generation of double-deckers. Until 1966 the law had demanded that all double-deckers have conductors, hence the Merlin and Swift single-deckers, but these, as we have seen, were far from satisfactory, and when the law was changed LT set about adapting the DMS to its requirements. Because of the bus grant from the government, which defrayed up to 25 per cent of the

cost of a new vehicle providing it was to a manufacturer's standard design, and because British Leyland wasn't prepared to produce a one-off for LT, the standard Fleetline chassis with a Gardner engine was chosen.

LT had bought its last AEC. The last Regent came off the production line in 1968, as the final

Above:
Two Hammersmith Line trains of C69 stock pass outside Paddington.

Below:
DMS111 in Commercial Road.

Routemasters were being delivered, and the Merlin and Swift single-deckers were a sad final chapter in what had been, for the most part, a glorious story – the collaboration between AEC and LT stretching back to the earliest days of the motorbus. The excellent Reliance continued in production and was chosen for the Green Line fleet until the very end, which came in 1979, when the works closed with the loss of over 2,000 jobs.

Just as London had ordered huge numbers of Merlins and Swifts without proper trials so, partly because of delivery delays, it did the same with the DMS and, surprise, surprise, ran into equally horrendous problems. Would you believe 1,967 were on the order books before the first had entered service. If the chassis was 'off the peg', the body was LT's own. There was a front entrance, divided so that passengers could either pay the driver or use the automatic machine and turnstile; the exit was amidships. There were seats for 44 upstairs and 24 downstairs with room for 21 standing passengers. The livery was the dullest yet seen on a London bus, red all over; thank goodness for adverts! AEC might be gone but Park Royal was still in business and it built the first DMS bodies. Tram replacement route 95 and trolleybus replacement route 220 were chosen to receive the first DMSs on 2 January 1971. As great a contrast as one could imagine was the RLH. This lowbridge double-decker seated only nine more in all than the DMS did on its upper deck alone. The last few managed to hang on into the DMS era, being withdrawn from Dalston garage and route 178 on 16 April.

Because of their vastly greater seating capacity, passengers were much happier with the DMS than with the new generation of single-deckers. Also, it has to be said, with the end of the overhaul cycle which had ensured an RT emerging from Aldenham was as good as new, these veterans were becoming distinctly shabby, inside and out.

Like the Merlins and Swifts the early DMSs had a public address system but it was little used and later

ones were not so fitted. DMS76 was given a broad white band above the lower-deck windows, which improved its appearance somewhat, and this became standard from 118 to 367. Meanwhile Chiswick Works fitted two instead of four-leaf entrance doors to DMS240 and painted them bright yellow (the surrounds, not the glass). This, together with a solid white bullseye logo instead of the rather insipid open one which was replacing the LT legend, was to become standard. The white stripe was omitted.

Decimal currency arrived more or less concurrently with the first DMSs – on 21 February 1971, to be precise as far as LT was concerned – and so all ticket machines, whether conductor-operated or automatic, on buses and of course machines at all Underground stations, were changed on that day, a massive though

Right:
Former GWR pannier tank, London Transport No L94 at Finchley Road, 7 June 1971.

worthwhile undertaking. DMS delivery continued right through 1971: RTs, RMs, Merlins and Swifts all being replaced, although only the RTs were actually withdrawn as a consequence.

Congestion was still growing, both in central London and the suburbs, but the socialists in charge of the GLC at County Hall were sympathetic to public transport and between 1970 and 1975 increased bus lanes from three to over 100. The steadily increasing number of OMO buses certainly didn't speed up traffic but was seen as the only way of holding down costs. It was expected that eventually conductors would disappear from the London scene and with them the now elderly RTs and the much newer Routemasters. LT had hoped that the larger capacity of the DMS would mean that it could operate rather fewer buses but because they spent so much longer at stops than the RT and the RM they soon had to settle for a one for one replacement policy; indeed on some routes more vehicles had to be scheduled when open rear-entrance buses were replaced. OMO was truly a necessary evil.

Royalty returned to the Underground when the final section of the Victoria Line to Brixton was opened by HRH the Princess Alexandra on 23 July 1971. Work was now well under way on the extension of the Piccadilly Line to Heathrow, sanctioned by the government in November 1970. Rather remarkably, although steam had disappeared from British Rail in August 1968, it survived on LT for another three years, former GWR pannier tanks continuing to work in dwindling numbers on engineers' trains. By the spring of 1971 only three remained and the end came on 6 June when a special last run was made over the Metropolitan between Barbican and Neasden by L94, formerly No 7752, hauling a train of engineers'

wagons. Large crowds turned out all along the route to watch; rather surprisingly, no one seems to have got themselves electrocuted and, 1971 being well into the preservation era, No L94 then headed off for a new lease of life on the Severn Valley Railway. A number of its fellows were also preserved and LT, realising the potential of all this, has since run many specials, hauled both by the preserved electric loco *Sarah Siddons*, and various steam engines, over the Metropolitan. It can honestly be said that steam has never really gone from this unique section of the Underground system.

1972

In order to ensure that all RTs and RMs could be replaced by 1978 (ho, ho, ho) that other stalwart LT body builder, MCW, began to produce DMS bodies, the first arriving on DMS1248 in March 1972. As with the RTs the two body builders were given separate blocks of numbers, thus the high number of the first MCW bus. Engines for the DMS were supplied not only by Gardner, but there were also a few from Rolls-Royce – very up-market. Of course, as we all know, you pay for quality and the Rolls-Royce engine proved to be a good deal more expensive to run. Neither did the name Rolls-Royce automatically mean higher quality any more than a minibus based on a Mercedes chassis guarantees a superior turn of speed. Following the addition of Daimler to the Leyland fold, and a shortage of Gardner engines, Leyland engines

Below:
DMSs, SMSs and one distant RM at Brent Cross.

Right:
London Country's AF4 pulls up the A25 westbound through Old Oxted.

Below:
London Country SMW11 on route 726 at West Croydon alongside an RML and RT1018.

were also fitted to Fleetlines. At first they were very noisy to the extent that, after the original DMS so fitted, No 1250, had been delivered in March 1972, the others were either put in store without engines or were given Gardner ones until the problem had been solved.

Although full scale overhaul of the RT had ended, recertifications and repainting still took place. By now only one RT route, the 197, was still operated by Croydon garage but evidence that the class was alive and kicking came in the spring when a number of members of the class emerged gleaming with a new coat of paint, which put members of the already shabby SMS class, alongside which they worked, to shame.

Meanwhile the problems besetting the OMO single-deckers continued. Some were already out of traffic but the entry of MBS4 into Aldenham for a pilot overhaul in June 1972 suggested that perhaps the class had a future. Virtually all the Merlins had been repainted by the end of 1972. Some variations on the standard livery were carried out, while MBA606 appeared covered in an overall advert – a phase LT was beginning to go through at this time – for Chappell's music store.

The last of the Swifts arrived in March 1972. By then it was obvious that the smaller engine, necessary on account of the reduced length of the bus compared to the Merlins, was very unreliable. It had been uprated but was still considered under-powered by many drivers. The automatic heating system was inadequate – there being insufficient warm air in winter, insufficient cold air in summer. I remember a particularly miserable ride in a Swift on route 115 through Purley on a damp winter's evening, although

the packed bodies of the steaming, standing passengers did help to heat things up a bit. Paintwork became less than pristine far too early in the vehicles' career and various body defects soon made themselves apparent, although these, just to make life even more interesting, varied from manufacturer to manufacturer. Repainting of Swifts began in October 1972 and, like the Merlins, there were some experiments, chiefly featuring variations of white, which, generally, improved the buses' looks.

Out in the wilder reaches of the Home Counties, ie London Country, great changes were afoot. Under the old regime secondhand vehicles were practically

unknown but the almost bewildering change around, which has become such a feature of modern bus fleets, had begun in 1971. Fifteen AEC Swifts, the SMW class dating from 1969-71, with bus bodies built by Willowbrook and Marshall, were transferred from South Wales Transport in 1971-2. The first three had uninspiring Willowbrook 48-seat bodies; the rest 53-seat Marshall bodies. These were built to the much more handsome standard BET specification, and were very similar to M&D and Southdown buses which they sometimes encountered in the course of their duties. Another Swift variation was the SMA. These also should have gone to South Wales but all 21 were

Above:
St Albans city centre with London Country Reliance RP2 of St Albans (SA) on the 727 and Garston's Atlantean AN103 on route 321.

Left:
GS55 in London Country ownership.

diverted to London Country before delivery. Very different in appearance, they had a double Celtic connection for their bodies which were built by Alexander in Scotland. They were put on Green Line service and had 45 coach type seats and spent most of their lives working route 725. The SMAs replaced RFs which were now being withdrawn.

None of the rear-engined Swift variations was really successful; the underfloor Reliance was vastly better, although in its early days this too had its problems. The first of the 90-strong RP class, Park Royal-bodied, 45-seat Reliances, basically buses but with coach type seats, went into service at the very end of 1971, on the 727. The rest arrived in 1972 and quickly replaced practically all the RMCs and RCLs in Green Line service. The only exceptions were three RCLs which Godstone retained for the rush hour and Sunday 709. This was drama indeed. Splendid as the Green Line double-deckers undoubtedly were, the doubting Thomases had been proved right. OMO, large capacity single-deckers were far more appropriate for the Green Line network of the 1970s.

The RT class was severely reduced in 1972, numbers being cut by around two-thirds. But a surprise was the sale of 34 RTs in September – to LT. New Year's Day saw RCLs arrive in Croydon on route 414 and the companion 405 got them on 25 March.

Now that I was living in Oxted, Godstone and Chelsham were my local garages and the former hit the headlines early in 1972. I was nosing around in the tin shed on the corner of the A22 and A25 at the end of January when I came across a brand-new OMO rear-engined double-decker, London Country's very first, painted in mid-green and a nasty mustard yellow livery. Yet another Celtic exile, it was a Northern Counties-bodied 72-seat Daimler Fleetline originally intended for Western Welsh. In all there were 11 of these AF class buses, and they took over from Routemasters on the 410, popping up on the 411 on Sundays.

Before spring 1972 was out another new class of OMO double-decker, one destined to be much more numerous and long-lived than the AF, appeared. This was the Leyland Atlantean, the AN class which is still with us. The first 90 had handsome Park Royal 72-seat bodies; the last 30, yet another diversion this time from Midland Red, were given similar MCW ones. They, too, appeared in the new green and yellow livery and brought about the end of great numbers of RTs. The first went to Hertford garage chiefly for routes 310 and 310A, and were soon a familiar sight in Croydon, being sent to Chelsham, Leatherhead and Guildford for the 408 and 470. By the end of 1972, 237 RTs had been withdrawn, most for breaking up although some found other owners.

The livery which London Country had chosen was rendered obsolete almost before the paint was dry, for by the autumn of 1972 the stranglehold of the NBC had dictated that, just as with the old Tilling companies, every concern within its huge empire should paint its buses either poppy red or leaf green and adorn them with its double N symbol and fleet name in corporate style. Thus the later Atlanteans appeared in this guise.

The vehicle most associated with the early days of the NBC was the celebrated Leyland National. This single-decker, still a familiar sight throughout the land, was intended to be Britain's standard bus for generations and had been developed by British Leyland in conjunction with the NBC. Not everyone would use the adjective 'celebrated' to describe it, but it is certain to become, if it isn't already, a classic bus design, the Model T of the bus world. London Country was destined to own more Nationals than any other bus company, in Britain or abroad. I met my first one autumn afternoon at Chelsham where it had arrived for crew training. It had a rather impressive front; from the side I thought it less attractive, while the pod on the roof at the rear, which contained heating and ventilating equipment, looked all the world like an old fashioned luggage rack.

As the first Nationals arrived so the last of the little GS normal control buses were taken out of service from Garston garage, when their last route, the 336A, was withdrawn. By 1972 we were well into the preservation era and, apart from some which continued on PSV work with other operators, a number have been restored to their original pristine 1953 condition.

The Victoria Line at last was complete in every detail when Pimlico, featured as the station for the Tate Galley on the north bank of the Thames, opened in September 1972. Meanwhile a new design of tube train was entering service on the Northern Line. It was very similar to the Victoria Line stock, which by now numbered 316 vehicles, but was designed for crew operation. 90 driving motor cars, 90 trailers and 30 uncoupling non-driving motor cars were ordered from Metro-Cammell. Withdrawal of the prewar, red-painted stock began with the delivery of the 1972 stock. Although this is now long gone elderly trains of 1956/9/62 stock can still be found on the Northern line.

1973

The rate at which the RT was being withdrawn suggested it would not see out 1973, certainly with London Country and perhaps not LT either. But this remarkable vehicle was not that easy to dispose of and LT took only 260 out of service that year, while London Country switched its withdrawal emphasis to the RF. At the end of 1973 there were still well over 1,000 licensed for service with the two concerns. One RT which did disappear that year was No 4325, the very last roof-box one which had been operating as a trainer until 9 November.

If the RT, dating back to 1939, was still needed; the Merlin, dating back to 1966, wasn't. The pilot overhaul of MBS4 had taken no less than eight months; the Certificates of Fitness for the class were coming up to expiry. Experience had shown that there was still a need for the double-deck bus whether crew or one-man operated, and all this, combined with the general unreliability and unpopularity of the Merlin prompted the GLC to announce in August that it sanctioned its gradual withdrawal.

Below:
Metro-Scania MS5 at Clapton. *Author's collection*

The prototypes had all gone by October 1973 and the first 15 production buses, MB16-31 were taken out of traffic; the rest lasted the year out.

Production of the Merlin's replacement, the DMS, continued in considerable numbers throughout 1973, although there was a hiccup when chassis production was transferred from the old Daimler works at Coventry to the Leyland one at Farington, Leyland. To most enthusiasts, Farington instantly brings to mind the final Leyland body design for the PD2, which bore this name with such distinction. By 1973 the once revered name of Leyland had become something of a musical hall joke, as the unreliability of its products

and periodic shortages of parts had reached epidemic proportions. Despite having a virtual monopoly of the British bus industry, and one or two excellent products, there was widespread dissatisfaction at its performance. The seeds of its own doom were being sewn and the market was being got ready, however unintentionally, for mainland Europe manufacturers.

One industry in which Britain has excelled in the latter part of the 20th century is that of exploiting its history, and not just olde worlde Anne Hathaway-type cottages, castles, cathedrals and such, but equally successfully its industrial heritage. The cynical might claim that, as we have become steadily less capable of making and selling products for home and foreign consumption, so we have excelled in demonstrating how good we used to be. It's rather more complicated than that: all of which is a roundabout way into recording the transfer of the LT Collection to Syon Park.

The Clapham Museum had been closed and the British Rail exhibits transferred to the magnificent new museum which was due to open at York – a laudable move away from London's monopoly of all things bright and historic but this left London's historic buses, trams, trains etc, looking for a home. Syon Park, belonging to the Duke of Northumberland, is beside the river between Brentford and Isleworth and on the opposite bank from Richmond, a very nice setting, if not terribly central or handily placed for public transport. The collection was housed in a modern building, and opened by the Duke on 23 May. Among the exhibits not seen at Clapham were two from the Underground, Q23 Metropolitan District car No 4248, and Metropolitan electric locomotive No 5 *John Hampden*, both only recently withdrawn.

If the Merlins were giving trouble the Swifts were no better, probably worse. Large numbers of them were unserviceable at various times throughout 1973, a combination of their many inherent design faults and shortage of spare parts from British Leyland. A vastly more successful single-deck class appeared in 1973. The local east London route, the S2, received six Leyland Nationals, LS1-6, in November. These were the precursors of a large fleet, many members of which are still at work in London, of which more anon. They worked alongside six Metro-Scanias, MS1-6, which had arrived a little earlier. These, too, were to have a considerable influence on LT policy in the years to come, although the vehicles themselves did not last long in the fleet.

Yet more variations on the single-deck theme had appeared in 1972, delivery continuing in 1973. Apart from the livery and LT roundels the vehicles of the FS class could not have looked less like the traditional London bus for they were tiny 16 seat Ford minibuses. They had bonnets and were thus the first

Left:
Ford Minibus FS11 on the B1 in Bromley.

Below:
Leyland National LN7 on Superbus duty at Stevenage in the company of an Atlantean and a United Counties Bristol/ECW RE.

Above right:
Bakerloo Line 1972 tube stock at Willesden Junction.

normal control red buses since the Leyland Cubs and were basically converted vans – 'Bread Vans' as the breed was instantly dubbed. They operated experimental services, at the request of the GLC, for a 10p flat fare, mostly along roads out in the suburbs which until then had never been served by public transport.

Congestion was getting steadily worse throughout London, and the GLC – sympathetic to public transport – continued to introduce bus lanes. Oxford Street west of Oxford Circus had been closed to ordinary traffic between 11.00 and 23.00 in October 1971, an experiment which led to the permanent exclusion of all except buses and taxis, while the most famous bus lane, the contraflow one along Piccadilly allowing buses to run from the Circus to Hyde Park Corner, came into operation in April. By the end of the year there were 45 in operation during the morning and evening rush hours. BESIs (Bus Electronic Scanning Indicators), looking like leftovers from an episode of *Doctor Who*, appeared at intervals along selected main routes which were able to monitor the position of each bus, direct radio links with drivers had begun in 1971, while Computer Assisted Radio Location Aids (CARLA) were introduced in 1973. These automatically pinpointed the position of every bus on a particular route. All these innovations were attempts to combat congestion and delays, although vandalism and assaults on crews were growing and there was an element of attempting to come to terms with this unpleasant phenomenon too.

The great London Country event of 1973 was the large scale entry into service of the Leyland National. The first four were already at work, on the Stevenage Superbus network, LNs1 and 2 carrying K suffix registrations, the rest being NPD-Ls. The first to appear in green livery took up work from Dunton Green on 1 January 1973; many others followed for bus work throughout the network.

The next innovation was the appearance of Nationals in Green Line guise, RPs being replaced on route 721 in February. From the outside they looked rather handsome in their two-tone livery, but

internally, where it mattered, they were a disaster. One wonders just what aberration persuaded London Country's master, the NBC, that the PVC-covered bus seats would be acceptable to passengers, particularly as the almost new RPs which they replaced had proper coach seats. Nevertheless more of the same was provided, although later ones did have a moquette covering but the seats were still basically bus ones and the National was quite definitely a bus, not a coach.

At the other extreme five proper coaches, the very first Green Line had owned, did enter service. Plaxton Panorama Elite II-bodied AEC Reliances, they were painted in standard NBC white coach livery and were used solely for private hire and tours. They were given no class or fleet numbers and were known only by their registration numbers, SPK201-5M.

The RPs moved on to other Green Line routes and these and the Nationals wrought havoc with the RF fleet which by September had no scheduled allocation on Green Line routes, other than from Chelsham on the 706. However RFs would pop up with perhaps not surprising frequency on Green Line services for several years yet.

It could only be a matter of time before the ECW/Bristol combination, so beloved by the nationalised companies, joined London Country; the breakthrough happened in October. While single-deckers and coaches had been growing longer and wider there remained a need for something a good deal smaller, in the tradition of the C and GS classes, and so London Country ordered a fleet of 35-seat ECW-bodied Bristol LHS6Ls – the BL class. They provided a further assault on the RF class which lost 63 members by the end of the year.

More new tube trains entered service from November. This was very similar to that of the previous year and was known as 1972 Mark II stock. There was a striking variation in the livery, the doors being painted red. The LT roundel, already appearing on buses, now appeared on trains. The large scale production of both marks of the 1972 stock meant that the long familiar 1938 stock now began to be withdrawn and scrapped.

1974

Withdrawal of LT's Merlins began in earnest in 1974; London Country would keep its fleet intact a little while longer. Indeed, in order to cover its chronic vehicle shortage, a number of LT's Merlins were hired out to London Country, a situation which continued to December 1976. The assault on the Merlins meant that although more than 400 DMSs joined the fleet, they mostly took over from the single-deckers. RTs were removed from four routes in January, 1974, but after that the type was left largely undisturbed so that only 118 members disappeared from the fleet that year: the drastic spare parts shortage resulting from the three-day week was one reason for this.

Not only were many RTs still needed but plans eventually to turn the fleet over to entire OMO were being put on hold, if not yet abandoned. In recognition of this it was decided to put a number of Fleetlines into service with conductors and class them as DMs. Some DMSs were already fulfilling this role, albeit with their OMO equipment intact. The first DMs proper took up work on route 16 from Cricklewood garage, replacing crewed DMSs in September, 1974. There were to be 400 DMs in all, numbered DM918-1247 and 1703-1832. The thousandth member of the class, DM1000, was the subject of a handing-over ceremony at Park Royal at the end of the year.

One of the routes which did lose its RTs was the 197, Croydon garage's last one. It had operated the type for over 26 years, since the very earliest days of the postwar RT when they had arrived in large numbers to replace the Tilling and General STLs and the STs which had more or less monopolised Croydon's routes. RTs were still to be found in the town, notably from Chelsham, Catford, Bromley, Thornton Heath, and Brixton garages, the two latter putting them out on the 109, the busiest route on the entire LT network.

Up north, on 19 October Dial-a-Bus began, operating amongst the leafy avenues of select Hampstead. Although the basic outline of the route, starting from Golders Green, was fixed, passengers could make bookings to the controller at Golders Green or hail the bus, an FS 'Bread Van', and it would make diversions to pick them up, providing they were not waiting in one of the many cul-de-sacs which Hampstead Garden suburb boasted.

Leyland had originally intended that the National would be produced with as few variations as possible in order to ease its production and keep costs down.

Below:
Newly overhauled RT537 in Croydon garage in May 1972.

One of the 7ft 6in wide Bristols, BN52 climbs Titsey Hill, the steepest bit of road anywhere on the London Country or London Transport network on its way back from working the 465 to Chelsham garage.

Just how it expected to maintain this rigidity is a puzzle, presumably it was devised by an expert in systems theory rather than a student of human nature; British Leyland certainly didn't seem to have employed anyone versed in the quirks and idiosyncrasies of bus passengers and operators. However it began to learn its lesson quite early on and in August 1974 a new version for Green Line service arrived fitted with proper coach seats and luggage racks. The series began at SNC116, WPG 216M. The S stood for short, the National being produced in two lengths, 33ft 10in and 37ft 2in. The longer ones were, naturally enough, given an L prefix.

A variation on the BL class appeared with London Country in August. This was a 7ft 6in wide version, and it was initially put to work along the narrow lanes of Surrey, Kent and Hertfordshire. Designated BN (N for narrow) the 30 members of the class went to Northfleet, Chelsham, Dunton Green, Dorking, Guildford, Leatherhead and Hertford garages, replacing RFs.

Although we are primarily concerned with vehicles we cannot ignore the wider context in which they operate and this might be an appropriate moment to consider some of the factors which determined the type of vehicles and their operation in the mid-1970s.

The cooling of enthusiasm for OMO, typified by the arrival of the DM class, is spelled out in the introduction to the LT 1974 Annual Report and Accounts: 'The problem of ticket issue and change giving, which increase [sic] the time that passengers take to board vehicles on heavily-used routes is one of the factors that limit – at least for the present – the number of buses that can be single-manned under London conditions.' Over 60 per cent of buses were still crew-operated. In a year when total passenger journeys were up by 1 per cent and staff shortages were down, although 'there was a shortage of skilled engineering staff,' a considerable restraint on progress was caused 'by a shortage of serviceable vehicles . . . delays in deliveries of new buses and . . . a severe shortage of spare parts for the bus fleet.'

The report then goes on to refer to the energy crisis and the 'staggering increase in oil prices. The fuel used in the Executive's electrical generation stations at Lots Road and Greenwich had sustained a more than fourfold price increase in nine months.' A particular statistic which sticks in my mind from this time is that the fuel oil being used by the great liner *France*, then on a cruise, had doubled in cost between the beginning and ending of its voyage. It was shortly after taken out

Left:
SNC138 at Chartwell, Sir Winston Churchill's former home whence route 706 was extended in summer. In the background is an elderly Bristol/ECW L5G.

Left:
RMC1480 of Dartford received an all-over advert for the Co-Op in 1974. It is seen here heading down the A23 for Brighton passing the preserved Southdown Leyland N of 1922 taking part in that year's HCVC run.

Left:
DMS1 after its first overhaul and transfer to Merton garage.

1975

of service, to be bought subsequently and re-engined and converted to the *Norway*.

Nothing as drastic as re-engining was proposed for London's bus and train fleet, but it was hoped that the steep increase in petrol prices would curb private motoring. For a brief period in December 1973 when there was a petrol shortage: 'bus mileage lost because of traffic congestion had dropped dramatically by 50%.'

The GLC had a policy of keeping fares down, highly commendable too, but difficult to sustain with such a dramatic increase in fuel costs. In November the GLC had accepted 'that there must be a major increase in fares' (they were to go up by a staggering 56 per cent in 1975). The report went on to note that there was: 'a recognition that the cost of providing an acceptable public transport system in London must be borne by the public one way or another, if not as fare-payers then as ratepayers and taxpayers.' This argument has been central to political debate, both at national and local level, ever since, the emphasis swinging first one way, then another. At its deepest level it reflects how one views society and how great a contribution the richer should make to improve the lot of the poorer. Though usually seen as a question of Right versus Left, it can cut across party lines and leaves many bus and train enthusiasts confused, torn between wanting to see a properly funded public transport network which invariably means a high degree of state control, but objecting to the uniformity and standardisation that this often entails.

In the spring of 1975 the first general fares' increase since 1972 took place, most bus and Underground tickets costing a third more. The cheapest 3p fare went up to 4p, the 5p to 7p, the 12p off peak maximum remaining, while the maximum at other times, 20p, was reduced to 15p. Red Arrow fares doubled to 10p. It was hoped that an additional £35 million would thus be brought in.

Two tragedies, different in scale, but both traumatic, clouded 1975. In January a conductor on a 77C bus, Ronald Jones, died as a result of an incident involving two 21-year olds. Both LT and London Country buspeople (no longer busmen for women were now driving London buses) had been protesting over the rising number of assaults on crews, and these protests increased dramatically, amidst much public disquiet about the situation. The press seized on every incident and there was a good deal of over-dramatisation and harking back to a supposed non-violent golden age, even if no one could quite recall when precisely this was; but for all that operating a bus in some parts of London and the suburbs had certainly become more hazardous. High level talks involving cabinet ministers, union leaders and the Chairman of LT took place; the police were given increased powers, and alarms and radios were to be fitted to vehicles.

On 28 February 43 people died when a Highbury branch Northern line tube train, instead of coming to a halt in Moorgate station, careered through it and crashed into the dead end tunnel just beyond. Carriages were telescoped and it took many hours for all the injured and dead to be extricated from the horrendously mangled wreckage. The driver was one of those who died and there has never been a

Left:
An Eastern Region Great Northern Line DMU bound for Moorgate approaching Farringdon station alongside a Metropolitan Line A stock train from Amersham to Aldgate.

Right:
Seen at Old Coulsdon, RCL2250 on the 709, the last regularly Routemaster-operated Green Line route, ahead of two Southend Corporation PD3s hired to London Transport for route 190.

Below right:
Ex-Southdown PD3 working for London Country from Godstone garage passing through Caterham on the 411.

satisfactory explanation of the accident. Somewhat ironically the branch closed later in the year in preparation for it to become part of the Great Northern section of British Rail's suburban electric network.

1975 was the year the RT was supposed to be taken out of service but hundreds were still needed and three-year re-certifications and some repaintings were the order of the day. Only one OPO conversion to DMS, route 183 at Hendon garage, took place, although other RTs were replaced by two man DMs and Routemasters.

It was the Merlin which, as in 1974, was the chief target for withdrawal. All the two-door MBs had gone by April and so rapid was the Merlin's disappearance that LT had to store them on the disused Radlett aerodrome. A total of 350 had gathered there by the end of the year, a rather extraordinary sight from passing trains on the Midland main line out of St Pancras.

Just about every bus company except LT was operating ECW-bodied Bristols of one sort or another and although the Lodekka never became a familiar sight on the streets of London – come to think of it that's not true, for Eastern National and Thames Valley examples did have regular workings on express routes into London but you know what I mean – LT jumped on the bandwagon in 1975 when six little 26-seat LHS6Ls arrived. Put into the BS class they were sent to Highgate to take over from the FS minibuses on the C11. They were painted in traditional red with white surrounds to the window frames and looked rather fetching. They were also adorned with the now almost white bullseye logo. RTs were the only class never to receive this, keeping the traditional gold underlined fleetname or, in a few cases, the later unlined version. Not everyone approved of the white roundel. It was my opinion that it simply showed how dull the old style had been. I know Gill Sans was ideal

for destination screens, clear and easy to read, but for a fleetname it was pretty uninspiring, not a patch on the handsome General which it replaced or, indeed, the very nice Stagecoach now to be seen on Upton Park's Routemasters for example.

After that dizzying leap into the past and then to the future, let us return to 1975. The shortage of buses, old and new, showed no sign of easing; if anything it was getting worse. BEA, along with its Routemasters, had become part of British Airways in 1973. Not all received the new corporate livery and those that didn't, 13 in all, were sold to LT in August 1975. They were classified RMA and were rushed into service, still in BEA orange and white, with no route indicators, merely a board in the nearside front window, and put to work from North Street garage on route 175. They had been given bells and used ticket boxes but no internal stanchions for passengers to hang on to and were clearly only a stop gap. They were re-certified and repainted into LT livery and lasted on passenger work until September 1976. Their story, however, was far from over.

As if orange wasn't a sufficiently different colour, 10 bright blue and cream double-deckers were next to join the fleet. These were handsome Massey and East Lancs-bodied Leyland Titan PD3s with exposed radiators, hired from Southend. Fortuitously they had three-piece indicators and were sent to Croydon, fitted with TC garage plates and from 22 September graced the streets of my home town on route 190. There was a sudden upsurge in the sale of sunglasses at Boots in North End Croydon around this time for, along with the red LT buses, the various shades of green of the London Country ones, and the Southend Titans, three more PD3s, this time ex-Southdown ones with Northern Counties bodies still in traditional Southdown pale green and cream livery, took up work on the 409 and the 411 from Godstone garage. London Country was having as many problems keeping its vehicles on the road as LT. There was yet more to come.

In order to replace its RTs on driver training duty, London Country bought 20 more Titans and painted them bright yellow. Undoubtedly the most famous of the many varieties of PD3 were the full fronted versions owned by Southdown and Ribble and it was from the latter company that the 20 trainers had come. By a remarkable coincidence both found their way into the London Country fleet and more than once I saw examples side by side at Godstone garage.

This was by no means the end of London Country's hirings and secondhand purchases. Only 30 new vehicles arrived in 1975, all Nationals, and, apart from hiring Merlins from LT, Bristol MW coaches came from Royal Blue and were sent to Dunton Green. As this garage worked the 483 to Croydon it is possible royal blue contributed to the kaleidoscope in the town. A second shade of yellow was certainly seen on some Bournemouth Corporation Fleetline double-deckers which worked in on route 408. Elsewhere on the London Country network there were single-deck Bournemouth Daimler Roadliners, brown and white Leyland Titans from Maidstone Corporation and blue and cream AEC Regent Vs from Eastbourne. Finally on the subject of London Country liveries we must record that two RTs still working in the training fleet, Nos 2230 and 2367, were repainted in National green.

The first section of the extension of the Piccadilly Line to Heathrow opened as far as Hatton Cross, serving the cargo terminal, in July 1975. New trains had been ordered from Metro-Cammell, hopefully for delivery in 1973, and they were designated 1973 stock, but in fact the first didn't enter service until the Hatton Cross extension was opened. They were some 6ft longer than previous tube stock, which they resembled in appearance. The red doors were abandoned but instead the front below the driving cab windows was painted red. In total, 196 driving cars, 175 trailers and 154 uncoupling non-driving motor cars were ordered. Because of the increased length of the cars they were made up into six rather than seven-car trains. There were a number of improvements and alterations compared with the 1972 stock but they still carried guards, rather than the one-man operation inaugurated with the Victoria Line.

Below left:
One of the 1977 delivery of ANs, AN157 bearing 'Watford Wide' logo, at Garston with derelict Swifts in the background.

Above:
A Bournemouth Corporation Daimler Fleetline on hire to London Country outside Leatherhead garage in the company of London Transport RT4286 and London Country former Green Line RF79.

Right:
A train of 1973 Piccadilly Line tube stock passing a District Line R stock train near Stamford Brook.

Left:
MD154 at Woolwich.

Below:
Crawley garage in March 1976 with, left to right, derelict RF and MBs, AN71 in all-over advertising livery, RCL2249 and former South Wales SMW1. NBC livery was now becoming widespread on London Country vehicles.

1976

1976 saw the sad Merlins disappear from all but the 500 series Red Arrow routes. They were all eventually sold, a good many for breaking up, but a lot found new owners. With them their careers varied; some lasted no longer than they had in London service but a few went on and served honourably for many years. This curious, almost inexplicable pattern was to be repeated with many former London buses from now on. In earlier times, certainly until the 1950s, London buses seldom worked as PSVs once their London service was over. The last prewar generation of buses and coaches had rather broken this tradition, and the postwar RT class, which had begun to be withdrawn as early as 1955, found ready buyers, not only in Britain but abroad too. These classes had, however, already proved their quality and reliability in London

service. What was curious about the generation of OMO buses disposed of prematurely by LT, was that the reception they received from their new owners varied so greatly. We will look at this phenomenon a little later in relation to the DMS. Which brings us back to this somewhat ill-starred bus

By 1976 it was proving as troublesome as the Merlins and Swifts. Among many problems were the engines which frequently overheated, while the gearbox was a disaster. The two-man DMs, which it was hoped would not only replace the RTs but the RMs and RMLs too, were significantly slower in operation than the older buses on account of their doors, and had to hand back such routes as the 16 and the 24 to Routemasters.

An attractive new livery, with white upper-deck window surrounds, appeared and the Daimler badge disappeared on new deliveries, the bus being now known as the Leyland Fleetline.

Meanwhile a new type of double-decker, the MD, entered service on 21 March from Peckham garage on the 36; I saw my first one outside Paddington station on my way back from spotting some of the last 'Warship' diesel-hydraulics and leapt aboard to try it out. With its white upper-deck window surrounds, the two-level windscreen, the rectangular headlamps, the chrome lower deck strip, the nicely appointed interior and the significantly lower noise level, I thought it a distinctly superior class of bus.

Although there were only 164 MDs and they were not very long-lived, they heralded the death, long drawn out though it was, of British Leyland. With so much dissatisfaction with that company's products, there was clearly room for other manufacturers and the MD was an integrally constructed vehicle built in Birmingham by Metro-Cammell and fitted with Swedish Scania-Vabis running units. They were the first such mainland European-powered buses to run in any quantity in London service. The entire class was allocated to the inner southeastern suburban garages of Peckham and New Cross and was generally to be found working the 36 group of routes, the 53 and 63. The last was delivered in February 1977.

Perhaps initially pleased with its MDs, LT announced late in 1976 that there would be no more orders for DMSs.

As in many other parts of the country the enthusiasm for dual door single-deckers soon waned and it was decided to convert a number of the SMs to conventional, single-door operation with increased seating. 42 seats were fitted and over 100 SMSs were dealt with, although not all actually re-entered service. The centre doors were simply sealed with a bar with 'no way out' painted on it fixed across them. It was crude and far below what LT would have tolerated in the 1950s.

Above:
Hounslow bus station with three Leyland Nationals and RF536.

Right:
Routemasters replace RTs on route 109. RM1449 and 1608 alongside RT3559 and DMS1689 in Thornton Heath garage.

Right:
A DM overtakes FRM1, both working the London Sightseeing Tour, followed by an RM in Trafalgar Square.

Below:
Grays SNB218 of London Country at Grays bus station alongside an Eastern National FLF with a Southend Corporation Fleetline in the distance.

As 1976 drew to a close LT owned close on 1,000 unserviceable buses, an horrendous state of affairs. Coaches had to be hired, as in the early postwar years, to help fill the breach, though after union opposition they only ran on two routes. The first of a batch of 51 Leyland Nationals began to arrive in May 1976, ostensibly as stopgaps while the problems with the Swifts were resolved. They were sent to Hounslow garage, being joined there by the original six in order to keep the type together. Over at London Country the much vaunted Superbus network at Stevenage was in trouble partly because Stevenage garage had to operate such a diversity of types.

By the autumn it was clear that the Leyland National, as London Country had discovered, was a much more reliable bus. As many as 24 Swifts were withdrawn in October, one being almost immediately sold to some unsuspecting soul in Fiji. At the end of the next month LT announced the Swift would follow the Merlin into oblivion. In December the GLC gave LT approval to buy 50 more Nationals.

Meanwhile the RT proved it was still needed and, to help fill the gaps, odd examples were allocated to a number of routes through the heart of London, from which they had officially been banished some while back. For all that the newest member of the class was 22

years old and their numbers inevitably continued to decline. In May they at last began to disappear from route 109, first from Brixton garage and then from Thornton Heath. I had ridden this route ever since it had replaced the 16 and 18 trams in 1951, 25 years earlier. A quarter of a century is an enormously long time for one type of bus to operate a route, in London or anywhere else, although it is a record which Routemasters have emulated on a number of routes since. Many of the RTs from both Streatham and Thornton Heath looked tired and ill-kempt with patches of exterior paintwork completely worn away in the worst cases, and that once magnificent interior still serviceable but much faded and discoloured with upholstery threadbare, a state far removed from the pristine condition in which they had been kept in earlier days.

The only new buses to enter service with London Country in 1976 were Nationals. Many types moved around as a consequence and the numbers of RTs and RFs in service was minuscule compared to their halcyon days. Scheduled RT operation was now in single figures, a mere seven, while the RF situation was scarcely better, just 10. Rather more than this were actually needed but clearly they were not going to last much longer.

1977

1977 was Silver Jubilee year and LT, as always at times of national rejoicing, rose to the occasion. Much the most up-front manifestation of this was the repainting of 25 RMs into silver livery. Silver-painted buses blossomed throughout the realm; London Country, for example, produced two silver Atlanteans, one of which, AN5, in the early part of the year was regularly seen passing through, and indeed stopping, at Oxted; the other, AN41, inhabited the frozen wastes of the North.

The 25 silver RMs were temporarily put into their own class, the SRM. I saw my first one at Waterloo in April, appropriately on route 1. The sun was out and it looked dazzling. Inside the SRMs were carpeted in pure wool, I kid you not, a wonderful touch made possible by the International Wool Secretariat (no connection with Southdown, baaa, as far as I know) and the British wool textile industry. The design on the carpet incorporated the Woolmark, the Celebrations Committee emblem and the LT Silver Jubilee symbol. The latter also appeared on the side of the buses alongside the legend 'The Queen's Silver Jubilee London Celebrations 1977'. The SRMs worked on many of the routes which passed through central London, Oxford Street seldom being without at least one, and often several at any time of the day. There were those of us who felt that it would have been a nice touch if 25 RTs could have been chosen

for the honour, the RM not yet having reached the cult status it now boasts, but in retrospect the right decision was surely made. The RMs honoured were from the series 1648-1922.

While on the subject of RTs, 1977 was not a happy year for the class. Its brief return to central London routes to help out RMs was now finished, while the last daytime route into central London to which it had been allocated in full, the 155 from Merton, went over to RM operation in January. Nevertheless RTs were to pop up in ones and twos more or less regularly on routes 1, 12, 29 and 47 right through the year and into 1978. By the end of 1977 the number of RTs scheduled for service was down to 236 on 16 suburban routes and two night ones from Barking, the N95 and N98, Monday to Friday.

Just about everyone assumed that 1977 would be the last year for the London Country RTs. Nineteen were still at work at the beginning of the year but their five-year certificates were all due to expire. You may thus imagine my astonishment when, standing at the bus stop by Redhill station waiting for a 410 one afternoon in April, what for a moment I was convinced was an apparition in the form of RT1018 hove into view. I don't think I had ever actually rubbed my eyes before to check they were functioning correctly but I did now. RT1018 gleamed in a coat of just applied

Below:
Two LT Silver Jubilee Routemasters in Oxford Street.

National light green, complete with all the appropriate insignia and grey wheels. One elderly lady stuck her hand out in the hope that this vision would deign to stop but it swept past on its way home to Chelsham. I assumed it was returning from overhaul at either Crawley or Reigate but records indicate this was carried out at Northfleet, so I don't quite know why it was returning in such a roundabout manner; perhaps it had been sent to Reigate for approval.

The National livery, whether red or green, then and ever since has found little favour amongst enthusiasts. When one thinks of some of the magnificent colour schemes and insignia it obliterated – of London's immediate neighbours Southdown and M&D immediately spring to mind – how right we were. Yet the new image sported by RT1018 won almost universal approval. Next month similarly-adorned RT3461 joined it, to be followed in sunny June by RT604. One wondered where this would stop but that was it. The three took up work on the 403 and sometimes on the 453 and many was the pilgrimage made from all parts of the Home Counties and beyond to view their magnificence. One suddenly realised

how dowdy the old Lincoln green had been. It had worked well when there was plenty of white or pale green to offset it but once from 1950 onwards there was nothing to relieve it beyond a thin cream band then it was pretty uninspiring. I never liked the vivid yellow London Country had introduced to go with Lincoln green, but National green might have been designed for the RT.

Inevitably RT604, HLX 421, became just about everyone's favourite. For, while all RTs were veterans, this was really old, nominally belonging to the very first batch of Country Area RTs, delivered to Hemel Hempstead garage in July 1948, 29 years earlier. I saw one or other of the magnificent three most days, but their final fling was brief, for in September RT1018 and 3461 were relegated to the training fleet. However RT604 continued to work from Chelsham into 1978. Reigate also had an RT, No 981, still on passenger duty, although this retained the old Lincoln green and yellow livery.

A total of 157 new vehicles joined London Country in 1977. Seeing that just about every other fleet in the country owned some ECW-bodied Bristol VR double-

deckers, it was inevitable that 15 should be delivered to London Country. Originally intended to take over route 403, these highbridge vehicles of the BT class actually went to Grays for the 370. Their career with London Country was brief. More Bristols, this time further members of the BN class, 14 in all, also arrived.

A somewhat curious new class, the RN, turned up. These were 10 Plaxton-bodied AEC Reliances, built for Barton in 1972. Although they had coach bodies Plaxton had somehow squeezed in three plus two

seating, giving a capacity of 64. London Country put in some luggage pens, which reduced seating to 60. As the class was regularly used on school runs it's quite possible the pens served other purposes too. Their other sphere of influence was the 418, operated by Dorking garage.

More Leyland Nationals arrived, swelling the ever growing numbers of this class, but the event of the year was the introduction of the very first, out and out coaches to serve regularly with Green Line. These were 30 Reliances. They were put into two classes.

Above:
RT1018 on its first day in service in National livery at Chelsham working the 403 express, 6 April 1977. To the right are two former Ribble PD3s in yellow trainer livery.

Right:
The Queen opens Hatton Cross Piccadilly Line station. *LT*

RS1-15 had Plaxton Supreme Express bodywork built in Scarborough, RB16-30 had Dominant II bodies built by Duple in the former Burlingham factory at Blackpool. Originating as they did from the seaside they were in the tradition of proper coaches as used on long-distance routes patronised by day trippers and holidaymakers, with high backed seats, full length luggage racks, forced-air vents and individual reading lamps. They were put to work on a variety of routes, immediately moving the Green Line image on to an altogether higher level and proving popular with passengers – even though, as with so many modern coaches, leg room was rather less generous than it might have been. As a consequence of the arrival of these coaches, many Leyland Nationals which had served in this capacity were down graded, and none too soon, to buses.

1977 saw the end of London Country's first Reliance class, the comfortable but unreliable RC, and the return of some of the hired vehicles to their owners. The four former M&D Harrington-bodied Reliance trainers, T1-4, were also taken out of service in 1977.

In contrast to the celebrity status LT afforded the RM, London Country's Routemasters were in a state of decline. Withdrawals began in October with 21 RMLs, RCLs and RMCs being taken out of service. Many had been unfit for a while and were to be seen dumped in corners of various garages, sad and neglected. Grays in particular was a last resting place for these once cosseted vehicles. LT took a very different view of the Routemaster's future and by the end of the year had bought back 16 from London Country, with many more to follow.

Meanwhile the final version of the DMS, the B20, appeared with a redesigned rear end and a much quieter sound. Older ones which were due for overhaul were taken out of passenger service, some being used as trainers. Only two, DMS1 and DMS118 had so far received overhauls, at Aldenham, the pair emerging from a very lengthy process in March and October respectively.

The long-established Round London Sightseeing Tour was always likely to throw up something out of the ordinary, none more so than the unique former Midland Red D9s, hired from Obsolete Fleet Limited

which had operated in open-top form since 1975. Seven convertible Weymann-bodied Daimler Fleetlines, the DMOs, were bought by LT from Bournemouth Corporation, now Yellow Buses, ready for the 1978 season. Another tourist attraction was route 100 which worked through the heart of the West End and provided me with my first ride on a Tilling ST since the 1940s for it was operated by the preserved ST922, also owned by Obsolete Fleet.

Merlin and Swift single-deckers were disappearing rapidly from the LT fleet, the only members of the former still at work being MBAs on the Red Arrow routes, but while Swift withdrawals also continued some of the class were recertified for another three years. More of the successful Leyland National and Bristol LH single-deckers were added to the fleet, the former reaching 107 members, the latter 95. These later LHs were longer, and placed in a new class, the BL. Many more Nationals were on order.

Below ground the big event was the opening of the Piccadilly Line extension to the centre of Heathrow Airport on 16 December. This didn't put road links with the centre of London out of business, which was no wonder for the tube extension was very much a compromise. Compared with what other European capitals offered, and Heathrow then as now was the world's busiest airport, it was a poor thing: a tube link which also served a considerable swathe of suburban west London, stopping at every station before the weary traveller from Tokyo, San Francisco, Birmingham, etc, was finally deposited in the West End.

On the surface lines a new version of the C69 stock, the C77, was put into production and, remarkably, actually entered service in the year of its designation. Although numbering only 11 cars C77 stock allowed

considerable alteration in the pattern of operation of the Edgware Road and Hammersmith & City services and meant that all C stock, whether on Metropolitan or District Lines, could be concentrated at Hammersmith Depot.

Above:
The last RF in traditional Lincoln green was RF684 of Chelsham which remained at work until May 1978. It is seen here heading across Limpsfield Chart on a bleak, February day.

Below:
RT436, nominally dating from October 1947, passing another RT on the North Circular Road at Edmonton.

1978

1978 saw the reappearance of green-liveried buses in the LT fleet. London Country Routemasters were now back on the streets of central London, although not quite in the pristine condition of their halcyon days of the 1960s. The RML buses were repainted and eight entered ordinary service in January alongside their brethren, which had always been red and from which they were indistinguishable. The former Green Line coaches took up work as trainers and, although they were gradually repainted red, many retained their green livery, but with the LT bullseye symbol, for several years. Others had been so robbed of parts that there was no possibility of them ever taking to the road again and they passed to that famous scrapyard, Wombwell Diesels, which if not in the sky was quite high up on the map of England – in Yorkshire, to be precise. Even so LT decided that it could actually save exactly half of the 38 which London Country had written off, while many parts were salvaged from the other 17 as they were being broken up.

As spring arrived the serviceable RMLs began emerging from Aldenham after a complete overhaul, rather than a quick repaint, their transmission altered from semi to fully automatic, and looking as good as new, inside and out. Nothing more vividly illustrated the different philosophies of LT and London Country – and both concerns, as is well known, employed a number of philosophers, full and part-time. While many of the RMLs which the latter disposed of in the late 1970s are still happily going about their business in central London and look set to do so into the next century, there are just two Routemasters in the possession of the many companies which once made up London Country, and these are cherished as vintage pieces of transport history.

1978 was the last year of London Country RT passenger operation. Reigate's No 981 went into the trainer fleet in February, leaving the celebrated RT604 to carry on at Chelsham. I stopped off at the garage one afternoon in June and found RT604 sitting in a corner at the back, all shipshape and shiny but minus one engine. Enquiries suggested that this would soon be restored but in the event it never was and so RT operation in what had been the Country Area of LT had finally ended. Astonishingly RT604 had seen it all, for it was one of the first batch delivered in July 1948 and had thus served for 29 years and 11 months; not a bad investment.

Time was also running out for the red RT. I had been taking pictures of this unique bus since the early 1950s but, as I realised how few opportunities were left, I took myself off to parts of London I'd never visited before to track down the last survivors. The last Enfield ones disappeared in January, many of Southall's went a few days later; then they disappeared from the North Circular Road with the conversion of routes 102 and 261 at

Palmers Green. They were still to be seen in some numbers in southeast London, bumping over the tram lines in Beresford Square, and speeding across the green open spaces of Woolwich Common and Blackheath. In April the RT lost four of these services, the 54, 89, 122 and 146. With the 54 gone this left just one RT operating in Croydon, London Country's RT604.

Also that month route 105 gave way to RMs from Shepherd's Bush and Southall. Perhaps surprisingly the veterans could still be found alongside Jumbo jets and Concorde at Heathrow – but not after 15 July when RTs disappeared from route 140. The last RTs departed from Catford and Bromley garages on 26 August and now there were just two routes left, 62 and 87, both worked by Barking. They had also worked the night services, the N95 and N98, but crews, feeling safer with doored vehicles, had had them replaced by DMSs at the end of May. One of the vehicles at Bromley was RT422, a favourite of mine for it had long been nominally the oldest bus in London service and had served for a good while from

Thornton Heath garage. Even now its career wasn't over for it was transferred to Barking.

The intention was that both Barking routes would lose their RTs in October. The 87 did, RMs taking over on 28 October. However route 62 crews raised several objections to the larger Routemasters and so the RTs remained for the rest of 1978 and, indeed, still put in appearances on the 87.

Two completely new classes of double-decker entered LT service in 1978. Prototype Leyland Titans had been undergoing extensive tests for some time. The second, registration number BCK 706R, most closely resembled the production vehicles. Various proposals for a completely new design of bus exclusively for London service had come to nothing and the Titan was the next best thing, a Leyland design with much LT input. A total of 250 were on order and the first batch entered service from Hornchurch Garage on 4 December. The body, built by Park Royal, was of distinctive design, with lower-deck windows larger than the upper ones and a curious rear end. It possessed the now standard front entrance, centre exit and central staircase layout. There were 44 seats upstairs, 25 downstairs and room for 20 lucky standing passengers. Originally entitled the TN it actually entered service as the T.

The other new bus was the Metrobus, or M (originally MT). Based on the MD, it was built exclusively by Metro-Cammell. It bore a strong resemblance to the MD but had a front-mounted

Below left:
RT4681 of Plumstead climbing Academy Road, Woolwich.

Below:
An elderly gentleman alights from Kingston's RF481 at Esher on a snowy March morning in 1978.

radiator. It seated 43 passengers upstairs and 28 down. Both the T and the M had Gardner engines and these two classes would become London standards. The T was originally concentrated in East London, the M in the west. The first Ms entered service from Cricklewood on the 16 and 16A.

Both types, although their numbers are somewhat reduced, are still familiar in many parts of London.

In the single-deck fleet Leyland National numbers had reached 267 by the end of the year. Other new buses were five Ford Dormobile minibuses, FS22-6. If the RT was almost gone, it had been intended that the RF class would go a year earlier. By the spring of 1977 it was working only two routes, the 218 and 219, appropriately from the heartland of the single-decker, Kingston. They stayed on here only because anything

longer on the Kingston garage inspection pits restricted the way through the bus station. There being no immediately obvious solution to this problem, 25 RFs were recertified, some of them losing their LT fleetnames and receiving the white roundel and lettering. The RF remained in remarkably good condition, both inside and out throughout its long London career, better on the whole than the RT, and Kingston's last examples looked virtually new right up to the end.

London Country was gradually reducing its dependence on the RF throughout the 1970s, but it was in no hurry to get rid of this famously reliable vehicle. It still saw regular Green Line service and the last survivors wore a bewildering variety of liveries. Chelsham garage operated not only the last RTs, but

Left:
Titan T81 preparing to head back to Romford from a deserted Trafalgar Square early one Saturday morning on the N98.

Below left:
Metrobus M1 at Victoria alongside RM1676.

Right:
Crew changing at Barking, 16 March. In the distance are an RT, a DMS and an RM.

also the last bus RF in Lincoln green. This was RF684 which regularly came past the end of our road on one of the Oxted local routes. It lasted until 20 May 1978, but another RF, 221, a coach in full London Country bus livery, worked from Chelsham until October. This left just one, RF202, which worked throughout 1978 from Northfleet on both bus and the occasional Green Line duties.

1979

The RT finally bowed out from passenger service with LT on 7 April 1979. Ironically the first members of the DMS class, the successor but two of the RT, had already been withdrawn for scrap. Barking had not, until the last months of 1978, featured high on many enthusiast's lists of places of outstanding public transport interest, but now they came from far and wide to ride, photograph and, sadly in a few cases, steal items from the last examples of what had become Britain's most famous bus.

By re-routing the 62 it was now possible for Routemasters to take over. Six RTs were scheduled to work on the last day, a Saturday, and LT, aware of the great interest in the event, had produced posters and organised a grand parade. The very last to operate was RT624, nominally the oldest, having entered service as a roof number box green bus from Hemel Hempstead garage in August 1948. It was sheer coincidence that the last RTs operated by both LT and London Country were in the early 600 series. RT624 returned to Barking garage at 13.45, no doubt to the great relief of the inhabitants of the block of flats opposite Barking garage, the balconies of which provided rather too many grandstand views over the last few months.

At 16.00 the parade got under way, featuring the six RTs bearing in their route indicators the legend '1939-1979 final run of the RT bus'. Many other preserved RTs joined them but the most unexpected sight, certainly for me and for many others, was the bus which led the parade. This was none other than RT1.

The survival of this historic vehicle owed a good deal to chance. Strictly speaking, not all of it was the prototype of 4,824 others, for in June 1956 RT1's body had been fitted on to the chassis of former Craven RT1420. In this form it served as mobile training unit 1037J and lasted no less than 22 years. Sold in 1978 it was supremely fortunate that it passed into the ownership of that pioneer preservationist, the late Prince Marshall. Re-registered as EYK 396, he had it restored to the condition in which it had appeared in April 1939 with polished aluminium horizontal bands and 164A route blinds. This was its first public appearance after restoration and it looked superb. RTs were out on the road for a little while longer, as staff buses and trainers, but by the end of the year even these functions had ceased, although a few still remained in LT ownership. The end for the red RF had come just a week before the last RT ran. By transferring the 218/9 a few yards down the road to Norbiton garage, Nationals could take over. Seventeen RFs operated on the last day, 30 March, the last scheduled bus being RF507. Crowds turned out, the Mayor and Mayoress appeared, there were ceremonial runs and many of the last survivors went, not to the scrapheap, but into preservation. This phenomenon was now in full flood and practically 100 RFs are still in existence, in various states of repair, quite a staggering total.

Large numbers of DMSs were withdrawn throughout 1979, Fulwell becoming the first garage to get rid of its entire allocation. It took to its replacement, the Metrobus, with enthusiasm, and still

Left:
London Transport's last passenger-carrying RT, 624, prepares to take part in the farewell parade at Barking Garage on 7 April 1979.

Centre left:
RT1 in the RT Farewell Parade, Barking, 7 April 1979.

Bottom left:
Shoplinker RM2171, Hyde Park Corner.

Right:
Shillibeer-liveried RM2153, Oxford Circus, 16 March 1979.

owns a considerable number. By the end of 1979 357 DMSs had been taken out of service. Metrobuses and Titans were proving more reliable with 1,000 due to be delivered by 1980.

The DM concept with two-man operation was of limited use, so a number were fitted with driver-operated ticket machines and reclassified D. 1979 marked the 150th anniversary of the first proper bus service to operate in London, that of George Shillibeer, and DM2646, the newest Fleetline, was sponsored by British Leyland and repainted in a handsome livery of dark green and cream with appropriate lettering and insignia. At the same time 12 Routemasters were similarly attired, while the replica Shillibeer horse-bus, built at Chiswick by the LGOC in 1929 for the Centenary celebrations, reappeared, although presumably not with the same horses.

If the appearance of RMs in the striking Shillibeer livery wasn't sufficient, only two years after the 25 Silver Jubilee buses, then 16 appeared in another equally striking guise – the Shoplinker. This service began on 7 April and ran between some of the principal hotels and stores in the West End. The livery was red on the lower deck and roof, the remainder bright yellow. Inside music played on both decks, interspersed with advertisements, in several languages. The 16 buses operated out of Stockwell garage. Shoplinker was a nice idea but it failed miserably, the buses carrying few passengers, and the service came to an end on 28 September. One spin off was that Londoners were becoming used to seeing their buses in other than the standard red, which was just as well, for in the years to come every colour combination known to man, would be seen on the streets of London and its suburbs.

On 1 May 1979 London's latest tube line, the Jubilee, opened. Like so many of its predecessors it incorporated part of an existing line, the former Bakerloo section from Baker Street by way of Neasden to Stanmore. Completion was delayed by two years, hence its title, but the new section was worth waiting for, much relief being provided as an alternative route to Bond Street, Green Park and, above all, its Charing Cross terminus. It was never intended that this would be a permanent end, but the government refused to fund the proposed extension southeastwards and it was only in 1993 that this was finally put in hand, to Docklands and Stratford. It is to be hoped that no tourist boards a Jubilee Line train sometime in the future with the intention of finding Shakespeare's lil' ole birthplace.

New trains, the D stock, for the District Line entered service in 1979 and they remain the newest surface stock. Their arrival marked the end of an era as surely as did the withdrawal of the last RTs, for completion of its delivery in 1983 brought about the end of the careers of the famous CO/CP and R stock.

The D stock consists of 450 cars, made up of three-car units, divided into A, C, and D types. Normally an A and a D unit work together, with driving cabs at the outer ends of the train, although at the opposite end of each unit, ie facing each other, there are simple controls which can be used to perform shunting movements. The 20 C units have driving cabs at both ends so that they can substitute for either an A or a D.

The D stock was built to metric measurements and the cars were longer than their predecessors, approximately 18m (60ft) against 16m (50ft). Although

somewhat similar to the C69/77 stock, there are noticeable differences. The sides are flat but taper slightly in order to allow the greater length of the cars to negotiate all curves on the District Line. Although given the usual aluminium finish this was relieved by a red panel at the front of each unit below the cab windows A new system of door control allowed passengers to open individual doors, although the guard could over-ride this and, of course, was in charge of the closing of all doors.

The last prewar-designed CO/CP, red-painted trains were taken out of service in March 1981, two specials being run on the final day, 31 March. A number of cars from this stock has been preserved in various locations.

London Country was determined to try and make the Green Line network viable and to help with this no fewer than 90 new coaches were taken into stock in 1979. They were repeats of the previous year's Reliances with Duple and Plaxton bodywork, and were leased for five years rather than bought outright. The old style of operation with services starting out deep in the Country Area, passing through the suburbs, central London, out through more suburbs and terminating on the outer fringes of the Country Area was no longer viable in the traffic conditions of the late 1970s and the last such services ended in 1979, either being curtailed or split, each section terminating in central London.

Jetlink 747, linking Heathrow and Gatwick airports by Green Line, not Jumbo Jet, began on 28 April with the Reliances in a special livery; standard Green Line livery had already departed from the strict NBC guidelines. The RF just lasted into this era, the last one, RF202 based at Northfleet, still occasionally appearing on routes 725 and 726 until it was withdrawn in July.

The 90 Reliances which Green Line put into service were a remarkable statement of faith in a company which had produced the great majority of London's buses and coaches for eight decades. But the last produced for LT, the Merlin and Swift single-deckers, had been a disaster; the rear-engined Routemaster had remained a sole tantalising example of what might have been, and even the last Reliances were called Leylands. On 25 May 1979 the AEC works at Southall closed.

1980

For the first time in our history we enter a decade without the RT. Around this time I attended a seminar given by one of LT's senior engineers at Chiswick Works. It was a fascinating experience; one could sense the hankering for the old days of certainty with a standardised fleet of Chiswick-designed purpose-built buses. Few doubted that the Merlins and Swifts suffered from severe design faults and were unreliable, but was the DMS really equally disastrous? We were told that it was simply incapable of standing up to the demands of day to day service in London and that's why it was being prematurely withdrawn and broken up or sold. But I couldn't help wondering if all the fault lay with the DMS. Could it be that LT simply didn't understand that it was a different sort of bus to the RT and the RM and needed to be dealt with in a different way? By then ex-London DMSs were in regular employment in Birmingham, Manchester (and still are, some 15 years on) and Glasgow; were conditions in these rural backwaters so very different to those in London?

One use London did have for some of its DMSs was as trainers, and 40 were so converted during 1980. The DMS trainer is still an occasional sight on the streets of London, although not from the original 1980 batch.

London's first Swedish double-deckers, the MD class, were taken out of service in 1980. Their career had been brief and not wholly successful – corrosion and lack of spare parts had caused problems – but they had led the way to the highly successful Metropolitans. The withdrawal of the MDs meant that the 36 group of routes went back to Routemaster operation. This was not the first re-conversion from doored buses; that had happened in March 1977 when RMs returned to route 29.

In contrast London Country had just 13 licensed Routemasters at the beginning of 1980 and they had less than two months to go. Chelsham, which had operated the last RT, very nearly operated the last Routemaster, managing to find work for RMC1515 on the 403 express until mid-February. It was outlasted by RMC1512 at Swanley on the 477 by a couple of days. RMC1512 and RML2446 performed a farewell tour on 1 March but this was not quite the intended end: Swanley unexpectedly used RMC1512 the following week, on 4 and 5 March, on route 477, to substitute for an unfit Atlantean. Next day, 6 March, it and all remaining Routemasters went straight into LT ownership.

Despite being anxious to get rid of the Routemaster, London Country had kept its prototype, RMC4, in ordinary service far longer than LT did its three, and it worked from Hatfield until May 1979. London Country had no intention of parting with this very special vehicle as we shall shortly see.

Meanwhile LT decided to put 26 of the RCLs to work as ordinary buses. This was done with great thoroughness: the doors were removed, a stanchion and grab rails fitted, the double headlamps converted to single, and the luggage racks removed. They were sent to the former trolleybus garages of Stamford Hill and Edmonton to work route 149. I had a ride on one, boarding it at Victoria, and was most impressed, not only by its immaculate paintwork, without adverts, but also by the deep, Green Line seat cushions, which were retained.

Below:
London Country AN184 and RMC1501 on rush hour workings of route 403, West Croydon.

RCL2221 was converted to a cinema and exhibition bus. I met it at a number of rallies including, somewhat unexpectedly, alongside former GWR 4-6-0 No 6000 *King George V* at Old Oak Common depot.

1930 had seen the beginning of the Green Line network and 50 years later this important anniversary was commemorated in some style. A handsome book was produced, written by D.W.K. Jones and B. J. Davis with help from a number of authoritative sources. The frontispiece was a handsome colour photograph of one of the original Green Line coaches, T211, working the C2 at Sevenoaks and couldn't have been taken later than 1938. Rare indeed – prewar colour photographs of any PSVs hardly exist.

Back to 1980. A number of the latest coaches were adorned with a large gold band and lettered 'Golden Jubilee', and the celebrations reached a climax on Sunday 13 July when a commemorative run took place from Golders Green to Crawley. Some 150 vehicles

took part, many of them with close Green Line associations. There were five prewar coaches plus CR14 which worked Green Line reliefs, a huge number of RFs, many other postwar past or present Green Line coaches, and RT and RM Green Line double-deckers. A sign of the times was DMS631, one of six of this type which London Country had bought to use as trainers and had repainted in NBC green livery.

As pleasant a spot as Syon Park is, it had not been the ideal venue for the LT Museum, not least because it was a long way from central London. Therefore it was with considerable celebration that the museum moved into new premises in Covent Garden and opened to the public on 29 March. As in Syon Park there was nothing like enough room to display the entire collection, but against this the former market buildings were themselves a delight and the venue could not have been more central. Not surprisingly both visitor numbers and takings at the shop soared.

On 6 October the Transport Act (1980) came into

Above:
Restored Tilling ST922 working Vintage Bus service 100 to the new LT Museum at Covent Garden, seen in Trafalgar Square with Routemasters passing by.

force. This was the first step in the encouragement of competition in the transport industry which was one of the cornerstones of the Thatcher administration – although the evidence suggested it was more a question of political dogma rather than a planned policy. Now coach routes longer than 30 miles were deregulated and Green Line vehicles began to make regular appearances in places well beyond what had for long been regarded as Green Line territory: Cambridge, Oxford and Brighton amongst them. With AEC no more, Green Line had to find other chassis suppliers and two Volvo B58s and two Leyland Leopards arrived for evaluation.

The Merlins and Swifts of whatever type, buses and coaches, LT or London Country owned, were fast disappearing and, although a number were scrapped, a great many appeared with new owners literally all over the world. I came across considerable numbers of both types in Northern Ireland, particularly in Belfast and Derry. The Merlin was quite popular but the Swift was not and many of the 80 owned by Citybus and Ulsterbus saw very little service. Some, inevitably, were destroyed in the Troubles.

1980 went out on a rather downbeat note; for the first time ever no buses or Underground trains ran on Christmas Day.

1981

The all conquering Leyland National conquered the last of LT's Merlins in 1981 – the last London Country ones had gone the previous year. The MBAs, latterly with some help from SMSs, had clung on to the Red Arrow services long after the type had been forced to abandon all others, but their end came in the spring and early summer of 1981. They were replaced by 69 10.6m long, two-door National 2s. The National 2, with its front-mounted radiator and bulging front end, was instantly recognisable. Meanwhile the prototype and early production Nationals were being overhauled at Aldenham, a process which was deemed much more successful than that of the Merlins, Swifts and Fleetlines.

LT simply couldn't make up its mind what to do with the Fleetlines. The previous year LT had decided

they would have to last longer than had originally been intended and overhauls went ahead on the Park Royal-bodied examples. Then, in 1981, overhauls of Park Royal buses were abandoned and the previously despised MCW version was taken into Aldenham. The very last pre-B20 DMS of any persuasion to be overhauled, No 1987, a Leyland-engined MCW-bodied bus, entered Aldenham in December 1981.

Meanwhile the Titan was having problems. LT was a good deal happier with this bus than it was with the DMS family but it attracted few buyers elsewhere. Without these the bus wasn't really an economic proposition for Leyland. Additionally there were problems at the Park Royal factory, that long time supplier of so many London bus bodies, and it closed down in 1981. Titan production was moved from there to Workington, but the move drastically slowed down the number of buses entering service so that by the end of the year London had only 370 Titans against 700 Metrobuses – hence one reason for extending the life of the Fleetline. London Country continued to patronise the handsome standard Park

Royal body for its Atlanteans until virtually the end.

Now that the DMS was no longer regarded as totally beyond redemption, it was used to replace some of the last remaining Swifts. A few worked Red Arrow services until the Nationals arrived, but otherwise the last was SMS771, which was taken out of service from Edgware garage on 23 January 1981. The last Red Arrow Swift was delicensed on 27 July. The London Country examples lasted a little longer, but Nationals had replaced practically all of them here too. The very last, SMA1, was taken out of service on 1 January 1982.

The saga of the Merlin and Swift was a sad one for all sorts of reasons, not least that it helped bring about the end of AEC, although the way the entire Leyland empire was heading it probably wouldn't have survived much longer anyhow – unless it had emigrated to Sweden or changed its name to Dennis.

London Country's RP class, another AEC type, was now on the way out and it lost much of its Green Line work in 1981. By the end of 1981, 34 remained licensed, including four in use as trainers.

Above:
SMS700, drafted into temporary Red Arrow duty, speeds across Waterloo Bridge. It is a pity that such a neat looking design was so unsuccessful.

Right:
A derelict Swift awaits its end at the back of Norbiton garage.

The XF was a small class always associated with East Grinstead garage. The last, and the last former LT bus to work in normal service for London Country, was XF3. It, and its garage, ceased to serve London Country on 31 December 1981.

A few years earlier it had seemed that the Bristol, seen in huge numbers in so much of the United Kingdom, might come to play a large part in the affairs of LT and London Country. In the event its popularity was fleeting. London Country disposed of its VR double-deckers in 1980, many of the services operated by London Country's LHs disappeared along with the buses through lack of patronage and county council support, and LT's BS and BL classes remained intact for only a short while. In the late 1970s and early 1980s it sometimes seemed that the paint was barely dry on a new bus before it was whipped off to a Yorkshire scrapyard, an American theme park or perhaps a third world entrepreneur.

London Country continued to put its faith in the Atlantean, particularly the later AN68, and the National – both these types are still operated in some numbers by London Country's successors – while the Leyland Tiger was the principal replacement for the Green Line Reliances.

Above left:
DMS2512 working the short-lived 616 has the advantage over a Swift around Marble Arch.

Left:
Godstone garage with XF1 prominent; AFs, ANS, an RML and a National play supporting roles in the background.

Above:
LS77 in the foreground, three Swifts very much in the background, DM1131 and DM1134 alongside, Thornton Heath garage.

Right:
London Transport's loss is Santa Claus's gain. Preserved RT4497 on the last leg of its journey from Lapland delivers him to Oxted County school's Christmas Fair.

1982

From time to time we have noted the vast discrepancy in size between LT and all other such undertakings throughout the United Kingdom. A perfect example of this was provided in 1982 when LT put in its order for new double-deckers to be delivered the following year. The 150 Metrobuses and 210 Titans amounted to a quarter of all double-deck buses on order in the UK – and 360 was small by earlier London standards.

A legal judgement at the end of 1981 was to have a huge impact on bus and underground services in London and is still quoted as a landmark. For those who argued that it was essential for a modern city to have a co-ordinated public transport system sufficiently intensive, convenient, safe and cheap to wean people away from the private car so that restrictions on the latter would not merely be tolerated but welcomed, the decision of the House of Lords that the GLC had unlawfully raised rates in order to subsidise bus and Underground travel, was a tragedy. The challenge had come initially from Bromley; a borough at that time considered by many obsessed with tightening the purse strings however dire the consequences. In fairness Bromley did have a point in wondering why it should subsidise Underground and tube travel when no part of the network penetrated the borough. The GLC won in the divisional court but lost on appeal. There was, inevitably, an element of party politics in all this, the Labour GLC being utterly opposed to everything the Conservative government stood for – and the Conservatives ruled Bromley.

Be that as it may, LT fares were generally doubled from 21 March 1982 and service cuts were planned. LT unions called the first general strike since 1926, and evidence was produced to show that, even taking into account the Fares Fair policy of the GLC, public transport subsidies in London were well below those of Paris, Brussels, Milan and New York. With the outlawing of Fares Fair the London subsidy fell to a derisory 12 per cent: Paris's stood at 56 per cent. As one who greatly admires the ever expanding public transport network in the French capital – buses, trams, Metro, RER and SNCF, I continue to be saddened by the short-sighted, miserable financial support Londoners and visitors to the capital receive.

Below:
M690 at Putney.

Right:
T119 in Piccadilly Circus.

Below right:
RM967 on route 11 pulls ahead of two open-top DMSs outside the National Gallery.

Inevitably the cut backs meant vehicle withdrawals and from 4 September 1982 some 500 less buses were on the roads during the peak hours. The first mass withdrawals of LT Routemasters took place, over 150 disappearing in August and September. The RM had been around over 20 years by then and its demise had been predicted long before, so in one sense it was no great shock. The Leyland-engined vehicles were the first to go. Many were scrapped but, as we shall see, changing times and the still sound condition of this remarkable bus meant that it was to have a far greater and more diverse afterlife than any other LT type.

A new type of double-decker entered service with London Country. This was the Olympian, destined to be the last new Leyland double-decker. As the successor of both the long-established Atlantean and, in a sense, the Titan, it had bodies by several makers, including ECW until it went out of business, Roe and Leyland. The Olympian remains the most modern type of double-decker in a number of the fleets which have succeeded London Country.

Left:
Open-top former Midland Red D9, OM1, working the London Transport Sightseeing Tour in Park Lane.

Below left:
A Berkhof-bodied Leyland Tiger BTL of 1985 at Victoria coach station working the Flightline 767 surrounded by the phenomenon of the 1980s, the double-deck coach.

Above:
A 1962 stock Central Line train leaving Blake Hall on the Ongar branch for Epping. *John Glover*

Atlanteans and Olympians also took over from what had been the first new class of double-decker delivered to London Country. So the AF, which like its predecessor – the front-entrance lowbridge STL – had always been associated with Godstone garage and route 410, disappeared from passenger service.

A development which would grow apace came into prominence in 1982. This was the takeover by London Country of a number of LT routes, following negotiations with the various county councils which subsidised them. All were out in the distant suburbs where the delineation between red and green bus routes had always been vague. There was also movement in the other direction: two of the routes in the traditional, north of the river 3xx green series, 313 and 347, passed to LT.

The vast increase in air travel, particularly by holidaymakers, continued to provide the Green Line network with much business, not just to and from Heathrow and Gatwick, but Luton as well. Some services were run jointly with Southdown and Alder Valley. A particularly cheeky one – joint with Alder Valley – was the Flightline 767, which ran non-stop between Victoria coach station and Heathrow's three terminals, competing directly with LT's double-deck airbuses. Another encroachment into the heart of LT territory was the use of two closed and two open-top London Country Atlanteans which were subcontracted by LT to help operate the Round London Sightseeing Tour, complete in full red livery with LT roundels.

Open-top bus tours of London were, like airport services, a growth area. I suppose it was a sign of my advancing years but I had always associated open-toppers exclusively with the seaside and I found the notion of citizens from Japan, Australia, the USA, Stow-on-the-Wold and elsewhere wanting to be shown the sights of London from an open double-decker rather disorientating. Very silly of me, for the number of tourists to London has increased manyfold since the 1940s, providing much welcome business for LT. In 1982 they contributed some £60 million to LT's income. I regularly take parties of schoolchildren from deepest Dorset on open-top Routemasters and they are entranced with this unique view of the sights. Probably the first RM to be regularly employed on sightseeing duties was former Northern General, EUP 406B, converted by Obsolete Fleet, which took up this work – with its top on – in 1982, while a year later, following changed legislation, Culturebus started the first hop-on/hop-off service using some DMSs. Initially these had a closed top but the open-top version soon appeared. It was as though the DMS had been created for showing off London to tourists for it has since appeared on these duties in a bewildering variety of forms and liveries with many owners, and continues to do so today. Much rarer was the fleet of converted Midland Red-designed D9s – a unique bus, much beloved by enthusiasts. Known as the OM class, Christmas 1982 found sufficient hardy souls to warrant using them, topless, on tours of the decorations in the West End.

The most rural of the tube services, the Epping-Ongar section of the Central Line, taken over from the LNER, had never been exactly a money spinner and in December 1982 it was reduced to a peak hours only service, a replacement bus service being provided at other times. Was this the beginning of the end for the Ongar branch? Read on and we will see.

1983

At the beginning of 1983 a new ticket, introduced the previous autumn, was proving popular. This was the London Explorer. It was valid for one, three, four or seven days and allowed unlimited travel on buses and Underground trains on much, although not all, of the network. The one-day ticket cost £4.50p. As I write this at the beginning of September 1995, I have in my pocket a Travelcard which I used yesterday, covering not only buses and Underground but also all the British Rail (or whatever this week's name for it is) network, and which 12 years later cost me just £3.30p. No wonder the Travelcard, which appeared as such in

1983 (although the Waterloo and City Line, which would eventually become part of the LT network, was the only British Rail line included in the original scheme) has proved enormously popular and has sent passenger figures climbing.

The GLC, refusing to admit total defeat in its praiseworthy attempts to make public transport economically irresistible, managed to find resources to bring about a 25 per cent cut in bus and Underground fares in May – 'Just the Ticket' – without incurring legal wrath. The fare system was now based on a series of zones, which was proving highly effective.

The Routemaster, while its numbers continued to diminish, was also celebrated in 1983 as we shall shortly see. OMO spread, two central London routes being involved, when the suburban ends of routes 77A and 134 went over to this form of operation. By 12 April London garages no longer employed conductors. Two famous garages which closed altogether in 1983, to general regret, were Mortlake (M), chiefly known for operating route 9, its buses being particularly well maintained, and Riverside, Hammersmith (R), which provided a large

Below:
Mortlake garage.

Above:
Two trains of C stock, a D stock train and an R stock set, the last of which ran in 1983, District Line, Wimbledon.

Below:
RT2189 on the famous Chiswick skid patch.

proportion of the buses operating the most famous route of all, the 11.

1983 was LT's Golden Jubilee, and for the rest of this chapter we will concentrate on the celebrations which marked 50 years of the world's largest urban transport authority.

Special events were held all over the capital, amongst the most notable being a thanksgiving service in St Martin-in-the-Fields in Trafalgar Square,

an Open Day at Aldenham Works and – probably the highlight – a Gala Weekend on 2 and 3 July at Chiswick and Acton works. Saturday the 2nd was a hot, cloudless day and LT, with the co-operation of many other bodies and individuals, put on a wonderful show. I brought my three boys up all the way from Dorset to have a ride, amongst other treats, on the famous skid pan. At least one RT was still employed for this purpose, giving me one last, short, spectacular journey in an LT-owned member of this famous class.

All sorts of one-off liveries appeared in Golden Jubilee year. Most appropriately, RM1983 was painted gold as was T747. Other double-deckers, including four Routemasters, were adorned in the 1933 livery of red and white with silver roofs and black lining and looked truly magnificent, emphasising how dull the virtually all-over red was. As it happened 1983 marked the beginning of the end

for this. When brand new and shiny the red looks fine, and the plethora of adverts which have always been a feature of the London scene, often enhance it, but I for one have no regrets that since 1983 liveries have become much more adventurous, although, of course, I hope – as I guess we all do – that the central London bus will always be predominantly red.

Many garages, or I should say many individuals with a real pride in being part of LT, took it upon themselves to cosset and take especial care of one particular vehicle, usually a Routemaster, and many of these showbuses were to be seen at Chiswick on 2 July 1983.

With a proper sense of the rightness of things, Croydon and Thornton Heath were amongst the principal focal points of the celebrations. There was a press launch at the Fairfield Halls, Croydon; the gold RM entered service from Croydon garage; D2629 was painted in the chocolate and cream livery of Croydon Tramways to celebrate 100 years of the town's charter; 1933-liveried DMS1933 was renumbered DS1933 and took up work on route 64 and then the 109 from Thornton Heath; and several Croydon

Above:
The unique single-deck RM1368 alongside LS194 in red, white and black livery, Chiswick, 2 July 1983.

Left:
The line up of the four prototype Routemasters, Chiswick, 2 July 1983.

DMSs, along with buses from other garages, received gold waistbands.

Many of these were all gathered at Chiswick for the great celebrations. There was a certain amount of controversy over one feature, the line up of the first eight Routemasters. It was an imaginative idea, particularly as RM1 had been somewhat neglected of late – I had come across it in the Chiswick tunnel looking sadly down at heel some years earlier – but it was claimed that RM5 was not the genuine article, the real RM5 being out of service at the time and RM555 substituted. Personally I couldn't see what the fuss was about: because of the overhaul system used at Aldenham virtually no production RT or RM came out with the same identity or, indeed, with many of the same parts, as it went in. Of course the prototypes were a different matter, and these, although modified over the years, were clearly what they claimed to be.

A very curious Routemaster which I had never seen before was the source of much interest. This was the single-deck – I kid you not – RM1368. Its top deck had suffered damage and it had therefore been neatly cut down to form a slightly odd looking experimental vehicle based at Chiswick.

Many preserved London buses were to be seen as well as those from other sources, AECs featuring particularly.

A similar event was staged at Aldenham on 25 September. Immediately afterwards the not altogether unexpected but nevertheless dramatic announcement was made that Aldenham works would close and the future of Chiswick was under investigation. If both went it was estimated that some £18 million would be saved each year – but at the cost of some 3,000 men and women losing their jobs.

1984

Orders for new Titans and Metrobuses in 1984-5 would, it was said, eliminate the DMS, although, please note, nothing was said about getting rid of the Routemaster. As it happened, surprise, surprise, there was still a number of DMSs at work on New Year's Day 1986 and by then production of the Titan had finished, the last, T1096, arriving in November 1984, although the highest numbered was 1125.

No concern as large as LT, operating in a capital city, can expect to steer clear of politics; nor indeed should it if we understand the political process to be

decision-making involving all citizens. The Labour-controlled GLC, headed by Ken Livingston, had been a severe thorn in the side of Mrs Thatcher's Conservative government, one such thorn being an illuminated sign set high on County Hall which flashed out the steadily rising number of unemployed across the river to the Houses of Parliament. Legislation was therefore passed abolishing the GLC, and devolving power to the various boroughs. In this London became virtually unique amongst capital cities in that it no longer had one overall authority. It was feared many services it provided would disappear, one being the free bus travel for old age pensioners. After much argument the government agreed to provide free OAP travel outside peak periods. Oh to be a pensioner

in the Republic of Ireland where my parents-in-law take themselves off by bus and train all over the country, for precisely nothing.

A London scheme which did have the wholehearted support, philosophical and financial, of Mrs Thatcher was the transformation of Docklands from the once busiest port in the world to a yuppie paradise. A little surprisingly it was acknowledged that there would be a need for public transport and in the foreword to the 1983 *Golden Jubilee Book*, published by the *Daily Telegraph* in co-operation with LT and written by Oliver Green and John Reed, LT Chairman Keith Bright referred to 'the "super-tram" – a new light railway which will link the City with Docklands and the Isle of Dogs.' In the meantime, while this was

Above left:
TP23, Green Line Plaxton Paramount-bodied Leyland Tiger at Hyde Park Corner.

Below left:
Green Line LRC3, an ECW-bodied Leyland Olympian coach from Northfleet, on the Embankment.

Above:
Another DMS finds a new owner, this time West Midlands. DMS1361 in New Street, Birmingham.

Left:
M1023 fitted with coach seats for Airbus duty at Shepherd's Bush.

being planned, a bus service – the D1 'Docklands Clipper' – began on 3 January 1983 with financial support from the London Docklands Development Corporation. Using six LSs in special livery, it ran every 15 minutes from Mile End station through the new developments to the southern end of the Isle of Dogs, opposite Greenwich.

The world was changing – not that it has ever exactly stood still – rapidly in the 1980s and the winter 1983-4 edition of the *London Bus Magazine* commented, 'The London Regional Transport Bill, at present in its Commons' Committee Stage, looks as though it will be the biggest thing to hit public transport in London since George Shillibeer put his first omnibus on the road one hundred and fifty-five years ago.' This was some claim but, with the possible exception of the setting up of LT, it proved to be perfectly accurate, as the following chapters will reveal.

In passing we ought to note that the 1983-4 registration introduced the A prefix. Titans and Metrobus double-deckers carried it, as did three prototype ECW-bodied Olympians, L1-3, and three prototype Alexander-bodied Volvo Ailsa B55s, V1-3, all put into service in 1984.

Amongst the London Country vehicles with A prefixes were a batch of Leyland Tigers, the TP class, used on Green Line service and adorned with the newly introduced, finely proportioned Plaxton P3200 body. Possibly the most remarkable vehicles seen on a Green Line service since the RTC, or even LT1137, was the LRC class, which appeared in 1984 with A prefixes. These extra-long Leyland Olympians were fitted with ECW bodies, quite unlike anything the Lowestoft firm had previously brought out. All windows were fixed, the vehicles being air-conditioned, and 71 high-backed coach seats were fitted. With their extra-high upper-deck front windows, striped livery and generally streamlined appearance, they were not the sort of vehicle you could ignore. I never got to travel on one in Green Line days but I did have a ride in one with its subsequent owner, Northumbria, some 300 miles away beside the North Sea in Whitley Bay. With its fabric interior covering, luxurious seating and soft ride it was a most impressive machine. Would you believe it, these double-deck coaches did not prove ideal for Green Line work, hence Northumbria's acquisition of some of them. However examples of these Olympian coaches can be still be seen in London as I write, for M&D still have at least two employed on their Invictaway commuter services from the Medway Towns.

On 29 June 1984 the London Transport Executive ceased to exist and handed over to London Regional Transport (LRT). This was all part of the vast changes of the 1980s; a key aspect of the new philosophy behind the setting up of LRT was that services would be put out to tender. Just what this would mean in reality we shall see. Strong opinions were held on whether the LRT was a good or bad thing; time would tell, but one initially hopeful indication was an agreement between LRT and British Rail extending the Travelcard to BR services in London.

Below:
T833 dwarfed by the towering masts of the Cutty Sark, Greenwich.

1985

1985 opened with LRT (we soon went back to calling it LT) still committed to getting rid of conductors – and that meant the Routemaster, eventually – and extending OMO operation to 75 per cent of its routes by 1987. A new type of OMO double-decker appeared, the Dennis Dominator. The revival of Dennis is a remarkable and heart-warming story, the fortunes of this long-established Guildford firm waxing as those of the once dominant Leyland giant have declined. Way back LT had owned Dennis vehicles, both double and single-deck, although all had gone by World War 2. The Dominator was not, as it happened, destined to dominate in London in the 1980s but the success of Dennis single-deckers in and around London, and indeed elsewhere, has been truly remarkable.

The Green Line image was changing rapidly. The leasing rather than outright purchase of vehicles encouraged this and allowed constant modernisation of the fleet, a contrast to the years when the seemingly indestructible RF had held sway. The coaches really

Above:
Hounslow bus station. Three London Transport Ms and a DM of London Buslines working tendered route 81.

Below:
Green Line Plaxton Paramount-bodied Leyland Tiger TP73 stands in front of the impressive facade of Tunbridge Wells West station, terminus of route 706.

were just that, rather than buses with certain refinements. The Reliances dating from 1979 were replaced by Plaxton-bodied Tigers of the TP class and the lofty Berkhof-bodied BTL Tigers. The livery, a mixture of stripes and bands in two shades of green and white, was a good deal more attractive than either the old plain Lincoln green or National Express white. A number of Green Line coaches were painted in this latter livery and worked National Express services; some appeared on Green Line routes in National livery while conversely Green Line-liveried vehicles

could be seen hundreds of miles away from London on National Express work.

The subject of liveries will exercise us increasingly through the 1980s and into the 1990s. Those who thought that LT's Golden Jubilee year and Green Line's stripes represented the ultimate divergence from the norm would have been well advised to put in an order for several powerful sets of sunglasses. LT vainly, and schizophrenically, attempted to hold back the inevitable by forbidding one-off liveries for showbuses while allowing specific services such as the Docklands Clipper and two routes through the heart of London, 15 and 23, to carry special branding and bright yellow stripes. The ban on showbuses was never rigidly enforced and in a number of cases the buses were bought by the staff who had cared for them as the Routemaster fleet declined, RM1000 at Croydon for example.

More remarkable was the putting out to tender of some suburban routes. Thirteen were won by other operators, who replaced the former red LT buses with their own vehicles in liveries which ranged from the

bright yellow DMSs of London Buslines, which took over the 81 from Hounslow to Slough, through the standard National green of Eastern National's VRTs on the 193 from Hornchurch to Romford, to the ivory-coloured minibuses of Crystals, operating the 146 from Downe to Bromley North station. All carried notices with the LT roundel and the legend 'London Regional Transport Service'.

Tendering was one of the most far reaching of the changes which the London Regional Transport Act of 1984 would bring about. No longer could the red buses of LT assume they would operate all services in the London area. The 13 routes of 1985 were only the first of many and not only in the suburbs. Soon famous routes operating through the heart of the West End and the City would pass from LT operation to a variety of other companies, each providing vehicles in their own distinctive liveries.

Back in my home town the long awaited 'proper' bus station at West Croydon was opened, on the site of the existing, temporary affair. Colourful and stylish, it offered greater and more comfortable undercover waiting areas and various other facilities, including an enquiry office.

Both Routemaster and DMS fleets continued to decline. Over 300 RMs disappeared in 1985 while virtually the only DMSs still in passenger service were the B20 variation, which it had been decided to keep for a while and have overhauled. Very little of this was done at Aldenham, it being found cheaper to contract out the work. The writing was on the wall not only for Aldenham but, unthinkable as it might seem, Chiswick too.

Right:
The Green Line network opens out. TPL92 at Oxford coach station about to set off for London.

Below:
One of the massive Green Line Leyland Olympian/ECW coaches, LRC12, heads along the Embankment.

1986

Aldenham works closed on 14 November 1986. Ironically one of its last contracts was to overhaul and repaint a fleet of Routemasters for operation in Scotland. On 26 October 1986 deregulation arrived in the United Kingdom, everywhere except London that is. The consequences were extraordinary. Any route which seemed to offer even the slimmest chance of a profit was fiercely fought for. Cheap-to-run minibuses became increasingly popular, while at the same time in many towns and cities full size double-deckers competed on the busiest routes. A bus with a conductor could save precious seconds on an OPO rival, especially a bus with an open rear platform. What could be more suitable than an elderly but well looked after and reliable Routemaster? Well over 100 were bought for work in Scotland and when I visited Glasgow in October of the following year I found the Routemasters of Clydeside and Kelvin Scottish perfectly at home there, one of their favourite gathering places being beneath the handsome iron and glass screen of Central station. All were RMs except for RML900 (sold in damaged condition), and I came across it working route 38, not between Victoria station and Clapton, but from Glasgow Centre to Johnstone adorned in a livery of red, yellow and white and the title *Oor Wullie's Special* after a famous cartoon character in the *Sunday Post*.

London's last new Mark I Metrobuses, M1439/40, were delivered in January 1986. Like their contemporaries the Titans, they have proved to be generally reliable and efficient and, although a few have been sold, the vast majority are still at work in London. Two Mark II Metrobuses, without the distinctive dropped windscreen, were delivered for evaluation trials in 1984: M1441 with a Gardner 6LXB engine and M1442 with a Cummins L10. These trials were intended to enable LT to choose its next generation of double-deckers and included the Leyland Olympians and Dennis Dominators mentioned earlier, and also three Volvo Ailsa B55s – one of which had two staircases. M1006-29 were delivered as Airbuses, linking central London with Heathrow via the M4, and were fitted with coach type seats, carpets upstairs, luggage lockers and, a little later, lifts for disabled access. The Metrobus proved very popular with provincial operators and some of these versions have subsequently appeared, secondhand, in London.

The vintage appeal of the Routemaster was recognised when 50 were put to work on the London Sightseeing Tour. Aldenham was given the £250,000

Above:
Aldenham in its heyday with a fleet of early RTLs – and one RT – waiting to take workers home to various parts of London and the Home Counties.

Left:
Clydeside's RML900 at work in Glasgow.

contract to carry out the conversion work. 11 were RCLs, 19 were standard RMs and, most interestingly, 20 were standard RMs converted to open-toppers. The latter proved very popular and helped increase LT's share of the much fought-for sightseeing market. A fascinating addition to the open-top fleet was one of the former Northern General front-entrance Routemasters, EUP 406B. Repainted, like the others, in traditional livery with gold, underlined fleetname and numbered RMT2793, it passed officially into LT ownership in 1987. Thus, finally, 25 years after the appearance of RMF1254, a member of the class entered passenger service with LT. It was not, however, the first front-entrance RM to operate the sightseeing service in LT ownership, for six former BEA RMAs were transferred from staff bus duties at the end of 1986, fitted with RCL-type front indicators, re-upholstered and brought up to standard in various other ways, ready for the 1987 season. The sightseeing fleet, based at Battersea garage, had by now become one of the most interesting aspects of the London bus scene. Over the years various Routemasters have come and gone from the sightseeing fleet; alterations and modifications have been made, none of which – as we shall see – has lessened its appeal, with the exception of some which

Above:
The former Northern General RMT2793 on sightseeing duties in the Haymarket.

briefly carried a fairly hideous all-over advert for McDonalds.

As startling as open-top Routemasters was the appearance of 25-seat minibuses in traditional red livery on a central London route. Nineteen Optare City Pacers on Volkswagen chassis entered service on 25 October on new route C1 from Westminster to Kensington. Classified OV, although this didn't appear anywhere on the vehicles, with D338 JUM-D356 JUM registrations, they operated from the basement of Victoria garage. I took a ride on one during the first month of operation, and although one's initial reaction was that anything other than a full-sized double-decker was quite out of order, I rapidly changed my opinion, not only on account of the quality of the interior appointments but chiefly the quality of the drivers. Not surprisingly the general public was somewhat bemused by the sudden, virtually unpublicised appearance of such vehicles in the middle of the West End. Outside Harrods one little old lady half entered the bus and then got into a long and confused conversation with our lady driver as to just where she, the old lady, wished to go, and whether the bus went there too. Our driver was patience itself and infinitely polite, as she was with a number of other enquiries all along the route. I was much impressed. The handsome little minibuses were branded Hoppas, a snappy title which caught on and was used elsewhere beyond the capital although, truth to tell, it would have been most appropriately applied to RMs with their open rear platforms on and off of which one really could hop.

More Leyland Tiger coaches, BTL34-53 with Berkhof bodies, and TDL46-65 with a new design of Duple body, entered London Country service in 1986, along with five more of the massive Olympian double-deck coaches, all wearing a variety of liveries.

These were the last vehicles to be ordered by London Country, for on 1 September it was split into four separate companies. This in part recognised that it was somewhat of an unwieldy organisation, operating as it did around the fringes of the red bus area, but more relevant was the Conservative government's determination to press ahead with privatisation. Among other large and long established companies which were ordered to be broken up were Midland Red, Ribble, United and Crosville. The minister concerned, Nicholas Ridley, declared that keeping them intact would 'undermine the development of competition'. When one considers how the industry over the subsequent 10 years has come to be dominated by a handful of vast, new companies, one can only comment, 'Ho, ho, ho.'

The four new companies were London Country North East, with some 340 vehicles and headquarters at Hertford; London Country North West, with 310 vehicles based at Watford; London Country South East based at Dartford and owning 220 vehicles; and the largest, London Country South West, with 360 vehicles based at Reigate. Crawley works passed to a new company, Gatwick Engineering, and a new marketing company was set up for Green Line.

With production of the Ts and Ms at an end, a new standard double-decker entered service with LT in 1986. This was the Leyland Olympian. Three prototypes had appeared in 1984. Strictly speaking it would have been more accurate to refer to the Olympian as a Bristol for it was developed at the Brislington works of the former Bristol Company and the first bodies were built by Bristol's traditional partner, ECW at Lowestoft. The Olympian bore some resemblance to the Titan but had rather more symmetrical proportions. Classified L by LT, the first members of the class entered service from Plumstead garage in March, being put to work from Bexleyheath (briefly), Sidcup, New Cross, Norwood, Croydon and Streatham garages. They seated 68 passengers.

Royalty put in one of its ceremonial visits to the Underground system on 1 April 1986 when the Prince and Princess of Wales opened the Piccadilly Line extension to Heathrow's latest terminal, number four. Around the same time orders were placed with Metro-Cammell for 16 six-car trains of 1983 stock to operate on the Jubilee Line and to provide additional rolling stock, for passenger numbers on the Underground were increasing, not a little of this welcome upsurge being due to the popularity of the Capital Card.

Below:
Olympian L138 passing the Old Vic in Waterloo Road on route 1. It carries a registration originally belonging to RM838.

1987

The first of the tube trains ordered from Metro-Cammell went into service at the end of November 1987. Known as the Batch II 1983 stock, they were in all respects virtually identical to their predecessors. OPO had been the aim of LT since the Victoria Line had proved its feasibility in the late 1960s, although it was not popular with the unions, nor with some of the general public who felt safer with a guard with them in the carriage. However, as with the buses, economics determined crew reductions where possible and stock had been built so that OPO conversion could be carried out fairly simply. The first conversions were the Circle and Hammersmith

Above:
AN236, a Roe-bodied Atlantean of 1980, at High Wycombe in London Country North West livery.

and City lines in 1986; as it was intended to convert the Jubilee Line in 1988, only the first five of the new 1983 Batch II tube trains went into service with two-man crews, modifications to the earlier batch for OPO operation starting in October 1986.

One of the worst disasters to hit LT, since World War 2, occurred on the evening of 18 November 1987 when an escalator caught fire at King's Cross Underground station and 31 people died. It sent shock waves through the system, led to a universal smoking

Right:
The Hammersmith terminus of the Hammersmith & City Line on a hot July day with a train of modified D stock at the platform.

Above:
Four London & Country Atlanteans at Chelsham, two ex-Northern General ones flank two ex-Southdown buses.

Left:
A Hampshire Bus ex-LT DMS2197 leads a Solent Blue Line VR ahead of Southampton City ex-LT RM1383, in Southampton city centre.

Above right:
London Coaches open-top RM1919 crossing a damp Lambeth Bridge.

Right:
London Coaches Duple-bodied Leyland Tiger LD2 outside Wandsworth garage.

ban and a drastic rethink of staffing, communication with passengers and safety generally.

LT and London Country coach operation was at this time extending further and further beyond the traditional Green Line boundaries and London Liner's involvement with what proved to be a short-lived express service to Birmingham, brought six-wheelers back into the fleet for the first time since the demise of the prewar Renowns, four 69-seat MCW Metroliners of the type familiar on many National Express routes being bought. They were classified ML. These, like the sightseeing Routemasters, belonged to the Commercial Operations Unit, set up in January 1986 and known from October that year as London Coaches. Apart from the Routemasters, the London Coaches fleet at the beginning of 1987 consisted of 14 varied vehicles, ranging from two East Lancs coach-

bodied Olympians and four modern DAF coaches, a type which would find increasing favour, to RT1530, the very last RT in LT's fleet, albeit unlicensed.

Chiswick works, now set up as Bus Engineering Ltd (BEL), had, in order to survive, to obtain works from sources other than LT and was now an agent and dealer for a number of transport manufacturers, Volkswagen and DAF diesel, for example.

If this took some getting used to, the London connection with the four new London Country companies was becoming even more diluted. London Country North East was the first to adopt a new livery – dark and light green and white window surrounds. All four companies were investing heavily in mini and midibuses, while London Country North West and London Country South West both took delivery of secondhand former Greater Manchester Atlanteans.

Left:
London United Leyland Lynx LX6
working from Hounslow garage
outside Richmond station.

Like LT they had three-piece indicators at the front but were arranged very differently. Their start was not auspicious with temporary and inadequate blinds, and some of the London Country South West vehicles even went into service on a route won from LT retaining their GMT livery. It was a state of affairs which did nothing to promote the image of deregulation. There were more and more operators appearing in the former Country Area and a mixed bunch they were, the quality of service and the vehicles varying from the excellent and up to date to the unreliable and antiquated.

London Country South East not only adopted a new name, Kentish Bus, but also a totally new livery, a rather stylish maroon and cream. In addition it began to renumber its routes, so that with the disappearance of many in the 4xx series, the break with LT was just about complete.

In the Central Area tendering was becoming more commonplace, with the various London Country companies taking over more former red routes, while other operators were also appearing, among them the long-established coach firm Grey-Green, which put former South Yorkshire Daimler Fleetlines on route 173 from Stratford to Becontree Heath. More Hoppas entered service in central London: C2 from Parliament Hill Fields to Regent Street and C3 from Chelsea Harbour to Earl's Court. C2 was operated by London Country North West with more Optare City Pacers which were owned by LT but leased to LCNW, and MBVs in traditional red livery. C3 had blue-liveried Ivecos and Sherpas. A minibus which was taking the country by storm at this time was the MCW Metrorider. Unlike some of the earlier 'Breadvans' it, along with the Optare City Pacers, was clearly designed from the outset as a PSV. Westlink, set up by London Buses in 1986 in the Kingston and Hounslow areas to bid for tendered routes, bought a considerable

number between 1987 and 1989, and still operates 33 of them as I write.

At the other end of the scale the final ECW-bodied L class Olympians entered service as yet another famous name, Eastern Coach Works of Lowestoft, went out of business at the end of January 1987. Many of the latest Ls went to Croydon garage and it was at this time that the first of a once quite unthinkable revival was seriously mooted, a new tram network for Croydon. This came in the form of a study carried out by LRT and Network SouthEast, advocating conversion of some BR electrified lines, street-running through central Croydon and a line to beleaguered New Addington, or 'Little Siberia' as this vast windswept development on top of the North Downs was known. Meantime the tram replacement 109 bus route became OPO and no longer served the Embankment, once a Mecca for tram enthusiasts but now virtually deserted due to the replacing buses, the 109's terminus becoming the more logical Trafalgar Square.

Routemasters were eagerly being snapped up and put to work all over England and Scotland. One of their earliest and most permanent new English homes was Blackpool. Decked out in a splendid version of the Corporation's prewar lined red and white livery, they took up work on the famous promenade, running alongside the trams, something RM1 had missed out in its home city by just two years. In 1987 they could be seen as far north as Perth and as far south as Southampton, and in London itself, although RMs were still being withdrawn, there were indications that they might yet have a future. There was opposition from many quarters to universal OPO in the capital and it seemed that London Buses itself was having second thoughts. Yes indeed. But not on Sundays. Many routes which continued to be operated by Routemasters Monday to Saturday went over to OPO on the Sabbath.

A bus which has become a great favourite of mine, the Leyland Lynx, replacement for the National and the very last in the long and generally highly honourable line of single-deckers produced by that once great firm, was beginning to appear in various liveries in London, although it never came anywhere approaching the numbers of its predecessors. Indeed a mere 11 wear LT red livery, the oldest being three delivered to Merthyr Tydfil in 1987 and brought back over the Severn Bridge from abroad two years later. London Buslines (Len Wright Travel) which had been in the very first batch of successful aspirants to run tendered services, taking over the 81 from Hounslow to Slough, replaced its DMSs with a batch of six yellow-painted Lynxes in 1987.

Many bus garages were closing at this time but an interesting acquisition by London Regional Transport was Victoria coach station, following the winding up of its previous owner, the NBC. Although red buses have never regularly appeared there Green Line coaches had already become a common sight.

1988

Yet more changes, as dramatic as any in LT's history, were forecast in the LRT Business Plan published in January 1988. Originally there were to have been 14-16 separate companies, but in the end there were fewer. One, Westlink/Stanwell Buses, was sold early, and another, London Forest, was disbanded in 1991, so that when the main privatisation programme came in 1994 just 10 remained to be sold. They were Centrewest, East London, Leaside, London Central, London General, London Northern, London United, Metroline, Selkent and South London. They would form the basis of separate, privatised companies, and would be in operation when privatisation arrived, which was expected to be in some two years' time. In other words LT, as it had been known since 1933, would disappear. If that doesn't warrant a new paragraph I don't know what does.

Privatisation arrived earlier than that in the former

Above:
Watford Bus DC6, a Carlyle Dartline-bodied Dennis Dart at Watford Junction.

Right:
On the Docklands Light Railway.

Country Area, London Country North East being sold to its management at the beginning of 1988. Inevitably a new livery was adopted, a not very lovely dark green and grey. A little later Kentish Bus and London Country North West went the same way, the former being bought by Proudmutual Ltd, a holding company for Northumbria. Very quickly exchanges began and vehicles previously at home on the Scottish border and Tyneside now found themselves operating in the Garden of England and vice versa. London Country North East went to Parkdale Holdings and Alan Stephenson, group chairman of East Yorkshire. It was soon split into two subsidiary concerns, based at Harlow and Hatfield. Meanwhile London Country South West adopted one of the most attractive of all the myriad new liveries appearing throughout the land, dark and light green with a red relief band.

The Docklands Light Railway, which was the nearest thing to trams seen in London since 1952, had been opened by HM the Queen on 30 July 1987, although it wasn't ready for the public to use for another month. This typified the problems this basically admirable but troubled innovative transport system was to suffer. Although set up by LT it operated as an independent concern and was to pass into the ownership of the Docklands Development Corporation in 1992, not without protest from those who felt that overall control of public transport in London was essential for the general good. For several years the DLR worked only Mondays-Fridays and not always then and buses have had to be used either as substitutes or in an ancillary capacity on countless occasions.

Despite the growing number of single-deck bus routes in central London, usually using small capacity vehicles, the pioneer Red Arrow No 500 ceased to operate in August 1987. It was replaced partly by Red Arrow 503 (not the original Waterloo-Victoria route which had vanished back in 1981) from Victoria to Paddington and the 73 which no longer ran to Hammersmith but turned south at Hyde Park Corner to terminate at Victoria. Its vanished western section was replaced by the revived 10 which ran from King's Cross to Hammersmith. Much the most interesting aspect of all this was that both the 73 and the 10 were operated by Routemasters. Truly it began to look less

Above:
Kentish Bus Park Royal-bodied Atlantean 685 in
Tunbridge Wells.

and less likely that OPO, whether single or double-deck, would become universal in the capital, whatever the provinces decided.

Routes were disappearing, reappearing, being rerouted and renumbered in and around London in a quite bewildering manner, while the companies operating them and the vehicles they provided were in a similar state of unpredictability. This wasn't necessarily a totally bad thing, for changing times – aren't they always – demanded changing public transport responses. The variety of vehicles, new and secondhand, could hardly have provided a greater contrast than the scene 30 years earlier when the RT and RF families had given London what was probably the most standardised fleet of any large city, worldwide. In modest numbers examples of both types could once again be seen operating in the LT area, the services of preserved examples being called upon from time to time to mark a route or ownership change or perhaps an anniversary, a phenomenon which both the preservation movement and operators were exploiting with growing enthusiasm.

After years of decline the Underground system saw a steady upsurge in patronage during the late 1980s. In this year 3.5 extra trains were converted from 1972

Mark I stock for the Victoria Line and a refurbishment programme was begun which has continued to the present day. One of the consequences of the terrible King's Cross fire was that in 1989 and 1990 Northern Line trains of 1972 stock were fitted with improved safety features and a public address system. Graffiti was reaching epidemic proportions at this time and LT was determined that it would not succumb as, for instance, New York had done. Various methods of removing the offending sprayed on paint were tried but these left marks on the unpainted bodywork and so experiments were begun with a return to painted stock. As one who had always thought unpainted Underground and tube trains were pretty uninspiring, I was delighted.

Two Victoria Line trains were given totally new interiors and externally the sides were painted in bands of white and blue with red ends and grey roofs. In both cases the result was excellent and it was decided that the entire Victoria Line fleet would be similarly treated. The work was done far away on the north bank of the Firth of Forth at Rosyth Royal Dockyard by Tickford Rail Ltd. Bakerloo and Northern Line 1972 stock has also been similarly refurbished, the programme continuing as I write.

Surface stock also began to undergo refurbishment and repainting. The seven units of A stock which worked the East London line were repainted in 1988-90, all with red cab ends and grey roofs and varying amounts of off-white, blue and red on the sides and doors. This was the prelude to the refurbishment of all the A and C stock.

1989

1989 was an eventful year on the Underground. Few of the trains were time expired but most were becoming dated and a programme of modernising them, inside and out, and improving safety on both the surface and tube lines began to make itself evident.

Passenger alarm facilities and public address systems were installed on the oldest, the 1959-62 tube trains, but otherwise there were no significant changes in livery or interior appointments. Withdrawal of this stock was expected to begin shortly, but only on a limited basis. Its replacement would be based on the three 1986 prototype tube trains, and an order was

Top:
Jubilee Line 1983 and refurbished Metropolitan Line A stock at Wembley Park.

Above:
Grey-Green Alexander-bodied Volvo B10M No 118 at Trafalgar Square bound for Hampstead Heath on the 24.

placed with BREL Derby for 85 trains for the Central Line. With these a new era would begin.

The first C surface stock unit working the Circle and Hammersmith and City lines, dating from 1970, to be refurbished, was dealt with at BREL Derby and went into experimental service in November 1989. At

the same time one of the 1961 A stock units, following on those already being refurbished for the East London Line, was sent to Metro-Cammell and returned in its new form for trials to determine whether any modifications would be needed before the main batch of units were dealt.

One of the highest profile examples of tendering occurred at the end of 1988 when London Buses lost the contract to operate route 24 and this was handed over to Grey-Green. The new year opened with the new dark green, pale grey and orange and white striped Alexander-bodied Volvo Citybuses already becoming a familiar sight wheeling around Trafalgar Square, heading down Whitehall and past the Houses of Parliament, successors of the many different types of red double-deckers which had worked this route.

Another remarkable arrival on the central London scene was Boro'line Maidstone, in other words Maidstone Borough Council, no less. It could be found initially operating a variety of secondhand double-deckers, later joined by some new Lynxes, on route 188 from Greenwich to Euston. Who would have

Above:
RMC1485 and a former BEA RMA of East London at Trafalgar Square on the X15.

thought that the successors of the ancient ginger-painted Crossleys, my earliest acquaintances in the Kent county town, would have had the nerve to oust London's own red double-deckers from such time-honoured haunts as Waterloo Bridge and Kingsway? The times were certainly changing.

1 April 1989 saw the various units, London United, London General, South London, etc, become limited companies, although wholly owned by London Buses Ltd. It was a big step towards privatisation. To the general public the change was generally only noticeable where special liveries were introduced. Those which attracted most attention were the East London vehicles which operated the X15, two RMs of London General and a Metrobus of London United. The latter brought out M1069 in an imaginative and most attractive version of the old London United livery as applied to its trams and trolleybuses, while RM89 and 1590 carried the red and white livery, with silver roof, of LT in the years 1933-9, virtually identical to that applied to the showbuses in the 50th anniversary year; it looked quite wonderful and might have been specially designed for them. Perhaps this said something about the vintage lines of the

Routemaster; more likely it was a reflection on the dourly unimaginative attitude to LT liveries since 1945.

The X15 was a new express rush hour route, the Beckton Express, running between Beckton and the Aldwych. It proved so popular that it was soon extended in the mornings to Oxford Circus with the return evening journeys beginning in Trafalgar Square. It was operated by six RMCs from Upton Park (U) garage, these former Green Line coaches being refurbished and painted red and gold. Immediately the route became the focus of much attention, something the East London company appreciated and fostered. The very last Routemaster, RML2760, which had spent all its career since delivery in 1968 at Upton Park, was later drafted to work it, as were former BEA front-entrance Routemasters, spruced up and restored to regular

Above:
South London Optare-bodied DAF DA1 at Trafalgar Square.

passenger service. The X15 and its parent route, the 15, were probably the most interesting in all central London, with RMLs, including 2760, standard RMs, two front-entrance RMAs and the RMCs all to be found working them. I was not a little surprised to leave Oxford Circus station a couple of weeks ago and, fighting my way through the assembled hordes of tourists of every hue, nationality and varying degrees of confusion, come upon an Upton Park RMC swinging into Regent Street sparkling in its just restored original Green Line livery. What next one wonders?

Around this time it became quite clear that the Routemaster had a future in the capital. London Coaches predicted that they would still be operating them into the next millenium while London Buses admitted that there would continue to be a need for crew-operated open-platform rear-entrance buses in central London for the forseeable future, and even talked about a possible successor to the RM. It also put out quite a silly statement to the effect that every Routemaster it withdrew was worn out and could not be put back into service. Various operators, not least London Buses itself, have disproved this on innumerable occasions since then.

We have seen how over the years the Green Line network had risen to the challenge of the ever increasing traffic demand for services to the various airports within its territory, which, of course, included Heathrow, the world's busiest, and Gatwick, which was not very far behind. In October a new company, Speedlink Airport Services Ltd headed by Nigel Gray,

former traffic manager of London & Country, was formed to operate these. Headquarters were at Crawley, while Staines garage was also taken over. 23 vehicles were transferred to Speedlink. By 1994 this number had risen dramatically to 61. Jetlink 747 and Flightline 777 have continued to sport a livery which is basically green and yellow, while the Speedlink service between Heathrow and Gatwick is operated by a fleet of coaches decked out in red, blue, white and yellow.

Mini and midibuses continued to flood into the fleets of the various operators in the London area, bringing in makes either never seen before or not for many decades. The ordering of 90 Renaults for Centrewest took one back to the earliest years of motorbuses in the capital, while the 28-seat body constructed by Wright of Ballymena, Northern Ireland, was a first, as was their Northern Irish registrations. At the other end of the scale a Celtic invasion from a different direction, which was gaining strength, was that of Alexander of Falkirk, its distinctive double-deck bodies becoming an ever more familiar sight on the streets of London. As I write they can be found on Leyland Olympians of Leaside Buses and London Central, London United's new Volvo Olympian Airbuses, and Scanias and Volvos of

Right:
London Buslines No 41, a Leyland Olympian with
Northern Counties body of 1990, Richmond bus station
with a Heathrow-bound aircraft overhead.

London Northern, while there are many single-deckers
with Alexander bodies, among the most interesting
being Selkent's distinctive 16 Dennis Lances.

The most striking looking single-decker to enter
service with LT for many years took up work in 1989
when DA1 – a DAF with Optare Delta 49-seat
bodywork – was bought for evaluation. I caught it one
afternoon in Trafalgar Square working the 109, a route
which never normally sees anything but double-
deckers. Optare, formed from the ashes of the Leeds
firm of Roe, has consistently produced the best-
looking double and single-deck bus bodies in the late
1980s and the 1990s.

The first of the new generation of Scania double-
deckers, S1-9 with Alexander bodies, arrived at
Potters Bar in July 1989 and took up work on the 263.

1990

Northern Counties, while long established, was not a
body builder traditionally associated with LT,
although it had provided bodies for the austerity Guys
immediately after the war; they were rather more
stylish than those of the various other suppliers for the
G class. These – Park Royal, Weymann, Duple and
Massey – had all fallen by the wayside over the
subsequent decades but by the end of the 1980s
Northern Counties, together with another long-
established Lancashire firm, East Lancashire, was
amongst the few surviving builders of double-deckers.
Both firms picked up sizeable contracts to supply
London & Country – which was how London Country
South West now styled itself – in 1989-91. East
Lancashire built bodies for eight Dennis Dominator
DDA1026s, Nos 602-9, and 48 Volvo B10M-50
Citybuses, Nos 610-622 and 648-684, while Northern
Counties put 21 bodies on Volvo chassis, Nos 623-43.

By this time the products of both firms were
becoming a very familiar sight in London, Grey-
Green, Kentish Bus, London Buslines, Capital
Citybus, Armchair – and London Buses – all owning
double-deck examples of one or other, sometimes
both manufacturers. The Northern Counties body of
the 1990 period was upright, restrained and rather
dignified but the East Lancs was stylish in the
extreme with sloping back upper-deck front windows,
married to a pronounced slope to the roof and dipped
side windows. It didn't appeal to everyone but it
could look very striking in a bold livery, which
London Country's two shades of green, red and black
stripes certainly was. It looked equally well in

Brighton, Hove and District colours, bringing back
memories of Tilling STs which worked in both
London and Brighton.

A notable feature of 1990 was the delivery of a first
order for 57 Dennis Darts. The first 27 had Duple
bodies, the next 30 Carlyle bodies and subsequent
years were to see more and more delivered.

The best looking Lynxes so far, half a dozen of
them, took up work in the London Country fleet in
1990. Numbered 311-16, examples can always be
found on route 289 which runs from Elmers End to
Croydon airport and Purley. It is remarkable that, 30
and more years after its demise, the pre-1939 London
airport still appears on bus indicators, but I guess that
this is because its famous control tower is a listed
building and the nearby Aerodrome Hotel also
remains. Much of the airfield is built over, part of it
being the Roundshaw Estate which FRM1 once
served, but a fair stretch of grass still survives and the
active Croydon Airport Society keeps the memory of
Croydon airport alive.

London & Country gained further former red bus
routes and its striking colours were being seen more
and more in central London. However a startling
reversal, at least for one who had known the 403 route
better than other green ones, was when London Buses
won the contract to operate it at the end of 1989, and

Croydon-based Olympians took over. I never did get used to red double-deckers parked beside the green at Warlingham. Chelsham garage, Mecca for so many spotting expeditions and where I encountered an NS on canteen duty, would soon disappear to be replaced by a superstore.

Twenty-three more Olympians arrived in the London Buses fleet in 1990. ECW being no more, these had Leyland bodies – not that these would be available much longer; the Leyland bodies were different in some respects, notably window arrangement. They had different route indicators, which were smaller, much less informative and of standard provincial design. Numbered L292-314, they bore the legend Riverside Bus and were sent to Stamford Brook garage to work the 237 from Shepherd's Bush to Sunbury. They are seen on other routes but I've only travelled on them on the 237 and then only when it has been raining, although I draw no conclusions from this about the weather in west London.

A one-time Croydon route which reached my home town no more, the 133, received 27 new Northern Counties-bodied Volvo Citybuses at the beginning of 1990. Running from its traditional City terminus at Liverpool Street, it headed southwestwards from Streatham to Tooting, which meant I could no longer catch it on my return home from the 67th Croydon cub pack meetings at the Endeavour in Melfort Road, Thornton Heath – although I hadn't actually needed

Above:
London & Country No 650, an East Lancs bodied-Volvo B10M Citybus of 1990 at Greenwich.

Above right:
L307, one of the Riverside Bus 1990 all-Leyland Olympians crosses the Grand Union Canal at Brentford.

Right:
ERM84 in Trafalgar Square.

to since 1948. The Volvos were numbered VC1-27 and took up work from Stockwell garage on 6 January 1990. A few months later they were joined by VC28-38 which were put to work on the 196, a route which did reach the Croydon area, terminating at Norwood Junction and serving the glorious Crystal Palace football ground, shades of Wright and Bright, before continuing on to Brixton where it has been known for misguided customers to get out and attempt to find a bus heading for Millwall. For a brief period at the end of 1989, after Cityrama with its blue Fleetlines suddenly gave up the routes, London & Country had operated the 196, Chelsham garage's Atlanteans providing rather more green than was

normally seen in that part of the world. With the contract passing to Stockwell, Chelsham garage finally shut up shop.

VC39 joined its brothers at Stockwell at the end of 1991, having possibly taken the long way round from Sweden. Not the least interesting aspect of the VC class is that although all of the VCs, apart from VC39, should bear G prefix registrations, many actually bear cherished ones nicked from RMs. VC3, for example, is WLT 803 and RM803, which was at that time operating out of GM garage, and was re-registered KGJ 24A.

There simply isn't space to note more than a fraction of the constant chopping and changing of routes and operators which has occurred since tendering arrived, but while passing through Croydon we must record that the 197 group of routes went green for a time, which was not so surprising as the southern terminus of Caterham was very nearly out in the country, a couple of miles inside the M25 periphery. South London's red Olympians ousted London & Country towards the end of 1989.

One of the most extraordinary episodes in the seemingly never-ending story of Routemaster variations was unveiled in 1990 when open-top ERM163 was shown to the public. This was a stretched version, the modification being carried out by Kent Engineering of Canterbury. An extra full-length bay from withdrawn RM458 was inserted in the middle of RM163, making it a five-bay 72-seater. Because of the modular construction of the Routemaster, such a sudden and drastic growth was perfectly feasible, resulting in the longest half-cab class of bus ever to run regularly in London. Nine further RMs were so treated that year and they have proved a valuable addition to the ever popular Original London Sightseeing Tour.

Few of London's once vast fleet of trams survived into preservation, principally because the preservation movement had hardly got under way by 1952, but one which did was the former prototype Feltham, MET No 331. Because of its centre door configuration it could not be converted to conduit operation when the rest of the fleet moved across the river to Telford Avenue in 1937 and it was sold to Sunderland. Ironically it was withdrawn from Sunderland service in 1952, the last year of trams in London, but its uniqueness was recognised and it was stored in various locations, eventually coming to that safe home of the British tram, Crich Museum. Even so its deteriorating state and complexity of construction gave little hope that it would run in the forseeable

future. Eventually the Gateshead Garden Festival of 1990 provided the spur and, with sponsorship from the Festival and British Steel, it returned to the northeast to work. The festival over, No 331 returned to Crich and was repainted in original MET livery. One golden October evening in 1995 I rode a Feltham for the first time in 44 years. The quality of the restoration, both inside and out, was quite breathtaking and as I sat gazing down the once so familiar length of the upper deck illuminated by brilliant shafts of the setting sun as we hummed up that Derbyshire hillside, all my notions of how advanced the Feltham had been for its time were confirmed.

In the workshops yet another amazing restoration, or rather re-creation, was in hand. The lower deck of former LCC E1 class No 1622 had been found years earlier and the car was now being put back together. The upper deck had to be built from scratch and the opportunity was taken to re-create 1622 as a rehabilitated E1r. This was an excellent notion as an original E1 already existed in the LT collection. The trucks had long since vanished but a pair of Feltham ones had been rescued from a field in Leeds. No 1622 had been wheeled out that day and, for the first time since 1952, one London tram had passed another. It was expected that restoration of 1622 would be complete in a year's time.

Below:
BL79 and a DMS at Richmond bus station.

Right:
SNB515, a former London Country National, working for Luton & District at Windsor.

Below right:
DWL8, a Wright-bodied Dennis Dart of Westlink at Kingston. The nose poking out of the bus station is a Westlink Metrorider.

1991

A sign of the times was the banning of smoking on all London buses from 14 February 1991. Long restricted to the upper deck, some companies had anticipated the effect of smoke on their paintwork by adopting a different colour scheme to downstairs – or inside as the lower deck was still sometimes known – but now society was sufficiently concerned about what nicotine was doing to the colour scheme of its lungs generally to go along with the measure. An extraordinary vehicle appeared on television screens at the beginning of 1991, advertising the ever more popular Travelcard. This started off as a DMS, changed midway to a tube carriage and finally decided it was a Network SouthEast train. Many wondered if it was the creation of a particularly ingenious computer graphic artist, but its appearance at several rallies proved that it did actually exist.

As one could write at the beginning of each new year in the 1990s, yet more mini or midi sized single-deck buses appeared on LT routes. The Dennis Dart

was to prove far and away the most popular bus at this period and 1991 saw further variations on the theme. Early in the year delivery of the first 8.5m batch with Wright bodies, the DW class, was completed, to be followed by some 9m long DWLs. Wright being a Belfast firm, most of its Darts received Northern Irish JDZ registrations, which was logical enough but for all that was not what one expected to be seen fixed upon red London buses. Around this time the BL class, which had put in some 14 years' service in London, ended passenger duties in the capital, the last being replaced by Darts. However, as I write, some examples can still be seen performing as learners, while many of the others were sold and have popped up all over the United Kingdom. Many other varieties of single-decker, particularly smaller ones, could be seen operating LT contracts, sometimes for quite brief periods. A real curiosity was the Talbot Pullman, which although far

Above:
CV7 of Westlink, an Omni designed to accommodate disabled passengers and partly owned by the London Borough of Richmond, on its way to Queen Mary's Hospital, followed by a Carlyle-bodied Dart.

from being a proper grown up bus, nevertheless sported six wheels.

Out in the former Country Area London Country North West had been bought by Luton & District in October 1990 but Watford area buses bore the legend Watfordwide and later Watford Bus, which was just as well for one cannot imagine the citizens of Watford and its environs putting up with having 'Luton' emblazoned on their buses. Seven all-Leyland Olympians delivered to Watford in 1991 suggested that the single-decker was not quite all-conquering; however at the time of writing they remain the latest double-deckers in the fleet.

Awareness of the problems the disabled have in coping with public transport led in the 1980s to the development of Mobility Buses, specially adapted to carry wheelchairs. The first would seem to have been National LS454 which took up work in Stratford and Walthamstow in 1984. A number of other Nationals were adapted with lifts and clamps for the wheelchairs down to 1991, although many subsequently passed out of London Buses' ownership. Other vehicles were purpose-built for these duties.

In March 1991 the Government published *A Bus Strategy for London*, which sent shivers down many a spine in that it promised deregulation. It promised a

number of other things too: nine things altogether, many of which on the surface looked as if they ought to command universal support – 'encouraging promotion of bus services', 'safeguarding . . . concessionary travel', 'making bus priority measures more widespread and effective', for example. The trouble was that few believed any Conservative administration of the 1980s or 1990s really had a commitment to better public transport and that when it talked of offering more choice it forbore to mention that it was almost inevitably the better off who were able to exercise the greatest choice. Regular bus users are not generally to be found amongst the most affluent and there was no suggestion of a serious intent to increased funding. Much in the final chapters of this volume is concerned with the working out of these changes, although they are nowhere near yet complete.

1992

Two of London's standard double-deckers, the RM and the DMS, suffered very different fates in 1992. Although withdrawal of the Routemaster was still going on, its continued place in the scheme of things was made abundantly clear when at the beginning of the year London Buses announced 486 RMLs would be refurbished. For many months previously experimental work had been proceeding on various members of the class and on 24 February 1992 the first production refurbishment, on RML895, was unveiled to the press, although RML2360 was actually the first to be completed.

Left:
A refurbished RML upper deck. The bus is working the 38 from Clapton garage.

Below:
Croydon DMS2306 passing Selhurst Park, home of Crystal Palace Football Club.

Back in the mid-1980s consideration had been given to a Routemaster replacement but the cost of such a one-off vehicle was far too high and so the refurbishment, about 20 per cent of the cost of a new vehicle, was embarked upon.

The modifications affected every part of the vehicle, mechanical, electrical and bodywork. The fitting of Cummins or Iveco engines had already taken place, producing a very different sound to that long associated with the Routemaster. Otherwise the most noticeable differences which met passengers were in the interior decor. This was a considerable improvement – many had long thought the RM inferior in this respect to the RT – with the seats retrimmed in a blue needlecord material, the sides below the windows lined to match, while the window surrounds and ceiling were white. This gave an

altogether lighter feel to the bus. Among other changes heating was improved, flooring and handrails were updated and reflective numberplates were fitted.

The standard RM soldiered on and, rather like the RT in the twilight of its career in the late 1970s, found itself reappearing in ones and twos on routes from which it had been long vanished, filling the place of RMLs away being refurbished. Initially the work was carried out by TBP Holdings, a West Midlands firm, South Yorkshire Transport (SYT) based in Rotherham and the London Buses subsidiary, Leaside Buses. Later Leaside also took on the refurbishment of its Tottenham allocation of RMLs. Before 1992 was out another unexpected twist in the Routemaster story led to the repainting of 24 of the refurbished buses into a completely new livery. On 9 December it was announced that Kentish Bus had won the contract to

operate route 19, which until then had been worked by Routemasters of London General.

For the DMS, 1992 offered far fewer new horizons, at least within London Buses. The year opened with the 21-year association of the type with Merton garage coming to an end on 4 January. This left only neighbouring Sutton, Thornton Heath and Croydon still operating the DMS in regular passenger service. In March Thornton Heath's allocation was replaced by Ts, Sutton's went in April, and by midsummer only DMS2438, 2480 and 2494 were still working from TC on the 68 (their last central London route) and the 130. From October DMS2438 worked alone but managed to last out the year.

If Irish-registered buses had taken a bit of getting used to, along with refurbishing of Routemasters in Birmingham and Rotherham, what were we to make of a former Green Line route being operated by coaches with Dutch chassis and Hungarian bodies? Take it in your stride was the answer, for now anything was possible. Route 726, Dartford-Heathrow, passed to London Coaches in February and for it were bought 10 distinctive looking Ikarus-bodied DAFs, DK1-10, painted in a red, white, grey and black livery with '726 Expresslink' branding. Three months later London Coaches became the first London Buses subsidiary to be sold, its management team gaining control. It continues to be based at Wandsworth garage.

The once mighty Leyland company, now owned by Volvo, became an even less distinct shadow of its former self with the announcement of the closure of its Workington factory. The Lynx, the last all-Leyland single-decker, would cease production as would bodies for the Olympian double-decker, although chassis production would continue at the Volvo factory in Scotland. At least Leyland's last products for London were not the ignominious failures AEC's Merlins and Swifts had been: the Lynx, although never seen in great numbers in and around London,

still has its part to play, while the Olympian, now labelled Volvo, is still in production.

Despite the popularity of the midibus, and particularly the Dennis Dart, there was still a place for the full size single-decker. Westlink especially continued to demonstrate its affection for the Leyland National and in 1989-90 had added nine DAFs with Optare Delta 49-seat bodies. Now East London added 25 more to its fleet. The Delta, with its purposeful, sloping expanse of windscreen, was the best looking of the many well-proportioned single-deckers in production, and the East London vehicles were further distinguished by a striking livery of red and silver. The Leyland National, and it will be remembered that London Country once owned more of these vehicles than any other company worldwide, demonstrated it was far from finished with London Country's successors when a barely recognisable rebuilt version appeared with London & Country.

Above:
Newly delivered DK3, Ikarus CitiBus-bodied DAF of London Coaches outside its Wandsworth home.

Left:
An East Lancs Greenway of London & Country at the Brentford terminus of the 117. A London United Renault-Dodge RW is in the background.

Above:
London Central's SP19, an DAF/Optare Spectra, in Trafalgar Square.

Below:
Slough bus station with Leyland Nationals of London United and Watford Bus.

This was the Greenway. Given a new 'green' Gardner engine and a complete body refurbishment inside and out by East Lancs in its Blackburn factory, Greenways would later appear in London Buses' red livery.

Among the ever more adventurous livery variations, notable was that applied to nine Alexander-bodied Scania double-deckers which were repainted red and white to operate a new rush hour express route, the X43 from North Finchley to London Bridge.

If the Delta was a handsome bus, what was one to say about its double-deck equivalent, the Spectra? Both proved conclusively that, even if a bus was basically a box, it didn't need to look like one. London's first DAF/Spectra, SP1, was shown to the public in September and the class took up work on route 3. As curvaceous as the Delta, the Spectra made all other designs look old-fashioned. Twenty-five were put into service in 1992-3. Surprisingly no others have appeared as yet in the capital, London Central subsequently favouring Olympians, and the infinitely smaller Wilts and Dorset fleet can boast more Spectras than London.

Garages continued to be closed and three long-established suppliers of many central London routes either gone or announced as going in 1992 were Streatham, only recently rebuilt, West Ham and Peckham.

1993

It still seemed scarcely believable but the prospect of trams reappearing on the streets of London came a little nearer at the beginning of 1993 with the appointment of a design team for the Croydon Tramlink. And the previous year trams had once again taken up regular operation in the streets of a British city for the first time since 1962 when the Manchester Metrolink had been inaugurated. So it could happen.

Early in 1993 the LT Museum closed for a £4 million refurbishment scheme. It was reopened by Michael Palin with a new mezzanine floor ingeniously squeezed in. Its home at Covent Garden might never have been an option, for the former fruit and vegetable market buildings had been threatened with demolition when the market itself had moved out to Nine Elms. That battle had been won and the continuing popularity of the whole complex of magnificent 19th century iron and glass structures is most heartening, but right from the start LT knew that, ideal though the location was, there was nothing like sufficient room to display its entire collection. The 1993 refurbishment has succeeded splendidly in creating more space while doing nothing to detract from the appeal of the building itself.

One of the best selling lines in the shop is bus models and it is remarkable how enormously popular these have become in the last few years. Some 50 years ago my friend Keith Ryde had a prewar tinplate clockwork toy bus approximating to an ST which I

coveted deeply and since the 19th century there have been many attempts to reproduce London buses, trams, trains and trolleys for the toy market. Those which still survive often have great charm – and a suitable price tag – but it was only in the 1980s that really accurate, mass-produced models appeared. There was, of course, the famous Dinky Toy STL dating from 1938; Corgi brought out a fairly accurate Routemaster in the 1960s as did Dinky Toys, the latter also in ready-to-be-assembled form, but rather surprisingly the French firm Solido was just about the earliest in the field with a near perfect replica, an O gauge 'Bus Londonien', an RT in both red and green liveries.

The real breakthrough came with EFE, whose first product was – surprise, surprise – an RT in 1:76 scale, OO gauge. I actually first saw one, and bought it, in Cardiff but such is the popularity of London prototypes that no doubt they sell equally well in the Outer Hebrides. In the December 1995 issue of *Classic Bus* its readers voted London liveries the most popular of all and, with Corgi's O gauge and Original Omnibus OO gauge models joining EFE, there is now a wonderful range of London prototypes (all right I know in some the sidelights are a millimetre too far to the left and the conductor has odd socks but I think

Below:
DMS2438, the last of its type in ordinary passenger service, at West Croydon bus station.

they're wonderful), although there's a strange dearth of trams and trolleybuses: I'd take out a second mortgage for a Feltham. The LT Museum has promoted several sets including one with an RM, a roof-box RT and a Red Arrow Leyland National which brings us neatly to the transformation of these latter vehicles – the real ones – into Greenways. Between 1992 and 1994, 42 Nationals were so treated by East Lancs. Interestingly, while other companies, London & Country for example, seldom get their own transformed Nationals back, all of London General's started out as LT Nationals and have, with one exception, kept their original fleet numbers, merely having G put before the LS. Three seat 38 passengers, the rest 24.

It is now well over 20 years since the first Leyland Nationals appeared, and although they had their faults, they seem destined for a very long life, in whatever form. Former London ones, both red and green, can be seen at work all over the United Kingdom; one-time provincial ones have been bought for use in London, and in the suburbs and the surrounding rural areas they are as readily come by as out of town shopping centres. Slough bus station – that architectural and environmental gem – is a particularly happy hunting ground where they cheerfully pump out clouds of diesel fumes in which I swear I've seem the faint outline of John Betjeman's ghost hovering more than once. Two successors to the National appeared on central London routes in 1993. Metroline purchased 31 Dennis Lances with Northern Counties bodies and installed them in Cricklewood garage whence they operate routes 32 and 113, while London General bought 13 Volvo B10Bs, also with Northern Counties bodies, for the 88, a route which now operates between Oxford Circus – where it meets its brothers on the 113 – and Clapham Common. The 88 has been rather imaginatively branded 'The

Left:
The man from the Clapham Omnibus at Clapham Common with VN4, a Northern Counties-bodied Volvo of London General.

Below left:
It could be a scene from the 1940s. In fact it's LT165, on a day trip from the LT Collection at Covent Garden, leaving Crystal Palace and heading for Brighton on the 1994 HCVC run.

Below:
'Fancy meeting you here.' Former LT Titan T612, Merseybus 2612, heading for a familiar destination, passes one of the original London Country Park Royal-bodied Atlanteans, AN36 of 1972, now North Western 480, in the centre of Liverpool.

Above:
The Cobham Bus Museum Open Day at Apps Court with STL441, RMs, an M&D Volvo Olympian and various London single-deckers in the background.

Below:
An RML in Kentish Bus livery crossing Chelsea Bridge on route 19.

Clapham Omnibus', after that favourite touchstone of generations of politicians.

The very last DMS in ordinary passenger service, 2438, performed a ceremonial enthusiasts' run on 2 January 1993 and was finally withdrawn from Croydon garage on 20 January, thus ending 22 years of DMS operation with LT which wasn't at all bad for a type once so reviled. A total of 37 remained in stock with London Buses and they continued to pop up performing various duties. The most commonly seen were the 12 B20 trainers of London General, many adorned with bright yellow fronts and some of which are still on learner service as I write, although probably not for much longer.

With the DMS gone it was now the turn of the next semi-standard London design, the Titan, to be disposed of. As the eldest was 15 years old this was not really surprising. Although it found few buyers outside London when new, the Titan had served London well and buyers of secondhand ones were readily found. Some stayed in London but the best place to find them in a new environment was on Merseyside. Merseybus has specialised, like its predecessor Liverpool Corporation, in ancient, rather scruffy double-deckers. I write as one who was regularly bumped and rattled around the city in what appeared to be not quite completed Regents and PD series Titans in the 1960s. It therefore came as little surprise to find hordes of ex-London Titans, some not only in London livery but even still bearing East London fleetnames and logos, bumping and rattling past St George's Hall and Lime Street in the autumn of 1993. Rather more surprising was the fact that they were fighting for road space with equally large numbers of former London Country Atlanteans now owned by North Western and Liverline, London Country and LT Nationals belonging to C&M Travel, former LT DMSs and Bexleybus Olympians of Fareway, and even a red Routemaster, RM1776, belonging to Liverline – who also owned yet more former London Country Atlanteans. I even saw a couple of former London Metrobuses which must have arrived only days earlier, for selling of these had also started, but only just. Two years later some Merseybus Titans were still in red London livery. Certainly one has no need to feel cut off from the London scene in Liverpool in the 1990s, a far cry from 30 years ago when the only ex-LT vehicles were a couple of Bedford/Scammell articulated mobile canteens – although in the 1950s St Helens Corporation ran its own fleet of brand-new RTs into the city. One of these has been preserved as has one of the mobile canteens which went to Liverpool, London number 702B, JXC 2.

This brings us to the home of 702B, Cobham Bus Museum. Founded back in 1966 as the London Bus Preservation Trust, the Cobham premises were acquired in 1972, and despite several ups and downs – typical of all preservation groups – the trust now hosts a quite magnificent collection of former London vehicles, built between the 1920s and the 1950s, complementing the official LT collection. Not only does Cobham possess the only Tilling ST, one of the original LGOC Ts, and a sit-up-and-beg STL similar to the one at Covent Garden, but it has also brought together the only two surviving roof-box STLs, surely the highpoint of the standard London double-deck design of the 1930s, as well as one of the front-entrance Country Area versions, which ended its days as an open-top tree lopper. None of the later STLs are in working order although STL2093 was active in the late 1960s and early 1970s and appeared on the HCVC London to Brighton run, while restoration of STL2377 is coming along nicely.

Although the Routemaster qualified for inclusion in Cobham's collection of vintage buses, its adventures in everyday service on the streets of London were far from over. The strikingly liveried Kentish Bus examples took over route 19 from London Buses earlier in 1993 and later a second Routemaster route passed to a new operator when BTS won the route 13 contract. Twenty-two refurbished RMLs and, interestingly, one RM, were leased from London Buses Ltd and repainted, though this time the livery was simply a different shade of red. Not the least notable aspect of all this was that, for the first time for several years, crewed buses once again operated in central London on Sundays.

In 1993 the elderly Network SouthEast units which worked the deep level Waterloo and City Line (the 'Drain'), designed prewar by Bulleid were replaced by six 1992 tube sets of the same design as the new Central Line stock. The following year, as a result of government discussion, the line passed into LT ownership.

1994

A strenuous campaign against the deregulation of LT had been mounted ever since the notion had been mooted. Many were the individuals and groups who felt that, just as London overall had suffered from the abolition of the GLC, so its transport infrastructure would deteriorate without a single authority being in charge. There was, therefore, much rejoicing when the Queen's Speech at the opening of Parliament in November 1993 failed to include a bill to bring deregulation about. Privatisation would take place in 1994 and all routes would eventually be put out to tender but LT would continue to have overall responsibility for public transport in the capital and the suburbs.

More new full size single-deckers appeared with Selkent, 12 Dennis Lances with Plaxton Verde bodies in a rather fetching red and white livery – not many perhaps but at least it proved there was still a place for the big bus in London. However any new vehicle deliveries were quite overshadowed by the long predicted sale of London Buses' 4,600 strong fleet.

First to go, in September, was CentreWest to a management buy out. London General and London United followed a similar path. That extraordinary set up, Stagecoach, of the blue, red and orange stripes, which 10 years earlier had begun far away in the Highlands of Scotland, bought Selkent and East London; the Tyneside based Go Ahead bought London Central. Cowie, already familiar in London with its Grey-Green operation, added Leaside Buses and MTL Holdings acquired London Northern. MTL also owned London Suburban Bus, which was in the same group as Liverbus, and already buses might one day be seen operating in Liverpool and a day or so later appear in service in London. By the end of the year only South London remained to be sold, a rather alarming proportion of its vehicles being in a less than satisfactory condition. Even that would go early in 1995, once it had got the spriggots rewired and the driver's uniforms pressed – to Cowie, which now owned more London buses than anyone else. Who would have thought it possible all those decades ago when Grey-Green was a coach company operating a fleet of Duple-bodied AEC Regals?

And so it had happened; the big one. Wow! No more LT or LT roundels on the side of buses after 62 years. All gone. It was all over.

Well, not really. The doomsday scenario of fleets of swooning enthusiasts confronted by Routemasters in

Below:
Titan T1101 of Bromley garage with Stagecoach Selkent branding at West Croydon.

Above:
A pair of London Central RMLs with route 12 branding in Piccadilly Circus.

Right:
South London's RM676 passing St Martin-in-the-Fields.

all over white with blue, red and orange stripes is never likely to happen, for it has been decreed that central London buses must remain predominantly – 80 per cent to be precise – red, although Ray Stenning has come up with snazzy motifs and variations: the Clapham Omnibus, the 12 and 36 branding amongst them. Ray and I go back a long way; I taught him art, briefly, back in the 1960s and he has probably done more to enliven British bus liveries than anyone else. Just how the 80 per cent rule will affect such liveries as the red and cream which South London applies to its elderly Routemasters operating out of Brixton on route 159 remains to be seen. These have become surely the best known buses in the land, for whenever a prominent politician is interviewed by the television cameras outside the Palace of Westminster there always seems to be a bright red and cream Routemaster going about its business in the background.

No doubt there will be many more changes of ownerships, yet more amalgamations and, should the national political picture change, then we may well see legislation and funding favour many more tram

schemes, Barking and North Kent for instance, and possibly for the first time ever, into the heart of the West End.

One London tradition which many see as being under threat is the double-decker. Virtually a British phenomenon – Berlin and Athens are the only other European mainland capitals I can recall where they are found, and they're rare elsewhere, certainly outside what was once the Empire – EEC legislation and a greater concern for the disabled pose problems for the future of the double-decker. The new generation of British trams, wherever they may be built, will be

articulated single-deckers and there have been far fewer double-deck buses bought in relation to single-deckers, particularly small capacity ones, in the last 10 years than ever before. For all that the high capacity double-deck bus is uniquely suitable for moving large numbers of passengers about our cities, Manchester has its doubts. Edinburgh does not and in 1994 orders were still being placed by a number of the London companies. London Suburban Bus put into service 10 Volvo Olympians with elegant, very comfortable Northern Counties' Palatine II bodies, very similar to the Optare Spectra. The Liverpool connection meant that buses might well be transferred from Merseyside to the capital and vice versa. Kentish Bus and Grey-Green were others who also bought new double-deckers and, inevitably, a variety of secondhand ones appeared and disappeared with bewildering frequency. Titans were snapped up by many London companies, London Suburban Bus, Westlink and London & Country for example.

On the Underground the Metropolitan has always maintained its individuality and something of the air of a main line concern. Throughout the 1980s steam specials out of Marylebone could be seen running parallel with Metropolitan tracks and it was perhaps not surprising that steam has returned to the

Left:
Preserved Metropolitan 0-4-4T No 1.

Below left:
One of three former West Midlands Metrobuses operated by Westlink on the 411 seen in Kingston.

Below:
0-6-0Ts Nos L90 and L99 together with Bo-Bo electric locomotive *Sarah Siddons* with a steam special from Amersham to Harrow-on-the-Hill passing through Chorleywood. *Brian Morrison*

Metropolitan itself with a number of specials operating over its northern section. The Metropolitan's own 0-4-4T, No 1 is based at Quainton, just up the line from Amersham and Aylesbury, while former GWR pannier tanks which once belonged to LT have reappeared in their old haunts, along with other classes of preserved steam locomotives. A somewhat different fate befell the Epping-Ongar branch of the Central Line, the most rural section of the Underground. It eventually closed on 30 September 1994. But immediately enthusiasts announced plans eventually to reopen it as a preserved railway.

1995

1995 began with the sale of the last London bus company, South London Buses, to the Cowie Group. The price, £16.3 million, was considered a bit of a bargain, the reason being that the company had a problem with vehicle maintenance, something which caused the Traffic Commissioner concern. As Cowie also owned Grey-Green and Leaside Buses it now possessed some 1,100 London buses, making it the biggest player in the game. The acquisition of County Bus in 1996 made it yet bigger. Throughout 1995 there were further sales, amalgamations, renamings and mergers, to say nothing of a liberal wielding of the paintspray.

In the northern reaches of the former LT Country Area the inappropriately named Luton and District rechristened itself the vastly less specific 'The Shires'. It then went on to set up very much more specific local identities: 'network Watford', 'the Stevenage line', 'Luton & Dunstable', etc.

By this date one would not have expected any raised eyebrows if a consortium with its head office on Mars had bid for a London bus company, so I suppose no one should have been surprised when

Below:
Formal handover of the final train of 1992 Central Line stock at ABB Litchurch Lane works, 13 March 1995. *Brian Morrison.*

Above right:
Three low-floor Dennis Lance SLFs with Wright bodywork of CentreWest with Uxbridge Buses branding at Uxbridge.

Below right:
The Green Line network now extends as far east as Maidstone. M&D No 2195, a Plaxton-bodied Leyland Tiger delivered to Bebb of Llantwit Pardre in 1992, newly adorned in Green Line livery with the Invictaway leaping horse, stands in Armstrong Road garage, Maidstone, alongside an M&D Northern Counties-bodied Volvo Olympian of 1995.

Westlink found itself owned by West Midlands Travel. Perhaps inevitably former Birmingham Metrobuses appeared working alongside their original London brothers in southwest London, although not for long as the three were soon sent to Coventry .

The London & Country garages at Croydon and Walworth joined with Kentish Bus's at Dunton Green to form LondonLinks. The livery chosen was very similar to London & Country's, while Kentish Bus decided on a vivid yellow and green for its buses outside London.

A further coming together brings our story right back to its beginnings in 1933. M&D had survived into 1995 as one of the very few large independents but in April it was sold to British Bus. It thus found itself in the same group as Kentish Bus and a joint M&D, Kentish Bus and LondonLinks administrative base was set up at Maidstone. In 1933 the formation of LT had seen M&D hand over its Dartford and Northfleet garages, the routes they operated, and 55 buses. Sixty-two years later Gravesend area rural routes passed to Kentish Bus, successor to LT. Since 1933 there had been a clear demarcation between where Green Line territory ended and the M&D express routes took over, although it was interesting that while Tunbridge Wells was exclusively M&D stage carriage territory, the express service to London belonged to Green Line. This came about because of

the transfer of the former Autocar M&D service to LT in 1934. Now M&D's Invictaway express routes between the Medway Towns and Maidstone and London became part of the Green Line network and by the end of the year practically all M&D coaches were in Green Line livery, although the Invictaway leaping horse symbol was retained, appearing alongside the Green Line branding.

Green Line might have abandoned its Eccelston Bridge home at Victoria but it had moved just a few metres southwestwards into a coach station in the Victoria Centre. From there it was now possible to take a regular Green Line service coach as far northeast as Norwich, as far north as Huntingdon and Milton Keynes, westwards to Oxford and Newbury, south to Brighton and east to its newly acquired Kentish termini. A variety of vehicles was used, all genuine coaches unlike the upmarket buses of earlier days; the now quite elderly but still comfortable Plaxton Paramount-bodied Leyland Tiger TP and TPL

class provided the backbone of the fleet, although many examples had been sold. I travelled on a Northumbria Tiger between Hexham and Corbridge on the River Tyne in May 1995 and came across another even further north in Princes Street, Edinburgh.

Former London Titans became equally well travelled. Westlink and London & Country snapped them up in some numbers, the red and cream ones branded for route 52 continued to operate for Metroline, while the acquisition of so many of the London Titans by Stagecoach meant that they began to be repainted into Stagecoach livery and posted to such far away places as Havant and Hastings on the south coast and Irvine in Scotland.

The new generation of double-deckers, curvaceous and comfortable, entered service in some numbers. Although there were no more of the pioneering Optare Spectras, Northern Counties Palatines and Alexander Royales appeared in various liveries, the most

luxurious being London United's fully air-conditioned Volvo Olympians with Royale bodies. These were airbuses and had luggage racks and wheelchair access downstairs and coach seats upstairs. They replaced many of the former Ms which were modified for ordinary service with bus type seats.

The low-floor single-decker, with the ability to kneel to enable elderly or disabled passengers and those in wheelchairs or mothers or fathers with buggies to board easily, had been a feature of 1994, many bearing striking liveries with a motif which looked rather like a zip painted around their middles. London United, CentreWest, Metroline, Leaside, County Bus and East London were already in the field. Although not all of them performed perfectly all the time, this very worthwhile concept was clearly here to stay. Four Dennis Lance SLFs with Wright Pathfinder bodies were put on the 408 by London & Country early in 1995 and 10 Scanias also with Wright bodies were delivered to Kentish Bus in November and December. I found them awaiting entry into service in M&D's headquarters garage, another example of the increasing links between the two companies.

What of the future? There is a lull for the moment in the delivery of new Underground trains, the last of the 1992 tube stock arriving in March 1995 and there is no need as yet for new surface stock. Construction is going ahead on the Jubilee Line extension.

As for the London bus, the great works which maintained it have both gone, first Aldenham and then Chiswick. The highly specialised London bus, often designed at least partly by its operator, starting way back before World War 1 with the B type and culminating with the Routemaster, is also very nearly in the past, although several hundred of the latter are still with us and some will survive in

various forms into the next millenium. The standardisation which LT strove so hard to achieve from 1933 onwards, and finally achieved in the 1950s, has gone for ever and privatisation has surely ensured it will not return, certainly in the forseeable future.

Deregulation, which once seemed a racing certainty, would seem to be a dead issue. After 10 years of it outside London a Parliamentary working party has declared it a failure and recommended the setting up of a regulator. Do I hear sighs of 'Why so long?' from passengers and local authorities? At the same time evidence worldwide has shown that the diesel engine is a primary cause of pollution. Stagecoach East London has experimented with low sulphur diesel and there are other initiatives around which ought to go a long way to solving the problem. But both this and regulation opens the way for the tram – and just possibly the trolleybus. Croydon Tramlink is happening and the climate is becoming daily more favourable for other schemes. Within these pages we have recorded the demise of both the London tram, in 1952, and the trolleybus 10 years later. Ten years on I would not be the slightest bit surprised to be recording their phoenix-like restoration.

Below:
Dunton Green garage in December 1995. A pair of Peugeot-Talbot 22-seat Pullmans flank Roe-bodied Atlantean 678 and a Volvo with its London Country fleetname showing beneath the not too-well applied LondonLinks fleetname.

1996

1996 opened on a tragic note when two Provisional IRA terrorist bombs exploded in London in February, the first resulting in the deaths of two people, these as in most such cases being innocent bystanders, who died near the Docklands Light Railway station at South Quay. Services between Canary Wharf or Heron Quays and Island Gardens were suspended for a considerable time while the damage was repaired. Later in the same month, London Central Titan T990 became the first London bus to be destroyed by a terrorist bomb when a device exploded on the upper deck; the young man who was carrying it with the intention of planting it elsewhere was killed. Dramatic pictures of the wrecked bus, on route 171 in the Aldwych, featured prominently in the national press.

A new, rounded, elegant look had appeared in the double-deck fleet with the arrival of the Optare Spectra in 1992, followed by the Alexander Royale in 1995. A third variation was the Northern Counties Palatine II, with a huge expanse of curved glass at the front, upstairs and down. Further examples, on DAF DB250 chassis, entered service with Cowie Leaside in February 1996. But it was the single-decker which picked up most orders and in particular the versatile Dennis Dart, the popularity of which continued to grow, the longer 9.8m version appearing in a number of London fleets. The Dart, which had started as a midibus, seemed, like many classic vehicle designs, to be capable of almost limitless stretching and modification. The low-floor, 10.6m Dart SLF with Plaxton Pointer bodywork was put into service by CentreWest, London & Country and Kentish Bus during 1996.

The London bus scene became more kaleidoscopic almost by the day as liveries became yet more varied and exotic. One of the most attractive was that adopted by London United, with a main body colour of red with a thin white line separating this from dark grey lower panels whilst the roof was light grey. A well-proportioned variation on the theme of red and white has always somehow seemed right for London, and London United's Lynxes and thirteen rejuvenated Nationals looked particularly fine. The Leyland

Left:
That Green Line stalwart, the Plaxton Paramount-bodied Leyland Tiger, was rapidly disappearing by 1996. One of the last survivors, TP74, now in the Guildford & West Surrey fleet, is seen at Hampton Court on its way to Guildford in May 1996.

Below:
Many other examples of the TP class remain at work with new owners. Former TP62 became Northumbria 242 and is seen, also in May 1996, crossing the River Tyne at Corbridge, on its way from Carlisle to Newcastle.

National was getting somewhat elderly by now, London's first new example having been delivered in 1973, the last in 1981.

There had been a time when double-deck buses resembled nothing more than a very square box, but by the mid-1990s this was all changing. The Optare Spectras delivered to London Central in 1992/3 were the first of the new generation of curvaceous, beautifully-styled double-deckers; one wonders why it took so long for operators to introduce further batches. It was left to the relatively small Wilts & Dorset to build up the largest fleet in the country. However, Optare's lead was soon followed, and in May 1995 London Central bought nine Olympians fitted with the almost equally elegant Alexander Royale body. Next came the Northern Counties Palatine II. In 1995/6 27 of these, mounted on Olympian chassis, entered the CentreWest fleet. Fifteen were painted in a special red and white livery, fitted with blue-backed destination blinds, and bore the fleetname Uxbridge Buses, and were put to work on the 607 express route between Shepherd's Bush and Uxbridge. They replaced a varied collection of vehicles including Leyland Nationals. The 607 had once been a trolleybus route. Interestingly, Corgi produced a model of a Royale-bodied Olympian on the 607, and also of a Q1 trolleybus which once worked this route. More Royales, 19 in all, with high-backed seats, were put into Airbus service by London United in 1995/6.

CentreWest Olympians turned up about as far from West London as they could get, when the company was awarded the contract for the 61 in the Orpington area, surprisingly taking over this route from Metrobus, which just about everyone had thought was doing an excellent job. Olympians, incidentally, were now produced by Volvo, the once-dominant name of

Above:
The Leyland Titan is gradually being disposed of, but has found ready buyers. A somewhat unexpected reappearance sees Londonlinks' former T411 back in the heart of London, crossing Oxford Circus.

Below:
The Kentish Bus livery would soon disappear from Central London. A Northern Counties-bodied Dennis Dart is seen in the City of London, amongst a typical mix of ancient and modern architecture.

Above:
Staines bus station, with a London Buslines Plaxton Pointer-bodied Dennis Dart of 1996 and a London United Leyland National of 1978, easily recognisable by its distinctive grey roof. London United is one of the National's last strongholds.

Leyland having been dropped and consigned to history.

At the other extreme in terms of double-deck technology, the highly historical Routemaster demonstrated its extraordinary longevity. The first crew route to come up for tender since privatisation was the 38 (Victoria-Clapton Pond), which was retained by Cowie Leaside in the face of fierce competition. The future of the Routemasters employed was thus assured for the five-year duration of the contract. Nevertheless, it was London Transport policy to encourage operators to invest in new buses, and as a consequence by late 1996 nearly 400 had been ordered by the 'red' companies.

The most famous of all London's routes, the 11, continued to be Routemaster-operated, Monday to Friday, from Waterloo Garage, across the road from the Old Vic. I came across the unique platform-doored RML2516, also known as DRM2516, parked there one sunny November morning, uniquely adorned with the legend 'GENERAL' in huge gold letters, looking as pretty as a picture. An interesting interview with Douglas Adie, Managing Director of London Central, was published in the Autumn 1996 edition of *The London Bus* magazine, in which he commented on graffiti, amongst other things. Having visited Italy in 1998 and 1999 and seen the appalling graffiti spreading like some uncontrollable fungus over public transport there, I can say that London is in far less desperate straits, thank goodness. Mr Adie said it was more of an issue in outer suburban areas, where the perpetrators were less likely to be observed. If it could, London Central contacted their parents, 'most of whom [perhaps surprisingly] are co-operative'. Regarding Go Ahead's control over its subsidiaries, London Central was, said Mr Adie, 'an essentially de-centralised operation with a very small head office'. Its 82 Routemasters were, Mr Adie considered, 'the best buses ever designed'.

1997

The year opened with information on London Transport services becoming available on the Internet. The older generation might wonder if this was little more than a gimmick (although to be fair, those in their late 50s and early 60s are some of the most enthusiastic users of the modern technology), whilst the school-age generation has grown up with the Internet.

A much earlier invention which has had a dramatic rebirth in the 1990s is the tram. Little did I think, when I made my final journey home from school on an E1 on route 18 on 6 April 1951, that I would ever again see trams operating in my home town. Yet, in January 1997, construction work began on a new system, work which would culminate in trams once again becoming a familiar sight in Croydon just over two years hence. We shall look in more detail at this extraordinary renaissance.

I could not have anticipated in 1951 that, 46 years later, I would again ride in a rehabilitated E1 — but I did. No 1622 was delivered to Poplar depot in 1911, and withdrawn from there in 1940. It was kept in reserve until after the war, and was then sold, to become a chalet on Hayling Island. In 1969 the lower deck — all that remained — was rediscovered, and eventually, in 1981, restoration began. It was decided that, as an original E1 existed in the London Transport Collection, No 1622 should take the form of one of the 150 rehabilitated cars. Parts from an E1 upper deck were discovered elsewhere in Hampshire, a new underframe was commissioned from a shipyard in Essex, and trucks from a Feltham car were obtained. Eventually (and that word takes the place of volumes of effort, painstaking research and money raised), on 5 July 1997, No 1622 emerged from the

Below:
A wonderful new opportunity for London tram enthusiasts was unveiled at Crich in 1997 when E1 No 1622, restored as a rehabilitated car from the mid-1930s, entered service.

workshop at the National Tram Museum, Crich, under its own power, for its first official public run in 57 years. Restored to the condition it would have been in, had it been one of the rehabilitated cars of 1935-7, it looked truly magnificent. Currently, no fewer than four London trams survive in Derbyshire, the others being No 106, the LCC four-wheeler of 1903, Feltham No 331 and the yet-to-be-restored LCC No 1.

One factor in the revival of the tram in Britain has been the smile it has brought to faces in the environmentalist lobby. An electrically-powered vehicle, capable of carrying well over a hundred passengers through the heart of a busy city, was the answer to many a prayer. However, there would always be a place for the diesel bus. It could, however, become more environmentally-friendly, and in 1997 various experiments were carried out to reduce the pollution from its engine. 250 Routemasters were fitted with oxidising catalysts, which enabled them to use ultra-low-sulphur fuels to minimise smells and smoke. There were other such experiments on various buses in the London area, around 100 of Cowie South London's Metrobuses being converted to operate on similar 'greenergy' fuel, for example.

The Routemaster, of course, is the speediest bus still at work on busy inner-city routes anywhere in Britain, thanks to conductors who collect fares en route, and so keep time at stops to a minimum. A letter in the *Guardian* around this time pointed out that putting back conductors was far and away the most sure and certain method of speeding up public

transport. I have recently spent a couple of days in Amsterdam, where a number of trams now carry conductors sitting at desks, not unlike the experimental system London Transport tried out on a handful of double-deck buses and trolleybuses immediately after World War 2.

One defeat suffered by the standard Routemaster in 1997 was its disappearance from route 139, operated by MTL between West Hampstead and Trafalgar Square, Dart SLFs taking over. These were the first low-floor buses to operate regularly into the centre of London, aside from the infrequent StationLink service. Elsewhere, however, the standard RM was assured of a future when London Central fitted 38 of its fleet with Scania engines.

Changes in ownership and liveries — the two not unconnected — were reminiscent of the 1920s and early 1930s, and keeping up-to-date with these changes became a full-time occupation. One of the most significant renamings was that of Cowie, which became Arriva. The company announced that, outside London, a corporate livery would be introduced, bringing it in line with the other 'Big Three' groups, Stagecoach and FirstGroup. The 80% red rule ensured

Above:
Slowly the attractive livery and the various fleetnames given to The Shires fleet are disappearing, now that it is part of the Arriva empire. A Leyland Olympian of Arriva The Shires heads towards Amersham station and High Wycombe.

Below:
RM1082, which entered service in January 1962 and is now owned by London Central, sweeps past Harris Bus 364, an East Lancs Pyoneer-bodied Volvo Olympian of 1998, in Lewisham.

that this would be less noticeable in London, although it soon began to make its presence felt in what had been the old Country Area. Ironically, it *did* have an almost immediate effect in the heart of London, for the dark green, pale grey and orange Alexander-bodied Volvo double-deckers which had given such a distinctive splash of colour around Trafalgar Square now began to disappear. Away from central London, the standard turquoise and cream Arriva livery, with a subtitle 'serving Surrey and West Sussex' (or wherever), soon became familiar. In central London the cream 'cow's horns', which relieved standard red, were often partly obscured by adverts.

The most colourful fleet of all belonged to Harris Bus. This West Thurrock firm gained the 108 route in April 1997, and allocated to it eleven stylish Optare Excels adorned in an equally stylish livery of dark blue merging into a pale green. The fleetname, Eltham Link, was picked out in white and pale blue with red and orange arrows on a white background. The following year the 108, which passes through the Blackwall Tunnel, would become the first route to serve the Millennium Dome site. Three more routes were won by Harris Bus later in 1997 and a further two in 1998. Double-deckers, in the shape of DAF DB250s with Palatine II bodies, and Olympians with East Lancs Pyoneer bodies, were bought for these, and all appeared in Harris's striking livery with either 'Ilford Link' or 'Lewisham Link' fleetnames. The contrast between the Pyoneers and the London Central Routemasters (the oldest dating back to 1959) which work the 36 is most striking when they stand together at Lewisham.

Heathrow, the busiest international airport in the world, has always been served by a plethora of bus

and coach services. By 1997, the days when it was served by once state-of-the-art, but latterly time-expired, shabby RTs were a distant memory, as a succession of new single and double-deckers had appeared on short- and long-distance routes in and around the vast complex of what was, in effect, a fair-sized town. The first motorway bus lane in the country was opened on the M4 spur road, although a couple of years later, Prime Minister Tony Blair, was reported to have pressed for its closure when his limousine was held up on its way to the airport.

Above:
North Greenwich. A Harris Bus Optare Excel, 322, stands beside the bus and Jubilee Line station, designed by Sir Norman Foster. In the background, a pair of Stagecoach Selkent Northern Counties-bodied Volvo Olympians are dwarfed by the Millennium Dome.

Below:
An enterprising initiative has been the Surrey Hills Leisure Buses, supported by Surrey County Council with the slogan 'The Green Way to the Best of Surrey on Summer Sundays and Public Holidays'. Vintage buses have been an added attraction, and here Nostalgiabus GS13 lays over at Guildford bus station on the 433, which serves (amongst other attractions) Leith Hill, the highest point in Surrey.

1998

As 1998 opened, more than half of all London buses were running on ultra-low-sulphur fuel. Arriva operated a DAF/Plaxton single-decker running on liquefied petroleum gas (LPG), the first gas-powered bus in London since World War 2. This time the gas was stored in tanks on the roof, a much neater arrangement. I travelled on a similar bus in Southampton which claimed to be not only ultra-environmentally-friendly but also quieter and faster than conventionally-powered vehicles. This was difficult to detect on a stop-and-start inner-city route, but clearly the technology had advanced greatly since the days of the underpowered, unreliable STs towing a trailer in the early 1940s.

In July the Government published its white paper on integrated transport, very much the brainchild of John Prescott, the Deputy Prime Minister. This proposed a number of measures which, it was hoped, would encourage people to abandon their cars in favour of public transport, and indeed, for the first time in 40 years, 1998 saw a halt in the decline of people using buses nationwide, and an actual increase in London. Much was written about making changing between various forms of public transport as effortless as possible. There had always been a number of interchanges in the London area — in the centre, the main line stations at Victoria, London Bridge and Liverpool Street, where bus stations adjoin them, immediately spring to mind, whilst further out are Stratford, Lewisham, Harrow-on-the-Hill and Morden. Many more were promised, the new Jubilee Line stations being examples of where this would be a priority.

Ownership was constantly changing. MTL London Northern, which often exchanged buses with its Liverpool operations, was bought for £41.9 million by

Metroline, and Capital Citybus was acquired by FirstGroup for a reported £14 million; its fleetname would change to First Capital. By now FirstGroup had a national market share of 21%, Stagecoach 16% and Arriva 15%. The corporate liveries were gradually being applied outside central London, although the 80% rule meant that the central area was becoming universally red; the former Kentish Bus Routemasters, for instance, rapidly lost their primrose and maroon livery. Kentish Bus had once been the largest operator of LT bus routes other than London Buses itself, but was now in decline. Its links with Maidstone & District, both companies having been absorbed by the Arriva Group, grew ever stronger. (There had always been an overlap in the Edenbridge, Tunbridge Wells, and Gravesend areas.) From 1998 the ex-Kentish Bus vehicles would bear the legend 'ARRIVA serving Kent Thameside', the ex-Maidstone & District ones 'ARRIVA serving Kent & Sussex'. The distinctive Southdown and East Kent liveries had already vanished, and now the third and last of the big companies south and east of London was to suffer a similar fate. Many regretted that the attractive deep green and buff livery with fleetname skilfully echoing that of BET days, which had only just been introduced by Maidstone & District, was doomed.

The first tram for Croydon Tramlink arrived in September. Built in Vienna by Bombardier Eurorail, it was a handsome, state-of-the-art car similar to Cologne's newest designs, a 30.2m, low-floor, articulated vehicle with 70 seats and a top speed of 50mph. But in two respects it paid pleasing homage to London tram traditions. The livery was red and white and its number, 2530 — and here someone revealed a real sense of history — followed on from the highest number of the generation of trams which disappeared in 1952, No 2529 having been an ex-LUT 'W class' car withdrawn in December 1935. No 2530 was delivered to the depot in Therapia Lane, situated between the former Waddon Marsh and Beddington Lane halts. Others followed and they began trials over the former West Croydon-Wimbledon railway line. In the meantime, construction of the street sections in Croydon and New Addington proceeded apace.

The ever-popular 'Steam on the Met' took place in late spring, the first day coinciding with the FA Cup Final between Arsenal and Newcastle United. It was a beautifully sunny day, more like mid-summer, and the area around Baker Street was awash with black and white striped shirts. You will probably have heard about the small zebra who was told by his mother that she couldn't afford to buy a new Manchester United kit every year and he would have to support Newcastle like the rest of the herd. Back to the plot. Some Newcastle fans, already well-oiled, looked very confused when they found themselves on a steam train heading north from Harrow-on-the-Hill instead of an electric one heading south to Wembley, but on

Above left:
London Country once owned more Leyland Nationals than any other operator in the world. By 1998 very few remained at work on former green bus routes. One of four still with Guildford & West Surrey was 242, new to Alder Valley in 1976. It is seen here picking up shoppers in Woking.

Left:
A trip down the Thames has always been a favourite with tourists, but once again attempts are being made to persuade commuters to take to the water and relieve congestion on the roads. To this end London Transport publishes a timetable of all the regular services which operate between Richmond and the Thames Barrier. One such service is seen passing a converted former World War 1 destroyer between Waterloo and Blackfriars Bridges, which, strictly speaking, are upriver from the Pool of London.

the whole the two events seemed to co-exist quite happily. I travelled from Harrow to Rickmansworth behind the preserved former LMS Stanier Class 5MT 2-6-0 No 2968, and at the latter encountered two newly-restored locomotives, 'B1' No 1264, one of a class of LNER-designed 4-6-0s which regularly worked alongside Metropolitan electrics from the 1940s to the 1960s, and former GWR 2-6-2T No 4144, a locomotive virtually identical to the '61xx' class which was associated with the London area for some 30 years.

New buses continued to be delivered in considerable numbers, both to 'red' bus companies and the outer London ones. Amongst them were some of the last of the long-lived Volvo (formerly Leyland) Olympian, which went to First Capital, Metrobus, London Sovereign and Metroline. The latter placed an order with Dennis for no fewer than 433 buses, the largest order by a London bus company for some 15 years.

1999 would be the year of the low-floor double-decker, but the first actually arrived on 5 November 1998, when Arriva London North put an Alexander ALX400-bodied DAF DB250 (DLA class) into service, the first of a number which took up work on the 168, 221 and 250 routes. The modest seating capacity, of 45 upstairs and a mere 17 down, was dictated by LT's insistence on a straight, central staircase, dual doors and plenty of standing room in the low-floor section to accommodate wheelchairs and buggies.

1999

The new generation of low-floor double-deckers made its impact in 1999, over 600 being due to enter service before the year was out, only 150 fewer than the entire delivery of both double and single-deckers in 1998, which was a good year in itself. Yet it hardly seemed any time since the double-decker's demise, assisted possibly by EEC regulations, had been predicted.

Before we look in more depth at the double-deckers of the next millennium, we'll step back seven decades and take a ride in a London double-decker of the 1930s. The Covent Garden Museum has never been large enough to accommodate all the buses in the London Transport Collection, and at the end of 1998 the reserve collection was moved from its home at Ash Grove garage to be displayed at Covent Garden for a day, before going on to its new home at Acton. I was lucky enough to receive an invitation to ride in whichever bus took my fancy. Types ranged from a

Top:
Preserved buses belonging to the reserve fleet of the London Transport Collection prepare to set off from Ash Grove garage to Covent Garden and their new home at Acton. From right to left are solid-tyred S742 of 1923, STL469 of 1934 (what a vast advance there had been in the intervening eleven years), RF537, GS64 and RT4712.

Above:
The Optare Solo is the state-of-the-art minibus of the late 1990s. Developed in close liaison with Wilts & Dorset, which wanted a low-floor vehicle with as much unimpeded floorspace as possible, the wheels set close to the extremities, an indicator as large as that found on a big bus, and various other refinements, it was soon taken up by many other operators. Travel London, part of the National Express Group, won the contract for the C1 (Victoria-Knightsbridge) and bought ten Solos. The first of these, 231, is seen appropriately parked alongside a Wilts & Dorset example at the 1999 Southsea rally.

solid-tyred, open-top S to a Routemaster. Tempting as the alternatives were, I had already decided on STL469, dating from July 1934. Thus I rode the streets of London in an STL, along Cambridge Heath Road, in parts hardly changed from the days when the type was a familiar sight in the East End, down the Whitechapel Road, home, now as then, to immigrants from many parts of the world, on round a much-changed Aldgate, and through the heart of the City, up Fleet Street, where newspaper men and women are now as scarce as tourists are commonplace, and thence to Covent Garden.

The list of preserved London buses grows and grows, inevitably of course as each type becomes obsolescent, and the Metrobuses, Titans and even early Olympians are rapidly heading for that category. I recently made successive journeys in an Alexander ALX400-bodied DAF of late 1998 and an 18-year-old Metrobus, and the contrast in the quality of the interiors was striking. I once invited my small son to

Above:
Brand-new Dennis Trident TN802 of First Capital, with Plaxton President low-floor body, stands in a traffic jam outside the Tower of London. It is about to be passed by the lady on a bicycle who has already overtaken the Big Bus Company open-top DMS, representative of an earlier generation of London double-decker.

Below:
Route 60, operated by Capital Logistics, linking Streatham with Old Coulsdon, went through a torrid time in 1998 and the early part of 1999 when a shortage of vehicles meant that all sorts of temporary arrangements had to be made, at one point a Routemaster coach being used. In March 1999 it suddenly became the most up-to-date route anywhere in the London area, when a batch of DAFs with low-floor Optare Spectra bodies took up work, immediately followed by more DAFs, this time with the very first Plaxton President low-floor bodies to enter service anywhere in the UK. One of the Optare buses is seen passing the Red Deer, South Croydon.

climb aboard a prototype Titan on display at Cobham in the early 1970s; he replied to the effect that he couldn't see what was new about it. I knew what he meant, for it could be argued that there was very little advance in interior appointments throughout the 1970s and '80s. The décor of production Titans, with bilious yellow, grey and white, and plenty of exposed screw heads, compares poorly with the new generation of low-floor buses. These have vastly better-designed interiors, with plenty of colour, fabrics where painted metal was once the norm, more comfortable seats, and a really smooth ride.

London leads the way in double-deckers, and has decided that front entrances and centre exits will remain standard, that staircases should be straight and well-lit, making them more easily negotiable and more likely to entice passengers upstairs where the majority of the seating is to be found. Indeed, seating downstairs is quite limited, in order to provide maximum space for short-distance standing passengers, wheelchairs and children's buggies, an interesting echo of the philosophy behind the Feltham tram design of 1931, although of course there were a couple of steps up into a Feltham. Seats are undergoing a radical rethink, with a move towards individual, high-backed ones which passengers prefer. Inevitably, not everyone thinks London has got it right. A letter from Croydon Retired People's Campaign complained of the soft suspension of the

new buses 'when they accelerate', and that 'hanging-straps are of little use to us, as they move when we move, so they do not provide the stability which is needed when we are standing'. London Transport said it would look into this.

The low-floor revolution has given the Optare Spectra a new lease of life in London. The very first production low-floor double-decker in the UK was a DAF/Optare, the first examples entering service in early 1998. A year or so later, Capital Logistics put six into service on the much-troubled route 60 between Streatham Common and Old Coulsdon, alongside ten Plaxton-bodied DAFs.

The problem of graffiti has not yet been totally overcome, some of the newest buses suffering from scratched windows within a few days of entering service. New York has led the way in conquering the problem, and it should not be beyond the wit of London to rid itself of this scourge. Apart from mindless (but hardly dangerous) vandalism, London Transport personnel are still having to risk life and limb on Saturday nights in some parts of the capital — particularly in certain, rather unlikely, affluent

suburbs. Drivers went through a hard time in the early days of tendering, when uneconomically low bids, dependent on reduced wages and working conditions, were accepted. There has been some improvement of late; it remains true that the average London bus driver is one of the most skilled and patient motorists on this planet, and Routemaster conductors, whatever their ethnic origin, retain their traditional wit and good spirits. Mind you, the odd employee still needs a crash course in customer relations, not least the inspector who, one June morning, took a nun to court. She belonged to a contemplative order whose members take a vow of poverty, and had fallen asleep after a night of prayer and been carried past her stop. Fortunately the magistrate had more sense than the inspector, discharged the nun and rounded on the inspector for his insensitivity.

The first section of the Jubilee Line Extension, from Stratford to North Greenwich, was opened (very late) on 14 May by John Prescott, the Deputy Prime Minister, and the man given responsibility for shifting the emphasis of the nation from private to public transport. It was worth waiting for, not least for the magnificent stations. It was Frank Pick who inspired London Transport in the 1930s to adopt a visual approach to everything it did, which, by 1939, had put it ahead of just about every other transport undertaking world-wide. As Nikolaus Pevsner said at the time, 'London Transport is the most efficacious centre of visual education in England.' The remainder of the Jubilee Line, on from North Greenwich to the centre of London to connect up with the existing line, would open a little later.

At the same time, the Docklands Light Railway was being extended under the Thames to Lewisham. It is to be hoped that proper pedestrian access (ie a footbridge and lifts and/or escalators from this bus/rail interchange to the busy shopping centre) will be installed. At present passengers have to cross four extremely busy roads, with lights which are unco-ordinated and designed to keep the traffic flowing rather than assist pedestrians on their way to the shops.

Frank Pick would have approved of the new Jubilee Line stations. All are splendid. North Greenwich, all deep blues and aluminium (which, being set alongside the Millennium Dome, has inevitably attracted the most attention and universal acclaim) is the work of Britain's most famous living architect, Sir Norman Foster. Stratford (ie Stratford East, not Shakespeare's half-timbered home town), which is basically a vast, airy, elegant space, is my favourite.

Elsewhere fragmentation might seem to be the order of the day, with bus liveries so varied as to put those of the 'pirate' days, immediately before Pick took over, to shame. Yet there is a still a visual theme running through much of the vast empire for which London Transport remains responsible, whether it be the excellent posters, the 80% red central bus livery, or the new Underground and Docklands Light Railway stations. A couple of quotes from the many wise words of Pick are as apposite now as they were in the 1930s: 'What is needed is someone to sort out the pieces and turn the jigsaw puzzle into something whole and plain'; 'labour is not civilisation unless it leads to leisure, and wealth without art is barbarism'. The latter might be thought particularly remarkable for a man who had a degree in law, and who was appointed to ensure that, above all else, London Transport was cost-effective, a task he pursued with total commitment.

Pick presided over a London which was determined to get rid of its trams, but he would surely have approved of their return in the very different world of the 1990s. By the summer of 1999, the track on the entire Croydon system was complete, all the masts were in place, and most of the overhead had been erected. The trams had been running over former railway track towards Wimbledon from their Therapia Road depot since the autumn of 1998. By the spring of 1999, all 24 cars had been delivered. It was a bright, midsummer morning when car No 2535 became the first tram since 7 April 1951 to run through the heart of Croydon under its own power, when it reached George Street and the approach to East Croydon station on Wednesday, 16 June.

Our story began with the formation of London Transport in 1933, one of its priorities being the replacement of its vast tram network. The trolleybuses took over with such determination that London's fleet became the largest in the world. World War 2 brought a halt to any further extensions of the trolleybus system and, when the replacement of trams recommenced in 1950, the diesel bus was chosen to complete the job. The world is very different now, and light rail, as the tram is often called, is seen as the best (if, in the short term, somewhat expensive)

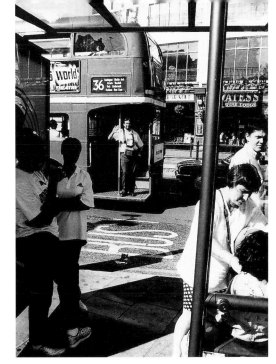

Above:
The Routemaster, that most traditional of London buses with its half cab and open rear entrance, will be with us into the new millennium. A Routemaster conductor strikes an equally traditional pose in Lewisham town centre as his New Cross-based bus is about to set off through inner southeast London, across the Thames at Vauxhall Bridge and on through the West End to Queens Park.

Below:
The new Stratford station. A Silverlink EMU is about to depart for North Woolwich. The Jubilee Line platforms are in the top right-hand corner of the picture, the Central Line and the Great Eastern platforms behind the photographer.

solution to spiralling congestion and pollution in our cities and conurbations, particularly if it can use existing railway tracks to achieve high speeds in the suburbs, taking to the streets, otherwise pedestrianised, in the town centre. Thus the inauguration of Croydon's Tramlink, following the Manchester, Sheffield and Birmingham/ Wolverhampton schemes earlier in the decade, is hopefully the first stage in the restoration of the tram to the parts of London where it was once familiar.

Above:
A Jubilee Line train at Stratford, about to set off for North Greenwich.

Below:
All eyes turn to watch one of the first trial runs by a tram through Croydon town centre. Tramlink No 2535 eases its way down the 9% slope of Crown Hill, a street never before served by public transport, on 3 July 1999. A month earlier, No 2535 had become the first tram to run under its own power in a London street for almost 47 years.